THE CAPITALISM PAPERS

THE
CAPITALISM
PAPERS

*Fatal Flaws of
an Obsolete System*

JERRY MANDER

COUNTERPOINT
BERKELEY

Copyright © 2012 Jerry Mander

Library of Congress Cataloging-in-Publication Data is available.

ISBN: 978-1-58243-717-0

COUNTERPOINT
1919 Fifth Street
Berkeley, CA 94710
www.counterpointpress.com

Interior design by David Bullen
Cover design by Daniela Sklan
Distributed by Publishers Group West

10 9 8 7 6 5 4 3 2 1

*This book is dedicated to the memory of my friend and colleague
Edward (Teddy) Goldsmith, visionary, activist, compassionate
inspirational leader, and the most charming, inclusive, kindest,
and entertaining man I ever met. He knew everything
in this book long before I did.*

Table of Contents

PART ONE: INTRODUCTION

PART TWO: THE FATAL FLAWS OF CAPITALISM

PART ONE

Introduction

QUESTION FROM THE AUDIENCE: *Jerry, do you mean my grandfather's furniture store is killing the world? Is he one of those capitalists? It's a nice shop. He's been there forty years, giving work to eight employees, and he pays a nice wage. With benefits. It doesn't seem bad to me.*

JERRY: *No, stores like that are really not the problem. We need to make distinctions when we talk about capitalism. The word covers too many different things. One distinction is this: Size matters! Small-scale local or family businesses, or community enterprises that make some money, pay salaries, send kids to college, and save a little, are not the problem, and never have been.*

But let's say your granddad had somehow made gigantic profits from his store forty years ago, so he decided to partner with another store owner and invest in big real estate, converting small farms and open lands into shopping malls. And let's say they started franchising shopping centers around the world, and were borrowing from big banks to do it, and then started buying banks, and buying other companies doing unrelated stuff, like shipping or mining or biotech farming, and then started getting their financing from Goldman Sachs. Then they "went public" and were listed on the New York Stock Exchange as SHOP AMERICA! and they became friends with congressmen, spent 10 percent of their business income lobbying in Washington to overturn zoning, dumping, and other environmental laws that were getting in their way. And they had their eye on export trade subsidies, and maybe some military contracts, and were desperate to keep their stock prices high and to keep their taxes down.

Well, then, you'd have to say your grandfather would be operating in a different world, with different values and drives, than he does now. At the beginning, it was all about furniture for local families and businesses, not the primary needs of nonstop capital expansion, growth, stock values, and distributions. That's the "capitalism" I worry about. That's what's consuming the world. Now it's all about growth, not furniture, not sufficiency, not community welfare. It's wealth, constantly seeking more wealth, to better seek still more wealth. That local store and those global businesses really shouldn't share the same name. They are different creatures.

I.

Economic Succession

This book anticipates the final failure of the global economic project that we have lived by, accepted, and treated as if it were nearly a law of nature for more than two hundred years. The capitalist system was able to thrive, on and off, during the eighteenth, nineteenth, and twentieth centuries, when we still lived in a world of richly abundant cheap resources, cheap (or slave) labor, myriad colonial interventions, and lots of developing markets. But it's now obsolete, nonmalleable, and increasingly destructive.

The system has reached a stage in its life span that is very familiar to ecologists and other students of natural evolution: A once thriving, even dominant species, in markedly changed physical circumstances, gives way to other species that are better adapted to current realities.

When applied to nature, it's called *natural succession*. When speaking of economics, however, the ecological philosopher Ernest Callenbach describes the process as "*economic succession*." I think he's got it right. The capitalist system had its day. If we care about the future well-being of humans and nature, it's time to move on.

The situation becomes especially urgent now that we're face-to-face with truly frightening macro-expressions of the limits of the earth's basic carrying capacities, which until only recently had been largely ignored. These include:

(1) *Climate change*, caused mostly by excessive carbon emissions, advancing rapidly in all regions of the planet. This brings with it the loss of lands from drowning—from ice cap runoffs and rising seas—or desertification, giant storms, loss of productive capacities, physical dislocations, and horrific new weather patterns.

(2) *Peak oil*, and the imminent global shortage of inexpensive, safe energy from any source, including coal, gas, and nuclear. Abundant cheap energy was the key underpinning of Western civilization and our economic system over the last two centuries. Large-scale industrial production, long-distance transport,

export food systems, complex urban and suburban systems, and commodities such as automobiles, plastics, chemicals, pesticides, refrigeration, and thousands of others are all based on the assumption of ever-increasing cheap energy. Alternative energy systems, highly touted now, can never become an adequate substitute, as we will explain.

(3) *The global resource depletion crises.* In addition to fuel, we face major oncoming scarcities of fresh water, arable soils, food grains, forests, biological and genetic diversity, wilderness, coral reefs, life in the oceans, and key industrial minerals including coltan, zinc, lithium, phosphorous, and rare earth elements. These shortages, among many others, put the survival of modern society in question.

(4) *A global population* now past seven billion, heading toward eight billion, exacerbating all other conditions.

(5) And *the social, environmental, and geopolitical chaos* that goes with all the above, already expressing itself in conflicts and wars over oil, water, and myriad other resources on land and in the sea, increased militarism, rising protests against systemic inequity, and fierce battles over increased cross-border migrations.

All of these crises share the same root cause: planet-wide immersion in a uniform economic system that requires continuous rapid growth and constant wealth expansion for its own viability, and in order to sustain the institutions and the people who sit at the top of the process. Such a state of permanent growth in turn requires never-ending expansion of resources, cheap labor, and unlimited waste disposal and absorption capacity. It also requires the universal promotion of a values system that equates perpetual commodity accumulation and personal and institutional wealth expansion with success and happiness. These are all impossible on a planet with finite resources and carrying capacities. The system is bound to fail.

The great tragedy of the moment is that the powers that be in our society have failed to recognize or acknowledge the fundamental fact that Earth has limits, which are already in view, and that our economic drives are now inappropriate. This is a profound signal that we humans have lost touch with reality, about who we are, where we live, and how we live.

The central questions come down to these: Can industrial society, consumer society, and globalization survive in anything approaching their present forms? Would we even want that, given the human and environmental costs and the sacrifices involved? Can capitalism be reformed, adjusted, or made relevant to this moment? If not, what comes next?

The Missing Link

Day after day we hear the economy discussed from all sides of the political equation in exactly the same way. Whether it's Obama or Sarkozy or Putin, or Hu, or it's Fox News or NPR, or Bill Clinton or John Boehner, or Mitt Romney or Larry Summers or George Soros, or Bill Gates or the Koch brothers, or Sean Hannity or Rachel Maddow, or Paul Krugman or Alan Greenspan, or Karl Rove, or even Robert Reich, *everybody* is now trying to figure out just one thing: how to revive and sustain rapid economic growth, which is equated with economic recovery and the larger visions of continued "progress."

Some say tax cuts, others say tax hikes. Some say stimulus, others say austerity; some say bailouts, others say no bailouts; some say jobs, others say investments; some say monetary policy, others say fiscal policy, and others say public works. *Everyone* is grasping for a magic elixir to revive rapid growth. Because without rapid growth, the mega-economic system that has functioned in this form for more than a century will collapse. They all agree on that point. How to build and sell more new cars? How to have more new housing starts? How to expand energy supplies? How to increase investment and bank lending? How to increase exports?

Perhaps most of all, how to increase *shopping*? This is the case not only in the United States, but in China, Spain, Chile, Russia, and just about everywhere else. How to get people to spend more money? How to commodify as much of life as possible? How to privatize what remains of natural resources, especially water, forests, open lands, biodiversity; and public services—social security, Medicare, the military, healthcare, prisons? Anything that has a chance to produce profits and increase economic growth.

But there's an important missing link in the discussion, ignored by everyone in the mainstream debate: *nature.* People behave as if our economic system were a self-contained separate entity residing in its own detached universe, unconnected to realities outside itself, rather than embodied in a much larger system from which it evolved and cannot escape. Nature *cannot* be left out. It is, in fact, the most important aspect of the entire discussion. Growth is made out of nature, transformed. What we call our economy is rooted largely in the process of transferring and transforming elements of the natural world into the tools and commodities of human activity, and then betting on the rates that we can continue to do it, nonstop, forever. To leave the source of it all entirely out of our concerns is, well, shortsighted.

Wherever you are sitting right now as you read this, please look around. Everything in your presence began as something from nature, mined from the ground, or harvested. The garments you are wearing, your shoes, the chair you are sitting in, the book or Kindle you are holding, the bed you sleep in. The car you drive and all its tires, wires, metals, parts. The phones you use. The walls and floor of the room, its carpet, the lights and the switches, the electrical line in the walls, the metals in your kitchen. All were once minerals that were dug up from the earth, then shipped around the world, transformed, assembled, shipped again to a store near you, and sold. Or else they were living beings—trees, plants, animals, fibers, corals—that had their own worldly existence, their own roles in living ecological systems. Even so-called "chemicals" and "synthetics" began as natural elements, later rearranged. Is your shirt made of polyester? Polyester is plastic. Plastic is oil. Oil used to be trees, plants, dinosaurs, sunlight.

The whole process of finding, recovering, and transforming these minerals, elements, energies, and beings into commodities that are shipped around the world and given economic value, and bought and sold, winding up in our homes, is what we call *economics*. The kind of economy we have come to depend upon, *capitalist*, was until recently highly efficient at delivering transformations, by using profits from previous transformations to do more of the same. And then wagering in financial markets on which part of these processes might grow and which might not.

But does this process go on forever? Can it? How can this possibly continue? Aren't we running out of resources? Where will the metals and minerals come from to build more and more cars, and where do we throw away the old ones? How many cars can be built and bought? How many roads can cover the landscape? How many new houses can be built on open land? Where will the food come from when the topsoils are overused and destroyed? How expensive will food become as transport costs continue to zoom? How much carbon can fill the skies? How much plastic can be dumped at sea? How many giant dead spots before the oceans give out? How much nature can be transformed into commodities and still remain viable?

"We imagined ourselves isolated from the sources of our existence," and we invented instead a "myth of endless progress," says the Dark Mountain Project, a new community of scholars, writers, and artists in the United Kingdom. "The fallout from this imaginative error is all around us: A quarter of the world's mammals are threatened with imminent extinction; an acre and a half of rain forest is felled every second; 75% of the world's fish stocks are on the verge of collapse; humanity consumes 25% more of the world's natural 'products' than the earth can replace—a figure predicted to rise to 80% by mid-century."

The World Conservation Union adds that extinction threatens 23 percent of mammal species, 25 percent of conifers, 32 percent of amphibians, 35 percent of mangroves, 20 percent of coral reefs. And that's before we get to the full effects of climate change.

South African environmental attorney Cormac Cullinan, author of *Wild Law*, reports on the UN Millenium Ecosystem Assessment, performed in 2001–2005 (including the participation of 1,300 scientists worldwide): The MA found that about 60 percent of "ecosystem services" are now threatened, including, for example, the ability of water to purify itself and of forests to contribute to clean air.

Economist Eric Zencey, of Empire State College, New York, says this: "In the standard view, the financial crisis besets an economy that consists solely of humans acting within formalized systems of their own creation—systems that have no connection to a larger world. That's why the standard views won't fix the problem. . . . [It's] what happens when an infinite growth economy runs into the limits of a finite world. The financial crisis *is* the environmental crisis . . . we can't solve the former until we start solving the latter."

Our society has blurred a most fundamental fact: Humans are completely dependent on the health of the natural world. In fact, we are part of the natural world, made of the same ingredients as the rest of life on Earth over which we have assumed dominion. But, having lost our connections to concrete reality, we don't grasp the predicament we are in. All of humanity begins to resemble the astronaut in space, spinning in our separate metal containments, millions of miles from the organic roots of our existence. We depend on nourishment that arrives from somewhere far away on ships or planes. We are disconnected from the sources of information we need, now brought to us only through processed images from distant places. We have no direct means of knowing right from wrong, or how to control our experience.

One thing is certain: We had better recognize this problem soon. Our horizons are not unlimited. There are boundaries to our aspirations. When we hear our political leaders renewing their race toward unlimited exponential growth, we realize they don't know what they are talking about. They themselves are lost in an obsolete set of mental frameworks, a thirty-centuries-long process to sublimate the most basic points of all: All of our economic and social activity depends on nature. We are not separate, and we are not in charge. Failing to grasp that fact while promoting ubiquitous economic strategies that remain unconscious of such realities may prove to be our most fatal flaw.

The "C"-Word

People throughout the world are already deeply concerned and talking about the problems of the capitalist system. However, most of them are not acknowledging that *that's* what they're talking about. Not long ago, I attended a speech by a leading environmentalist friend articulating the depth of the depletion crises we now face. He brilliantly described the problems inherent to our system—social, political, and environmental—and he spoke of the need for new economic paradigms that accept the limits of the earth's carrying capacities.

The talk focused on the urgent need for a revised system of economic values to modify the "present system," a term he used several times. But what "present system" did he have in mind? Why not name it? Did he mean "infinite growth" was the system? Are we worrying about a system called growth? There is no such system. The drive to destructive, never-ending growth is an intrinsic, fundamental expression, a *subset*, of an economic system named *capitalism*. I'm for naming the system.

In November 2010, I heard a speech by Bill Moyers, who quoted Socrates saying this: "If you are going to remember a thing, you must first name it." I like that a lot. Naming something diminishes its amorphousness and stimulates focus—what it is, and what it is not. On the other hand, Moyers didn't name capitalism, either, though he did put a name on the system: "plutonomy." That's a good name for what's going on now, but, like "growth," plutonomy is a subset of capitalism; capitalism *produces* plutonomy.

Another colleague, a leading liberal economist, last year said to me, "Jerry, I hope you're not really going to write that book about capitalism. Nobody even knows what it is. It has so many forms; it defies single definitions. Anyway, if you critique capitalism, per se, you'll only marginalize all of us, as socialists, or worse." On a previous occasion, during a conference we both attended, called "Is Capitalism Soon Over?" the same colleague said that if the assembled group of economists and activists took a public stand against capitalism, he might have to leave. And yet in reading his writings, I can find only the most blistering critiques of the unnamed system, and very little that suggests that large-scale, free-market capitalism, as we know it, has any chance of surviving for much longer.

Nonetheless, he is exactly right to ask: While we are discussing the "C" word, what, exactly, are we talking about? The word is applied to many different iterations of similar economic practices.

The standard definition of capitalism goes more or less this way: *An economic system dominated by private [as opposed to community, or public, or state] ownership of capital, property, land, and the means of production and distribution.* Some definitions add that the system requires freedom from regulation, freedom of movement (geographic mobility), and unfettered free markets. All of those encourage continuous pursuit of financial self-interest, profits, growth, and economic and political autonomy (aka "laissez-faire capitalism" or "free-market fundamentalism").

American-style capitalism is probably the closest example in the world to the ideals of laissez-faire capitalism—the least government regulation or intervention of any developed nation—except for those times when governments provide helpful subsidies, privatization schemes, military contracts, or other forms of supportive largess to corporations. The whole system focuses on the primacy of corporate expansion and profit. If government tries to initiate any kind of regulatory steps—an environmental law, for example, or regulations on the freedom of banks to invest depositors' money in risky ventures, or taxes levied on profits—these are often met with cries against government powers, as they are seen to defy the primary freedoms and drives of the system.

Another definition of a capitalist system comes from Yale University scholar Immanuel Wallerstein. In his book *World Systems Analysis*, he cuts to the chase:

"We are in a capitalist system when the system gives priority to the endless accumulation of capital.... Endless accumulation is a quite simple concept: It means that people and firms are accumulating capital in order to accumulate still more capital, a process that is continual and endless."

That's the crux of the matter, I think: *accumulating capital in order to accumulate still more capital ... continual and endless.*

Or perhaps we should turn to the words of film director Oliver Stone: "Money never sleeps."

There are many international variations on the system. For example, there is considerable diversity of "state capitalist" expressions (in China, Russia, Saudi Arabia, Japan, India, Vietnam, Venezuela, and others) where countries permit capitalist enterprises to operate for private profit and to compete within domestic and international markets. But they permit this only within certain pre-defined spheres of activity, and not others, and with a high degree of central planning, regulation, and control. In most of those cases, the state continues to operate the most crucial industries, such as energy, transportation, banking, education, security, and others. Some of these countries describe themselves as socialist; others don't.

Another set of variations on the theme are the mixed economies of Europe, especially northern Europe, where capitalism operates freely in most economic domains, but within a context of considerable state regulation, higher taxes, and the extensive provision by governments of free or very low-cost social services—lifetime healthcare, education, transportation, childcare, eldercare, guaranteed incomes, and assured worker benefits like vacations, maternity leave, etc. Europeans call this "social democracy." Republicans in the United States call it "socialism."

Then there is the crucial matter of *scale*. Most economists these days, the media at large, and the general public do not make clear distinctions between large-scale domestic or global capitalism versus local, *small-market* capitalism. The former operates in diverse, far-flung markets and regions, with extensive infrastructures, gathering resources or engaging in production and distribution, wherever on Earth they can do so profitably, especially after the boost provided by corporate globalization after World War II. Or else they *franchise* their activities broadly beyond their initial community. Large national and global corporations—especially those whose stock is publicly traded—are *obliged* to seek constant growth, constant profit expansion, and the absolute primacy of short-term self-interest, no matter the social, political, or environmental contexts or effects. Making profits for shareholders is the primary, if not the only, *legal* and practical obligation of corporate structure. If they do not succeed in that, businesses fail.

On the other hand, small-market local businesses like the furniture store in the opening paragraph have the option to operate in far different ways. Private, small-scale, locally owned and oriented businesses that operate in single markets—especially those that are *not* listed by stock markets—are usually more directly involved in community life; their customers may also be personal friends or neighbors. Such businesses can set priorities and retain options that large-scale capitalist enterprises cannot. For example, privately owned, small-market businesses can opt out of any legal imperatives to continuously expand, nor do they have to pay dividends to anonymous or dominant shareholders. This is also true of family or community-based businesses, as well as worker-owned and operated businesses, coops, and "not-for-profit" corporations of various kinds.

Small enterprises will usually continue to seek profits, i.e., the excess of income over expenses. But their smaller-scale and community-embedded ownership allows them at least the possibility to operate from entirely different hierarchies of value than their megacousins operating nationally or globally. They can more easily avoid the intrinsic pitfalls that derive from serving the hungers of large-scale, growth-oriented, stock market–driven enterprises. (This is *not* to say that smaller-scale businesses always behave morally or that they necessarily place the interests of community or nature ahead of personal gain. But the smaller and more local the scale of the operation, the greater the *opportunity* for more pro-social, pro-community, and pro-environmental values, and an acceptance of limits to growth.)

A family-run store, or a restaurant, or local service business, even when it seeks a profit, is a very different entity from a national or global resource company or bank or manufacturer or hedge fund. They are structurally and functionally different from large-scale or global capitalism, with mostly different motivations and drives—not really even cousins. They should not both be called "capitalist." I think the word "capitalism" should not be used to cover nearly the territory it now does. If local entrepreneurs were the only "capitalists" in the world, I would never have thought about this book. They are not the problem.

This Book

The Capitalism Papers takes a different path than most popular critiques of the system, which tend to focus on *reforming* or *controlling* negative behaviors of the corporate executives who steer the central drives of the economy. They promote the goal of introducing more ecological or "pro-social" values among corporate and banking players; to convert the executives and their institutions from "greed to green," as it were, or to make rules (in the rare cases when a government is willing to do so) that limit negative activities among giant economic players.

But to publicly suggest that those approaches are ultimately doomed to be largely ineffective, and that the capitalist system itself is the core problem, *not* the people who express it—after all, people in corporations are merely following the inherent drives and rules of the system ("grow or die," "profit comes first")—is rarely heard in political debates about the situation we face.

The idea that large-scale free-market capitalism may eventually be revealed as simply a temporary short-term experiment, appropriate perhaps for relatively brief moments of human history but now out of date, is rarely discussed openly. And the idea that capitalism is ultimately not amenable to reforms, not sustainable, inherently flawed—that it's the system that's greedy, not the people—and that it may need to be abandoned in the interests of planetary survival, remains heretical to mainstream worldviews. It has effectively become a kind of "third rail" of discourse—forbidden to touch. Such observations bring charges of impracticality, at the least, or "socialist," or "communist." It remains okay to critique certain aspects of the system—that it often causes pollution problems, for example—but not the system itself, as if global capitalism occupies a virtually permanent existence, like a religion, a gift of God, infallible.

Disclaimer

For the record, I think it will be useful to get a few questions out of the way. I am not a communist, or Marxist or socialist, and never have been. You really don't have to be any of those things to find major flaws in capitalism's inherent design and begin to be alarmed about its downside performance. You just have to be awake. Neither am I an academic, and this will not be an academic work. And I don't claim this book as the definitive case against capitalism—I will leave that to the Marxists—it is really only *my* case against capitalism, mixing in my own observations, experiences in business, some journalism, and conjectures from years in the commercial advertising business (including also lots of political campaign advertising), as well as from ecological activism, the foundation world, and a more recent career over two decades as an anti-globalization activist. And as an author.

Neither is this book meant to be a definitive answer to the present recession or how to get out of it, except to point out that similar recessions have been a constant of capitalist form for two centuries. They are routine, not exceptional, though they feel exceptional when you're in one. Economists have names for the problem. If they're conservative, they call it the "business cycle." If they're leftist, they call it the "boom and bust cycle."

In either case, when something in the market gets really popular and hot—a commodity that takes off, or a stock, or a desperate need for more housing—profit-seeking money flows toward that like a raging flood tide, eventually satisfying the need for investment and the profit opportunity, but then continuing to flow beyond the point of saturation. Once you have sold X million MacBooks, or housing prices have doubled, or stock prices have exceeded their expected potential, how much further can they go? The process can quickly lead to one of those "investment bubbles," wherein the values of a product, or the market for a whole industry, or a whole expression of a form of technology, are dangerously inflated. The saturated bubble starts to leak or burst. The value declines and starts to evaporate. Opportunities for investors start to deplete. The smartest investors spot the leak early and quickly sell off their holdings, thus accelerating the leakage. Other, less sensitive investors experience their wealth disappearing, reducing also the excess profits they have available for new investments, and stimulating the next round of the downward spiral. Many people may lose a high percentage of their net worth, which turns out to be amorphous. Stocks fall, jobs are lost, businesses close. It's traumatic, but, viewed over a long term, this is business as usual. That's just the way it goes. The trend is always up, until it's not. It's close to gambling.

If you are going to have capitalism, you are going to have such patterns. Normally, the system gets through them efficiently. *This* time, however, is different. We are not going to rise out of this one, at least not totally, because the current economic crisis has been amplified by a terrifying contextual factor: The raw materials the economy depends upon, from nature, especially cheap fuel, have been depleted. The supplies that remain are more difficult to extract, far more expensive, and less efficient. And despite our tendency toward techno-utopianism, there will be no technological solution that will enable society to continue on its present growth path. There may be bursts of growth within certain categories of production—certainly for local food production and distribution, and for local alternative energy systems—but overall, the situation will get worse over time. We are running out of nature. We have overdone it. We have expanded beyond the carrying capacity of the planet. The physical basis of the system is disappearing. Systemic adjustment is required.

Structural Arguments

The central focuses of this book will be on a substantial list of *intrinsic* characteristics: specific, and sometimes overlapping, drives and effects of global capitalism that make it no longer viable as a long-term model for global sustainability, equity, democracy, or even its own survival. These arguments against capitalism as a sustainable system are *structural*; they are very resistant to reform. They will include:

- *Amorality.* Capitalism's only purpose and mandate is the expansion of individual and corporate wealth. It has no other job, and no interest in "right or wrong," or human welfare, or communities, or in the well-being of the natural world, except as resources for itself.

- *Dependence on growth.* This is the most fundamental problem, though it is the least noticed, and is rarely included in mainstream economic and political discourse: The entire system and its practitioners, like all of modern society itself, have become seriously oblivious to any connection with nature and its limits, or to the realization that human activity is embedded in a larger natural system that has been under deadly assault for centuries. No solutions to the crises today will be possible if the system ignores this most fundamental reality, or is unable to correct it.

- *Propensity to war.* This includes buildup to wars, innovations for wars, rebuilding after wars, and forward basing for defense against future wars. It encourages what some now call "permanent war" and is viewed as a highly effective economic strategy, good for both wealth creation and jobs. Where others see destruction, capital sees opportunity.

- *Intrinsically inequitable.* In every fiber of its structure, from its strictly hierarchical structural forms to its practical performance, the system expresses and expands inequity. The central function of capitalism is to help people with wealth to seek more wealth and greater dominance; the separation between rich and nonrich within countries and among them inevitably becomes steadily greater. We have achieved plutocracy. The Occupy movement's people are on that case.

- *Undermines democracy.* The system has an *intrinsic* need to dominate and undermine democracy, and also public consciousness, so as to control its rules, benefit more easily, and advance its primary self-interest: expanding growth, profit, and wealth. Governments become subordinate, and democracy is destroyed.

- *Capitalism does not bring happiness.* Societies based on a constant quest for external satisfactions, such as wealth advancement, commodity accumulation, competitive advantage—quests for "prosperity and power"—do not tend to achieve overall well-being; quite the opposite. Happiness and well-being are rooted in other values and behaviors.

There is nothing original about these arguments. Many books have been written about each. But when we compile them all together, as the essential ingredients of a larger system, it reveals a picture that is far worse than the sum of its parts. Far more deadly, and also far more fragile. What is exquisitely clear is that the inherent aspects of capitalism, especially when operating on a large scale, make it structurally incompatible with the survival of nature, the well-being of humans and of the society we have tried to build around it.

We should think of the whole system as a kind of technology. Get it rolling, and it does the same things everywhere, over and over, nonstop. Its root drives and behaviors are woven directly into its fabric, aided by a (derivative) ideology that puts its faith squarely on values of never-ending wealth accumulation, laissez-faire governance, the free movement of capital, strict hierarchies, and manipulation of all political contexts that might otherwise seek to control it.

If there was ever a time in prior eras, at earlier stages of economic development, when this kind of system made sense, that time is gone. Now it is doing far more harm than good. In any case, economic permanence is an illusion, as we have seen historically, especially if it is based on never-ending expansion. The Romans could have told us that. It's time for *economic succession*.

Efforts to apply short-term tweaks to this system or its institutions only delay better, more encompassing solutions. This increases the urgency for systemic replacement by more modern, *post-capitalist* economic designs that are no longer oblivious to the limits of the planet.

The good news is that thousands of people and organizations on every continent—from protestors to "new economy" think tanks—are already fully cognizant of these facts and have been working to thrash out alternative ideas that may have a chance to function successfully and far more equitably within the boundaries of nature. So far their ideas are not generally taken seriously by the powers that be or the mass media, who still have their bets on *no change*. But the mood is shifting. Starting with the huge democracy uprisings on many continents and then, in fall 2011, with the bursting forth of the Occupy movement in the United States, there is growing evidence that people will not sit still for what the system has brought us. Even the initial silence of the Occupiers was eloquent, seeming to say, *It's all so corrupt, dangerous, unfair, and unsalvageable, we may not be able to fix it. Maybe we have to start all over. Meanwhile, join us.*

But envisioning more democratic, sustainable systems is really the easiest part. We all have good ideas on what sustainability, fairness, equity, community, and sufficiency are about, and there are literally hundreds of new ideas increasingly on display. We will discuss some of these in Chapter XII. People have begun to see that transformation may not be achievable within the current frameworks. Change is inevitable.

It would surely be useful to prepare ahead for some positive options, if only to forestall a global chaos that might otherwise come. But how do we get from here to there? The chasm is wide. Many of us are trying to see across, but there are no bridges. It may be up to us to build them.

II.

Growing Up Global

I was born in 1936 and raised in a new middle-class suburb in Yonkers, New York, and I lived through all the anxieties of World War II. I watched my worried parents fixed to the radio every evening. Desperate to know the plight of European Jews in particular, they were glued to every word from Walter Winchell, Lowell Thomas, and Edward R. Murrow about all the political and military goings-on.

Both of my parents had come to the United States in the first decade of the 1900s as children, immigrants from Eastern Europe. They understood and deeply feared the madness raging in Europe, and that it might yet engulf us. My father had been medically disqualified from the draft, but every day we worried about his brother, Alex, who was flying bombing missions over the Pacific. We were all proud of him.

Nationwide food rationing had been invoked. My mother, who had never touched soil in her life, joined many of our neighbors who tended their backyards daily to grow vegetables and fruits in very spectacular "liberty gardens." The volume of food those women grew was impressive, and they routinely shared the bounty with each other's families. Meanwhile, my father kept things afloat with a small garment-district business in New York City, manufacturing collar canvas, piping, and waistbands—portions of the interior linings for coats and suits. A substantial part of his business during World War II was subcontracting with manufacturers of military uniforms. We lived a comfortable life, but those were anxious times.

Of course, the world had already been through a terrible series of traumas even before the onset of World War II. Following the nightmares of World War I came the Roaring Twenties, a spurt of capitalist energy and indulgence (much like our 1960s–1980s) that soon burst its bubbles and sank into a terrible, worldwide depression lasting from 1929 through the 1930s. Many historians believe that the extreme right-wing nationalist, militaristic movement in Europe was a reaction to the global economic crises brought by the Depression. This was concurrent with right-wing expansionist zeal in the Far East, leading to a cataclysmic global war on two fronts.

Before World War II broke out, President Roosevelt sought to ease the Depression by increasing government spending on infrastructure, and even the arts, to stimulate the economy. He had notable early success. But when he tried to continue that policy for a few more years, he was stymied by conservative Republicans. When the war came, the Depression did subside, mostly because of massive military spending. Since then, even in the absence of war, military spending has continued to be a familiar economic strategy.

World War II ended in 1945 but that brought only the briefest calm. The world quickly drifted into a new global realignment that split the countries of the world into communist and noncommunist blocs, and produced a dangerous Cold War that would last for nearly a half century. Would these new tensions convert into an even more terrible war—this time against Russia and the communist countries? Those were the days we had weekly air-raid drills to protect ourselves in case of atomic attack. In my Yonkers grade school, P.S. 21, my classmates and I were told to dive under our desks, as if that could have any benefit. Suddenly we learned to hate a new mortal enemy—the Russians, and communism.

This history of trauma was fresh in the minds of global leaders (and populations) midcentury, as they tried to see their way forward. One important positive step was the creation of the United Nations in 1945, which gave hope that future crises could be cooperatively resolved, and I think it has had some success in certain areas since then.

However, more to the point for us today was the second step: the creation of a new global economic experiment, a plan to integrate all national economies of the noncommunist world within a single global megasystem, later called economic globalization.

A New World Order

Some people argued that globalization was nothing new. Global trade had existed since before the voyages of Columbus and was now even more logical, given the evolution of technology, especially transport and communications, advanced by military innovation.

But this globalization was something different: a unified, *centralized* economic vision; a global supersystem with "free market" rules, that would interlock all economies on the planet. In fact, the modern globalization era had a birth date and birthplace: Bretton Woods, New Hampshire, July 1944.

That's when the "free world's" leading economists, scholars, corporations, and governments gathered to outline the new, "permanent," "one world" free-market economy. All countries were meant to accept the same rules, structures, and values—in an all-out push for new mechanisms of growth. This would prevent the world from sliding back into the Great Depression. The conferees thought of themselves as do-gooders enabling global banks and corporations to accelerate the redevelopment of nations that had suffered during the war, and to modernize and develop the poorest nations. They would be helped to rise from poverty, the theory went, by becoming the source of new resources, cheap labor, and expanding markets. Bretton Woods would bring a "rising tide that would lift all boats," stop wars, and launch a new era of permanent global prosperity. Expectations were high, despite the fact that no representatives from communist countries were included at the meetings.

The economic goals of Bretton Woods were aided significantly by the 1948 U.S. Marshall Plan, a $13 billion aid program designed specifically to support European recovery from the war. But the Marshall Plan contained other important, less-noted conditions. These included that a high percentage of spending among European countries would go to an expanded military (which ultimately evolved into NATO in 1949); that European countries would reduce trade barriers in their region and with the United States; and that a high percentage of the money granted to Europe would be used to buy goods and services from U.S. companies. This last condition was an early prototype of future U.S. Agency for International Development (AID) programs to Africa and elsewhere. Development aid was conditioned partly on the necessity to hire American companies to do the work, effectively reducing benefits available to the recipient country. So, instead of its being an unconditional grant to poor countries or to Europe, it served partly as a stimulus plan toward American growth.

Soon after Bretton Woods, new institutions were formed, like the World Bank (at first called the International Bank for Reconstruction and Development) and the International Monetary Fund (IMF), that made enormous inroads into the rights of national sovereignties. These institutions demanded that countries—especially poor ones—abandon their own then-prevalent self-sufficiency strategies and allow global banks and corporations to effectively take over their economies. Part of the plan was to accelerate an evolution toward a future centralized global economic governance. That was the big idea still to come.

Forty years later, the World Trade Organization (WTO) was launched. Renato Ruggiero, president of the WTO in the late 1990s, went so far as to call it "the new world government." Though it tried to fulfill that destiny, by 1999 in Seattle the WTO faced enormous opposition by labor unions and environmentalists, and a newly unified resistance from the world's poor countries. By Seattle, the poor countries "got it"—they had come to understand that globalization was good for rich countries' corporations, but not for them. The WTO never fully recovered after Seattle. By January 4, 2011, Gideon Rachman was proclaiming in the *Financial Times* that even Americans and Europeans "are ill at ease with the 'new world order' that emerged at the end of the Cold War . . . a backlash against globalization is forming—and it is likely to grow in strength."

But in the 1950s, global banks and corporations were considered the best "neutral" arbiters to drive an accelerated development process, even if they profited enormously from those developments. So, with all the ducks nicely in a row—except for that pesky "Cold War" with the communist half of the world— the "free world" leapt forward, to an extravagant, indulgent half-century-long party. With all the new opportunities for economic intervention in the poorest and weakest countries of the world, rapid growth was quickly fueled for the richest countries, which grabbed and gobbled all the local resources they could.

Meanwhile, in the United States, by 1950 the efforts at "recovery"—in both economic and "spiritual" terms (i.e., the confidence to be able to start over)—were well under way. This was the decade in which consumerism was first declared to be equated with patriotism. Television was launched, joined at the hip by an exploding advertising industry—a marriage made in consumerist heaven. Suddenly it was possible to project fast-moving, idealized imagery of the joys of consumption, nonstop, into millions of passive brains, implanting the notion that commodity accumulation was the bottom-line necessity for happiness.

Still, no one was yet anticipating that consumer spending could ever reach the heights it would over the next two decades. No limits were anywhere in view. Only now, sixty years later, do we clearly see the end of the line for a process totally dependent upon infinite resource supplies and rapid economic growth. Today—as author Richard Heinberg puts it in the title of one of his books—*The Party's Over*.

What has not slowed down, despite the resources crises, is another aspect of the "economic miracles" of the 1950s and 1960s—the grand merger between the consumer economy and military economy. In April 1950, in the midst of Cold War fears, the U.S. National Security Council under Paul Nitze announced— and President Truman approved—an overall national economic strategy that, for the first time, officially integrated military goals with national economic goals. That put the United States firmly ahead of all other nations of the world in terms of military spending—a position and a policy that we have never relinquished. In fact, military spending in the United States is by now greater than that of all other countries in the world *combined*. But there remains, even today, little open discussion of the degree to which this policy, launched sixty years earlier, is as much an economic strategy as a defense strategy. But we'll save that discussion for chapter VIII. Let's go back to Yonkers.

From Yonkers to Wharton

The 1950s were my "coming of age" years. I graduated high school in 1954 and headed for the Ivy League. But if the world around me was giving birth to some kind of profound economic transformation, you could never have learned about it from me. I was mainly interested in golf.

It was only pressure from my family that pushed me to the University of Pennsylvania's Wharton School of Finance and Commerce. My interest in academics was zero at that point. I was a mediocre student. My only passion was devoted to being part of the university golf team. In fact, my only real undergraduate achievement was that in my senior year (1958), I was captain of the team, and my "match play" record, 17–1, was best in the Ivy League. But actually, I wasn't even the best player on the team. That honor went to a young sophomore, Don Norberry. He was destined to become a great professional golfer, until his early death a few years later.

It had always been clearly understood in my family that I would eventually go into business. Graduation from a prestigious university was part of the plan. My father, born in Poland, had lived his own coming-of-age years on New York's Lower East Side and had only two years of college at City College of New York, which offered free tuition at that time. My mother, from Romania, had no college at all.

My family was very impressed with the American Dream. By the mid-1930s, my father had built a successful small business against great odds. But despite his modest achievements, he had far bigger aspirations for me. "Never work with your hands" was his considered advice. He enormously admired and respected America's big businesses and deeply hoped I would find a career with a giant corporation, so the Wharton School was the logical place for me.

When I later began a career, I realized that the only truly useful things I learned while at Wharton were how to dress really well—in those days, mainly Brooks Brothers suits and button-down shirts with ties (worn even to class)— how to use business-appropriate jargon, and how to be charming. I could shake hands sincerely and impressively and convincingly convey *pseudogmeinschaft* (false friendship). But let's be clear: My lack of other benefits from Wharton had to do only with me, not with the school. I was just not yet interested in what was on offer.

My next stop was Columbia University's Graduate Business School, where I advanced to become an A–B student and in one year achieved a master's degree in international economics. This allowed me to call myself an "economist," but, as it would turn out, my actual business career was mostly in advertising.

While I was at Columbia in 1959, Fidel Castro achieved his revolutionary victory in Cuba and came to speak at the United Nations, and also at Columbia. Castro was staying in an apartment on 125th Street, in nearby Harlem, where he famously brought hundreds of live chickens and other foods from Cuba in order not to be poisoned by the CIA. That seemed to me *so* paranoid at the time, but it proved prescient. In later years, it was revealed that the CIA was indeed hoping to poison Castro, apparently because he had abruptly ejected from Cuba some U.S. casino owners and big sugar corporations, nationalizing several of their projects. But the U.S. agents couldn't get near his chickens or his cigars. Castro, we were warned, was some kind of socialist or communist, so we were supposed to hate him. Aside from assassination plans, of course, there was that secret planning for the upcoming U.S. invasion fiasco at the Bay of Pigs.

When Castro came over from Harlem to speak at Columbia, more than ten thousand people gathered on the central mall to hear about his revolution and his intentions. I was not among the crowd. I was in a golf tournament at Bethpage, Long Island.

New Dawn for Business

My years at Columbia were not entirely as wasted as they'd been at Wharton. For example, I developed very interesting and useful relations with several prominent professors of international economics, including Émile Benoît— the man credited with launching the term "fourth world"—and, most notably, a remarkable and charming man named John Fayerweather, who turned out to be among the leading intellectual gurus of a newly blossoming economic trend beginning to be known as "corporate globalization"—an idea that was sweeping through the halls of academe and the businesses sector in the 1950s. We learned in class that domestic industries had been transforming themselves increasingly to take advantage of the growing postwar emphasis on globalized activity. Fayerweather achieved a leadership role in advising and training businesses for this transition. He focused on the practical underpinnings that businesses needed to be effective in globalizing their thinking and their activities.

I became Fayerweather's devoted student. He asked me to become the business manager of a new quarterly "digest" magazine that he and his wife started up out of the dining nook of their apartment in Riverdale. They called it *The*

International Executive. To give you an idea of the way things were discussed in those days, here are just a few of the articles we carried during the brief time I was working there in 1959:

- "Labor Problems in the Industrialization of India"
- "Can Capitalism Compete?"
- "How to Maintain Productive Working Relationships with Overseas Managers"
- "What Makes a Russian Manager Tick?"
- "Trade Union Development and Labor Policy in the Philippines"
- "The Communist World as Customer and Competitor"
- "Protectionism or Trade, Not Aid"
- "How Much Bribery?" (A Special Section)
- "The Moslem Rulers and Contractual Obligations"
- "New Americans in Old Societies"
- "The Anthropology of Manners"
- "Worker Control of Industry in Europe"

Fayerweather told us that we were at a new dawn for American business, and that executives needed training in how to move through bumpy foreign terrain and how to deal with foreign governments and cultures and differing ethical standards—for example, alternative standards on practices like bribery, or differing religious concepts, or with the different roles of women, labor conflicts, and cultural restrictions on loan practices and interest rates.

On the other hand, in some places where traditional farming practice or artisanal production remained popular, local populations needed to be "re-educated" to appreciate the greater benefits of large-scale export-oriented industrial production. They had to be taught to accept specialization, mechanization, and monocultures, rather than diverse crops for local and regional markets, in keeping with theories of "comparative advantage." Farmers were told they would do better by giving up their own small farms to become part of giant, multinational, industrial agribusiness enterprises that were destined to take over farming.

Many foreign countries were still clinging to traditional subsistence-agriculture models and the idea that a country's economic priorities should be toward national self-sufficiency in all crucial economic sectors, including food, energy, basic manufacturing, and transportation systems.

But in 1950, for the new breed of global economic planners, national self-sufficiency was not acceptable. The world was headed at top speed in the opposite direction. Far better if farmers could be trained in new modern economic models, where most benefits came from mass production of luxury products for export markets. They could make more money by getting a great job working for a large transnational agricultural company. This sales point for globalization turned out to be fictional. Highly mechanized agricultural production is notably absent of human labor. The transition set off huge migrations from subsistence farms to cities and across borders that are still going on today, causing immigration battles now rampant within many countries.

All of the new global instruments and philosophies of the period shared a central ideology that everything would get better if we moved real economic power away from the control of local communities and economies and away from the petty interests of nation states. National interest needed to be replaced by a universal, centralized, export-oriented model, controlled by multinational banks and corporations.

The pillars of this model, introduced over the next four decades, included: *free trade* (the end of protective tariffs), *increased mobility* for capital and corporations (but not labor) to move freely among nations, *deregulation of corporate activity*, *privatization and commodification* of the natural commons, and liberalization of rules governing *intellectual property rights*—so that natural resources (such as plants with potentially lucrative medicinal properties) could be more easily harvested from indigenous lands, and patented.

New *centralized dispute settlement mechanisms* were introduced, designed to overrule efforts by democratic nations to defend their own labor, environmental, or investment laws that these countries saw as working in their national interest. Hundreds of challenges to "restraints on trade" worked their way through various venues of new global bodies, especially the General Agreement on Tariffs and Trade (GATT), the Agreement on Trade-Related Aspects of Intellectual Property Rights (TRIPS), and the World Trade Organization. These challenges gave rise to: rulings against elements of the U.S. Clean Air Act; rulings against the U.S. Marine Mammal Protection Act; rulings against small Guatemalan banana growers in favor of the U.S. multinational Chiquita; and the overturning of the European Union's efforts to ban the import of U.S. beef injected with synthetic growth hormones.

As recently as September 2011, the WTO ruled against China's attempts to limit its export of "rare earth" minerals. The agency determined that China must keep exporting these materials even though the country's supply may run out within a decade. Any decision by a government to conserve its own resources may have consequences for global industries—in this case, for U.S. high-tech and military industries. *Not allowed*. But China quickly appealed the ruling.

Together these and many other elements advanced a formula that globalizes the kind of free-market principles that had formerly operated mostly domestically.

Global economic integration and homogenization promised to accelerate economic growth all over the planet and bring on that familiar "rising tide that lifts all boats." I heard that phrase every day during the late '50s, especially at Columbia. Fayerweather himself kept repeating that the beneficial instrument to achieve all this would be global corporations. As they grew, the benefits would all "trickle down." I heard that every day, too. The benefits were expected to go on forever.

Under the banner of globalization, countries with cultures, economies, and traditions as varied as India, Sweden, Thailand, Kenya, Indonesia, Bolivia, Brazil, Canada, and a hundred more (excluding the communist world) would soon all enjoy the bounty of the same few global corporations—the same fast-food restaurants, hotel chains, and clothing outlets. They would soon all wear the same kind of jeans and shoes, drive similar cars, watch the same films and TV shows, enjoy the same music, and live in the same kind of urban landscapes. They would rely on the same kind of corporate agriculture and development schemes that had come to dominate the world, *and* they would come to share personal, cultural, and spiritual values similar to those we espouse in the United States—global monoculture! If you have traveled much, you have surely noted the trend. Every place is becoming more and more like every place else. Cultural diversity is going the way of biodiversity. Soon, there will be little reason for tourists to travel anywhere at all.

Such a homogenized model directly serves the efficiency needs of the largest corporations. Acting on a global plain allows them to duplicate their production and marketing efforts and achieve the many efficiencies of scale that go with borderlessness. It's like the standard-gauge railway of earlier times, or, in today's terms, "computer compatability." It was among the primary purposes of the global, regional, and bilateral trade agreements, such as NAFTA, CAFTA, ASEAN, TPP, and others, to make rules that assured no blockages in the flow of commerce.

But the Columbia professors forgot something: We live on a small planet. It has very limited space, land, and resources. You can design an economy that depends on constant expansion, but it won't last forever. During my whole time at Columbia, the subject of long-term ecosystem survival was never raised once. In those early days of globalization, we didn't notice that little point. A half century later, we *are* noticing.

Robert McNamara, Enforcer

The new structures of postwar economic globalization succeeded in engineering not just a conceptual change but also a very real power shift over the latter half of the twentieth century. Economic and political power moved further away from the controls of individual nations, states, local governments, and communities, and toward global corporations, banks, and bureaucracies. But major challenges continued: How to enforce universal conformity? How to overcome sovereign democratic initiatives? How to advance the privatization of the natural commons—water, forests, biodiversity, atmosphere, genetic structures? And how to privatize public services like healthcare, the military, prisons, Social Security, and Medicare?

Sovereign governments were sometimes inclined to resist pressures to conform, and this resistance was slowing down the process of globalization. It remained the explicit job of the Bretton Woods institutions to eliminate "impediments" to the free flow of the system. National laws to protect environment, resources, public services, intellectual property, the natural commons, and the rights of workers became anathemas and were increasingly subject to legal challenge.

This effort to achieve global conformity was particularly heightened during the reign of Robert McNamara as head of the World Bank (1968–1981). Many believe that McNamara actively sought the job at the bank to try to recover his reputation, which had been badly damaged by his disastrous career as defense secretary, running the Vietnam War for John F. Kennedy and Lyndon Johnson. Now, his goal was to do "good." But McNamara arguably did more harm at the helm of the World Bank than he did in Vietnam.

During his tenure, McNamara crisscrossed the world to issue explicit threats against countries that were slow to revamp their economies to conform to the new rules of economic integration. He threatened nonconforming countries with boycotts and exclusion from the global trading system if they didn't change their policies to comply with the bank's strictures. Poor countries were especially vulnerable, as it eventually became very difficult for them to get loans or financial aid from the World Bank or International Monetary Fund without first opening their economies to invasions by global banks and corporations, not to mention the severe austerity agreements they would have to sign.

McNamara's most important targets were countries that tried to retain traditional economic systems that emphasized local or regional self-reliance. Such ideas were extremely subversive to free trade, economic globalization, and corporate expectations of hypergrowth, which all depend upon maximizing economic steps and processes—for example, transport, processing, packaging, retailing, advertising, which all involve separate exchanges, each with the promise of profits. Local and regional production operates on an inherently smaller scale and has far fewer opportunities for "value added" interventions, thus limiting overall growth, especially among global corporations and banks.

Earlier in the 1900s, many countries of the world had only recently emerged from under colonialist yokes. They had been actively trying to do the *opposite* of specialization—to *diversify* their industrial and agricultural systems—

precisely in order to recover from the colonial period, when monocultural systems had been imposed by outsiders, destroying sometimes successful traditional, local agricultural and craft economies. During the 1800s and 1900s, traditional economies—those that featured many very small individual producers, or village-based enterprises—were forcibly replaced by industrialized pineapple, sugar, coffee, and banana plantations, and, in more modern times, fancy flowers for rich northern markets. Native croplands and forests that were not transformed into plantations were often destroyed by mining and oil-drilling operations or cleared to make way for mass industrial production for export.

Agricultural countries understood that specialization in a few export crops made them extremely vulnerable to the shocks and whims of foreign markets, the vagaries of commodity pricing and trading systems, and the repercussions of unexpected political decisions made abroad. It also left them with large swaths of export crops exposed to loss from unpredictable seasonal weather patterns, pests, or disease. Providing food for foreign markets often left traditional farmers unable to take care of their own basic needs and those of their local communities.

The drive toward local self-sufficiency was at the root of the terms "national self-reliance" and "import substitution." These concepts were advocated increasingly by South American countries and by others among the less industrialized nations—not getting rich, but getting along. But since self-reliance is the archenemy of globalized integration, such schemes were labeled with the dreaded accusation of "isolationist" or "protectionist."

For globalized economies, conformity is a life-and-death matter. If local populations or countries can satisfy their own needs internally or regionally, there are far fewer chances for global corporations to intervene and profit. Success in a globalized model requires that economic activity move constantly back and forth across oceans, mining here, producing there, exporting, importing, reworking, then exporting again, with thousands of ships passing each other in the night, while building hundreds of profit steps in the economic chains of events. Each of these steps brings a new level of "value added" to the production process, more and more movement of capital, and greater opportunity for corporate profit. It's such "make work" processes that build global economic growth fastest and provide added opportunities for capital investment and corporate operations.

For example, in the half century since Bretton Woods, the explosion of global trade has produced a twenty-five-fold increase in transport activity worldwide. The Wuppertal Institute of Germany published a famous series of studies during the 1990s on the distance that food travels from source to plate. It reported, for example, that the different ingredients in a typical 150-gram package of strawberry yogurt travel about 1,200 miles from the fields where they are harvested to the factory where they are combined to the stores where they are shipped to be purchased by consumers. Wuppertal found that the strawberries came from Poland, the corn and wheat flour came from Holland, and the jam, sugar beets, and yogurt were sourced from Germany. The yogurt's plastic and paper containers and wrappings came from various other places.

Similarly, the ingredients in the typical plate of food on American dinner tables travel, on average, about 1,500 miles from farm to fork. Of course, every mile of the increased transport activity in the globalized economy has tremendous costs to the environment—costs that remain "externalized" in our current measures of efficiency, i.e., costs to the environment that are subsidized by taxpayers. But every mile, and every step of that transport process, brings added opportunity for "value added," profits, and increased overall economic activity as measured by gross domestic product (GDP).

As global transport increased and the distance from resource base to market expanded, the growing demands of worldwide commerce required grand increases in global infrastructure development: airports, seaports, oilfields, oil and gas pipelines, new rail lines, high-speed highways. This was good for Bechtel and other large contractors. And it was good news for the transport companies that did the shipping and handled the paperwork. But it was bad for the environment. Many of these massive construction projects were built in areas that were rich in biodiversity. Pristine wilderness, untouched forested areas, intact coral reefs, and sustainably managed rural and indigenous areas were disrupted and replaced by concrete, steel, and asphalt.

The damage has been especially tragic in the Amazon, the Andes, and other wilderness regions of South and Central America. Often these intrusive mega-development projects trigger angry resistance from native communities located in the targeted areas. This is particularly the case with indigenous protests against oil, pipeline, and forest development in the "less developed" world, but the problems are also obvious in the developed world. In England, for example, there was a mass series of protests by two hundred thousand people opposed to the rapid development of huge new highways that were being jammed through rural landscapes of the English countryside so that truck drivers could better service the global trading system. The indigenous people of the Amazon Basin and the rural defenders of the English countryside were both protesting the same thing: the destruction of local environments by globalization.

McNamara's pressure mostly worked, producing in the 1960s and 1970s new rounds of invasion by foreign corporations and banks, in search of lands, resources, cheap labor, and new markets. Some of the countries' GDP numbers did improve, except that they mostly reflected gains for a tiny, elite class of millionaires and billionaires who sprang up to run the export businesses and skim the fat off the sale of commodified resources.

But McNamara finally got most countries of the (noncommunist) world to go along. He often bought them off with huge infrastructure loans. As an unannounced outcome, however, many of them found themselves suddenly in far greater debt than ever before, unable to repay IMF or World Bank loans without instituting horrific austerity programs, later evolving into those highly dreaded "structural adjustment" commitments.

The tide, however, has now begun to turn. Some countries, especially in South America, have demanded cancellation of all debt stemming from those times. They have made a sharp course reversal, away from any dealings with the World Bank and IMF, and have begun to reemphasize those old "import substitution" programs. This is most clearly the case in places like Peru, Ecuador, Bolivia, Paraguay, and to some degree Argentina, Brazil, and Venezuela. The new goal has become the old goal: self-sufficiency, as much as possible, certainly in the fundamentals of food, shelter, transport, energy, and security. Local economies have become primary.

Meanwhile (and perhaps predictably), the countries that did *not* go along with McNamara and the World Bank and insisted on retaining most of their self-sufficiency goals all along—Singapore, South Korea, Formosa—actually performed far better, and more stably, than those who submitted to the Western corporate and banking takeovers pushed by globalization.

Forty Years Later

For me, it wasn't until forty years after my college days were over that I began to revisit global economics. My early career path in the 1960s had taken me through an incarnation as a theatrical "press agent" promoting movies, theaters, nightclubs, and Hollywood actors—and then into commercial advertising, as a partner at Freeman, Mander & Gossage. Both of those careers were a lot more glamorous and fun than economics! But it *was* the 1960s, so political and cultural upheaval was everywhere obvious in the San Francisco Bay Area, where I lived. By 1972, my commercial ad work had morphed into full-time political and advocacy advertising, partly because of the influence of David Brower, the great environmental leader of that time and director of the Sierra Club. I worked with him on numerous campaigns. During that time, I also cofounded Public Interest Communications, which evolved into Public Media Center in San Francisco, working for nonprofit activist groups that included Greenpeace, Friends of the Earth, Earth Island Institute, Planned Parenthood, and several antiwar groups.

But it wasn't until the 1990s that everything I had been taught in the 1950s came flooding back into my consciousness, this time during my work for the

Foundation for Deep Ecology and the International Forum on Globalization (IFG). By then, I was seeing globalization through a set of prisms exactly *opposite* from the ones we used during the 1950s post–World War II era at Columbia Graduate Business School. The 1990s saw huge bursts of resistance to globalization. These came from thousands of farmers in Asia and Europe, and from trade unions, small businesses, and environmentalists everywhere. By the time of the 1999 WTO meeting in Seattle, IFG was hosting mass public teach-ins in Seattle's Benaroya Symphony Hall, and 80,000 people were out on the street in opposition to the WTO takeover.

By then it was clear that the benefits of globalized capitalism *don't* trickle down; for the most part, they trickle *up*. The rising tide does *not* lift all boats; it lifts mainly yachts. The purpose of globalization was never to lift the global poor. Instead, it has brought the greatest separation between rich and poor in history, both among and within countries. The purpose of the global corporate experiment was to find, free up, and control new territories, new resources, and new markets in order to sustain high growth rates and accelerating profits. That was and remains the only priority of corporate capitalism. The whole project was based on false advertising, which, over the latter half of the twentieth century, consumed the world, until it started feeding on itself. Despite its promises, globalization wasn't nearly the answer to our social and economic problems. It was the cause of many of them, and it was killing the planet.

The whole hyperactive globalized economic project was in service to an idea, an ideology (a fantasy, actually), that began in a postwar panic but offered a rare (if temporary) opportunity to broaden the impacts and controls of global corporations.

In the 1950s, we thought of globalization as a rational process for global economic improvement, when actually it was only a wild experiment based on an equation that failed to include some of the most important ingredients: the limits of nature, the positive need for equity, and the negative effects of undermining national culture, sovereignty, and democracy.

One might grant the benefit of the doubt to the mid-twentieth-century architects of this global experiment, including my teachers at Columbia. I believe they meant well. They thought that corporate globalizations would produce a kind of rapid exponential growth that would be truly beneficial to all. But in their wisdom, they were wrong. A half century later, it is obvious that to keep arguing that such a system, dedicated to expanding growth in a finite system, can survive much longer amounts to capitalist utopianism.

III.

The Copenhagen Conundrum

At the 2009 United Nations Climate Change Conference in Copenhagen, we witnessed the most tortured dances by governments trying to avoid the conflicting realities of our time, and to circumvent profound conundrums we face as a society. The performance was largely duplicated a year later in Cancún, Mexico, with a similarly pathetic outcome, and then again in Durban in November 2011. Each year, the wealthiest countries continued to blame developing countries for the impasse. At this point, there is still no visible sign of any meaningful breakthrough. In fact, we saw significant backtracking in Durban.

Let's start the three-year story with the struggles of President Obama in Copenhagen, December 2009. Obama has sometimes exhibited what looks to me like a serious understanding of climate change, as the global megaproblem that most spectacularly expresses the limits of nature and that is driven directly by industrial society's overconsumption of energy and material resources. But the President has allowed himself to get caught within a terrible dilemma. When he occasionally expresses the need for lower emissions limits, he simultaneously tries to make moves to somehow revive a weak economy that shows sluggish growth, or no growth, and provides insufficient jobs. He argues for accelerated industrial growth and consumption, particularly in such climate-deadly industries as oil exploration, private automobile manufacture and sales, road construction, coal extraction, nuclear energy, and "new housing starts," among numerous other heavy industrial expressions. He also continues to coddle large private banks and financial institutions, which are supposed to stimulate the rest into action.

Watching from a distance, we really don't know if Obama understands the contradictions in this pattern, how one effort cancels the other, or if he has simply made a "safer" political choice. If so, it is safer only in the very short run, given that the growing global resource crises of the planet are creating unsolvable problems, threatening the viability of industrial-consumer society and capitalism itself. Some enlightened political leadership and transition strategies would be helpful. But, for the moment, the main point is this: In a choice between addressing the stresses of the planet and addressing the stresses of corporate capitalism, the President always chooses the latter.

Of course, he is not alone in this choice. Nearly all domestic politicians, and nearly all governments of the world, exhibit similar conflict and timidity, and did so especially in Copenhagen, in Cancún, and then again, in Durban, a year later. Even those with an apparently true desire to reduce carbon emissions feel that their first priority is to somehow help stimulate economic growth for their own industries, at all costs. Without growth, businesses whither, and so do national economies, and jobs. And yet, as we discuss repeatedly throughout this book, continuous systemic growth is impossible on a finite planet nearing the end of its resource base. It is already largely stymied, putting the entire capitalist project in danger.

Carbon Debt

A lot of blame for the failure of Copenhagen talks in 2009 was directed at the G-77 and China (representing 130 developing countries), for resisting any deal that did not recognize their historic victimization by the G-8 (the wealthiest industrial countries). The G-8 countries have been by far the largest carbon emitters for a century. The poor countries argued that since 80 percent of historic carbon emissions have come from G-8 countries—which comprise only 20 percent of the global population—a "carbon debt" to the poorer countries must be recognized as an important factor in how wealthy countries became rich while poor countries stayed poor.

But two years later, at the United Nations Climate Change Conference in Durban, 2011, the wealthiest countries (led by the United States) refused to budge. They focused ire particularly toward China, which has been categorized as a "developing nation" but, with the largest population, has become the planet's largest aggregate carbon emitter. Rich countries demanded that China agree to reduce emissions at the same rate as the wealthiest G-8 countries. This demand emerged despite the fact that China's *per capita* emissions are only about one-fifth of U.S. *per capita* emissions. And a very high percent of its emissions result from its industrial export work for U.S. companies like Apple and Walmart, among many others. China continued to insist on the carbon-debt formula of the G-77 developing countries.

A contributing factor that was frequently cited as having helped produce the extreme imbalance between countries was the high degree of foreign ownership by the corporations and banks from wealthy countries of the raw materials and energy resources of poorer countries. Now that global economic growth is stunted, perhaps permanently, there were many calls for special measures, including financial and technology transfers, to support countries mired in poverty to at least advance, if not nearly to an equitable level, at least to a formula that allows for their survival. But the representatives of wealthy countries, including Mr. Obama, steadily resisted such a formula, agreeing to some mild mitigation efforts only, unless high-emitting countries, including China, India, Brazil, et al., agreed to equal commitments.

What finally resulted in Durban was a loose, nonbinding agreement to complete some kind of unspecified deal by 2015. No one so far trusts that the negotiation will succeed in identifying and agreeing to a low enough emissions level to prevent catastrophic climate change. Whatever they agree on in 2015 will, in any case, not go into effect until 2020. So the greatest achievement of Durban was really that the talks didn't break down entirely, and nations will show up again next time. It's a very sad story.

Releases of WikiLeaks documents in late 2011 that focused on the climate negotiations confirmed the degree to which wealthy countries tried bribery, sometimes successfully, to get grudging support from poor countries. After Copenhagen, for example, the United States apparently went so far as to inform several countries that had not supported the U.S. position from that meeting that aid to those countries for climate mitigation would be henceforth eliminated, a ham-handed move reminiscent of more explicitly colonial days.

Then, more recently, after Durban, EU climate action commissioner Connie Hedegaard was quoted as saying that the Alliance of Small Island States (some of which might soon go underwater) "could be our best allies, given their need for financing" to avert catastrophe. And according to South Africa scholar Patrick Bond, of the University of KwaZulu-Natal, one of the small island states, the Maldives, a leader in the campaign for low emissions targets, "suddenly reversed course." According to Bond, this was "because of a $50 million aid package arranged by U.S. deputy climate change envoy Jonathan Pershing." This led to a wave of small countries' accepting buyoffs from Washington. One wonders what they will do with the money when the waters rise and they are on a boat going somewhere else.

But the fact remains that no individual country or group of countries was to blame for this tragic failure of climate talks over the last three years. The real deal killer has been the overriding central commitment of nearly all countries to try to stimulate corporate growth *everywhere* and to placate giant global oil companies, while at the same time claiming to seek emissions cuts. That was the impossible burden of Copenhagen and the real dead end. The same problem doomed negotiations in Cancún and Durban.

Nowhere among the assembled nations (with the notable exceptions of

Bolivia and Ecuador) were there expressed any significant national emphases on "conservation"—that is, to actually seek economies of *lower* production and *lower* consumption of energy and materials—and the reshaping of economic systems to live within the realities of a depleted planet; a *postcapitalist* model that could be embedded within the limits of nature and still serve the need for greater equity. Such steps could have directly and dramatically reduced carbon outputs and provided an opportunity for nature to begin to revive. But such moves toward extensive conservation would have required economic transformations that few corporate powers, bankers, or heads of state can accept; they would certainly defy the bases of free-enterprise capitalism.

Governments are left with a profound dilemma. How to solve one problem without exacerbating the other? While some efficiencies and innovations may have beneficial effects around the margins, they can never be sufficient to solve the megaproblem we face. So, we are forced to choose between drastically cutting emissions, thus reducing climate change, and supporting the demands for corporate growth and profit as the primary drivers of our system, its raison d'être, the heart of the capitalist enterprise, thus increasing emissions. Given the inherent needs of that system, it seems impossible to have it both ways.

Cochabamba, Bolivia

In April 2010, six months after the first round of failure in Copenhagen, president Evo Morales of Bolivia convened a *post*-Copenhagen meeting in Cochabamba, Bolivia, gathering some thirty thousand of the Copenhagen protestors, whose viewpoints had been largely ignored. Morales found significant support from other South American countries, all of which are part of the G-77, in attempting to redefine economic strategies to deal with climate change. One of the countries, Ecuador, had for several years been arguing in favor of such concepts as "The Inherent Rights of Nature," which had recently been added as a new article in Ecuador's national constitution. Since then, this movement has gained significant traction, as even the UN General Assembly has recognized the concept, proclaiming April 22 to be International Mother Earth Day.

At Copenhagen, Ecuador had put forth a mitigation strategy for poverty-stricken, though resource-rich, countries—the Ecuadorian Amazon is one of few places in the world still rich in oil reserves—that would incentivize nations to keep their oil, and other scarce resources in the ground, undeveloped. To achieve that, however, would have required compensation from the richest countries toward the "climate debt" of the poor countries, thus making it possible for poor countries to forgo development of their untapped wealth. Thus far, wealthy countries have refused to support that idea.

Meanwhile, Bolivia's President Morales, who is the only head of state from an indigenous heritage in the world, made his own positions clear, first in Copenhagen, and then again at the opening of the giant (April 2009) event in Bolivia: "We have a stark choice between capitalism and survival," he said. "The countries of the world have failed in their obligations. . . . Either capitalism lives or Mother Earth lives."

Morales has proposed three main ideas: (1) Nature should be granted rights that protect ecosystems from annihilation—a Universal Declaration of Mother Earth Rights, with enforcement powers, (2) poor countries should receive compensation for a crisis they are facing but had little part in creating (that concept is called "climate debt"), a position close to that of the G-77 and China, and (3) there should be a continuing "World Referendum on Climate Change," open to all people.

He went on to denounce the system-wide dependency on economic growth and overconsumption for being inherently harmful to the earth, and he advocated a return to the wisdom of indigenous peoples, many of whom have continued to live in a sustainable manner for millennia. He pointed out that more than 50 percent of surviving global biodiversity is now on indigenous lands, and praised the indigenous concept of "living well," or *buenvivir*, rather than "living better" by overusing their resources.

Morales's remarks at Copenhagen and Cochabamba were surely the first such remarks by any national leader in many decades, if ever, and I was eager to learn more of his thinking on the matter. It was not easy to find out. Not one American mainstream newspaper or television report gave any background details or amplification of these remarks; most did not mention them at all. The only exception was Amy Goodman's *Democracy Now*, on the Pacifica Network, reporting directly from Cochabamba, which featured a forty-five-minute interview with Morales.

During it, Goodman included a question about ongoing mining activities in Bolivia—silver, lithium, and natural gas. (Bolivia has the world's largest remaining lithium supply, a crucial ingredient for the manufacture of modern batteries, especially for electronic car batteries and other equipment.) Those lithium mines, operated by giant Japanese multinational corporations, were the subject of highly visible protest activities by many indigenous peoples during Morales's Cochabamba summit.

Morales admitted that he himself is not entirely free from the very same conundrums that face other nations. Bolivia, one of the poorest nations on Earth and one of the most historically exploited, desperately needs export cash, Morales said, though he bemoaned that need. He suggested a commitment to study "the long-term effects to Mother Earth" of these extraction operations, and of the "time it will take us to regenerate the lands" to their natural condition.

He also indicated that the "plurinational state of Bolivia" was changing its relation to such practices. Bolivia would no longer take a backseat role to giant transnational corporations, and would no longer accept the historically feeble royalties of prior times in South America. The country will now demand controlling interest of all such mining operations. "We welcome foreign investment into these projects, and corporations can make some profits, but we retain 60 percent ownership"—a statement, alas, that looks actually to the outsider like a giant step toward something like "state capitalism."

The *Democracy Now* interview offered few further explanations as to Morales's interpretation of the workings of his new semicapitalist approaches, or how Bolivia might balance industrial extraction activity with the opposing desires of the indigenous population, as well as protections for the natural world. Does Morales have a new set of economic structures in mind? Was Bolivia to become a kind of mixed economy, accepting capitalist participation when desirable, but within a state-run socialist framework, à la China? Or does he really have in mind an eventual return to indigenous economic models, and, if so, does that imply a minimum of modern economic development on any meaningful scale? Of course, beginning to address and answer such questions as these was the essential stated mandate of the April meeting in Cochabamba.

In November 2010, the Japanese Oil, Gas and Metals agency and the government of Bolivia announced plans to jointly develop the large deposits of lithium at the Salar de Uyuni salt flat. The Japanese state-owned corporation provided testing equipment and personnel for a pilot plant being built by Corporación Minera de Bolivia, Bolivia's state-owned company. Mitsubishi Corporation and Sumitomo are also making overtures toward the project. (According to the U.S. Geological Survey, Bolivia is home to about 5.4 million metric tons of lithium, enough to make batteries for 4.8 billion electric cars.) Similar deals are being worked out in Chile and Argentina, which together with Bolivia are said to have about half of the world's supply of this crucial mineral, making them "the Saudi Arabia of lithium." However, as we go to press, Bolivia continues to insist that it will be its own state-run enterprise that will run the mining operation in that country.

The Cancún Conundrum

By December 2010, when the next stage of the UN climate process story shifted to Cancun, most heads of state stayed away. Their absence helped enable a dramatic shift toward lowered expectations, and low achievement is exactly what everyone got. Some felt "progress has been made," in the words of May Boeve of 350.org—the most radical of the U.S. mainstream climate groups, headed by Bill McKibben—though Boeve was commenting on a vague new "feeling of momentum" and hope, rather than on anything concrete toward lower-emissions agreements.

"It's tempting to overlook the fact that delegates mostly avoided the real crux of the negotiations," Boeve added. "Exactly how much will countries reduce their planet-heating emissions? The 'pledges' contained in the Cancún negotiating text are still grossly inadequate, leaving the planet on a crash course with at least four degrees Celsius of temperature rise—a terrifying prospect that would put us closer to 750 ppm than 350 ppm. That's very far from where we must be."

According to Victor Menotti of the International Forum on Globalization, "there were *no* real binding 'pledges' but only voluntary targets from national delegations. And the idea of a cap on emissions was specifically blocked and excluded from further discussion by the United States delegation. Everything is now voluntary." That lack of formal commitment continued through Durban.

Bolivia's UN ambassador, Pablo Solón, called Cancún "a step backwards. *Non-binding* commitments to reduce emissions by around 15 percent by 2020," said Solón, "simply cannot stabilize temperature at a level that could sustain human life and the life of the planet."

After Durban, Meena Raman, of the Malaysia-based Third World Network, expressed even greater disappointment: "The mitigation paradigm has changed from one which is legally binding—the Kyoto Protocol, with an aggregate target which is system based, science based—to one which is voluntary, a pledge-and-review system."

Patrick Bond summarized the situation, blogging that "even if the unambitious Copenhagen and Cancun [and now Durban] promises are kept (a big 'if'), the result will be a cataclysmic 4–5%C rise in temperature over this century. And if they are not met, 7 degrees is likely. Even with a rise of only 2 degrees, scientists generally agree," said Bond, "small islands will sink, Andean and Himalayan glaciers will melt, coastal areas such as much of Bangladesh and many port cities will drown, and Africa will dry out—or in some places flood—so much that nine of ten peasants will not survive. The politicians and officials have been warned of this often enough by climate scientists, but are beholden to powerful business interests which are lined up to either promote climate denialism, or to generate nation-versus-nation negotiating blocs destined to fail in their race to gain most emission rights."

Meanwhile, what some called "progress" after three meetings had mainly to do with the advance of a *capitalist-driven* climate process. Whatever "solutions" are instituted, they must somehow add to national growth and corporate profits simultaneously. So, rather than seeking any real emissions cuts, the process is aimed at somehow achieving lower aggregate emissions through a complicated blizzard of schemes that promoted carbon markets, exchanges, offsets, and the like. Moreover, the success of these schemes would remain subject to unknown and possibly variable actual pricing/trading practices—yet another intrusion of Wall Street into markets not meant for their unhelpful participation.

As for the possible deals for new, more "efficient" technologies, these of course were encouraged by G-77 countries and were also being promoted by the new burgeoning "green tech" industries, which see much to be gained in delivering technological conversions.

Some of these proposed "solutions" could sidestep the actual necessity for *any* carbon-producing countries to actually reduce *any* emissions—or try to change their national industrial priorities. They could instead permit the carbon-producing countries to maintain their polluting industries while paying cash (and/or technology) to poor countries and indigenous communities, among others, to protect their forests (carbon sinks) against development.

One could argue such steps bring no gain whatsoever in overall emissions reductions, and thousands of activist groups make that case. Meanwhile, the deadly climate clock keeps ticking. John Vidal, the environmental editor for the *Guardian* (U.K.), put it this way in an interview on *Democracy Now* (December 10, 2010): "All of these talks in the end have nothing really to do with climate change. But they have enormous geopolitical significance. The talks are really about money, about capitalism, about the future of regional blocs and countries' economics over the next twenty, thirty years. That's why so much is at stake. That's why they can't get agreement. That's why the talks could fail."

The Morales Conundrum

The only head of state who did show up to the second UN meeting in Cancún was, yet again, Evo Morales. On December 9, 2010, he addressed a plenary of attending nations and amplified his comments from the previous year:

> We must look at the cause of global warming, which is capitalism. We talk about effects and not causes of the multiple crises we face: the climate crisis, the food crisis, the energy crisis. These are crises of capitalism. If we address these crises, we are being responsible to our sons, grandsons, future generations. If we are responsible, we must change policies. It is an obligation of large powers to pay their ecological debt. But more important is to change the causes of global warming.
>
> Nature is our home; land is our life. I am convinced that human beings can't live without the planet, but yes, the planet can exist without human beings. We are not in the epoch of class struggle anymore; we are debating how to live in harmony with Mother Earth. Mother Earth has rights. In past decades, the UN approved human rights, then civil rights, economic, political rights, and finally, a few years ago, indigenous rights. This new century is

the time to debate and discuss the rights of Mother Earth. These include the rights to regenerate biocapacity, to have a clean life without contamination, the right to equilibrium. If governments don't guarantee this, we are all responsible for ecocide.

We came to Cancún to save nature, forests, Planet Earth, not to convert nature into a commodity. We did not come here to revitalize capitalism with carbon markets. Forests are sacred for indigenous peoples; we can't have policies which merely help capitalism survive.

That's a very thorough and interesting statement. But, back at home, the Morales government has continued to make moves that are sometimes contradictory. Some seem to support the ideas of his public speeches, but others do not. For example, according to a report by Mattia Cabitza in the *Guardian* (U.K.) (June 21, 2011), the Morales government will "invest some $500 million in sustainable policies that guarantee the local self-sufficient production of high quality food, while preserving and respecting the country's immense biodiversity. A key part of the proposals in this 'food revolution' is Bolivia's intention to produce its own seeds." According to the article, Morales's move is designed to reduce Bolivia's dependence on expensive imported food, and to reduce the corporate control of seeds.

Ciro Kopp, an agricultural engineer at the National Council for Food and Nutrition, is quoted as saying, "Bolivia's priority should be to guarantee food sovereignty and security for its people. About 20 to 25 years ago, 70 to 80 percent of what we ate was produced locally in Bolivia," Kopp said, "but then we embraced the agro-industrial model, and now 70 to 80 percent of what we eat comes from the agro-industry, which makes us dependent on technologies and price controls from abroad."

However, the *Guardian* article also quotes Demetrio Pérez, president of Anapo, an association of more than fourteen thousand wheat, soya, and corn producers in the country's fertile eastern plains. He hails the development of local seeds, but his aims seem different than Kopp's. "If we use the latest technology and have a good harvest," said Pérez, "we can convert Bolivia into an exporting country." *Exporting country*? Is that what the government is aiming for?

American author Chellis Glendinning, now living in Cochabamba, has reported on these internal struggles in Bolivia, especially the controversies over the lithium development project, as well as the prospect of very large new hydroelectric dams, "requiring the replacement of rural villages" (*Counterpunch*, December 10, 2010). She also cites a new nine-hundred-mile gas pipeline with Argentina; new iron mines as part of a joint development project with Jindal Corporation of India; new highways running through eco-reserves; vast new telecommunications networks; and, most recently, new uranium mines, bringing at least the possibility of development of nuclear power plants.

Local opposition to such projects, especially from the indigenous communities, has reportedly increased and includes some former indigenous supporters. Among them were Oscar and Marcela Olivera, the brother-sister team who led the successful revolutionary protest movements of the 1990s against water privatization. This movement succeeded in evicting Bechtel Corporation from its control of Bolivia's water and brought Evo Morales to power. According to Glendinning, the question being asked by Marcela Olivera is whether there are two Moraleses, "the one who makes international proclamations about Mother Earth, and the other one at home, who is pushing dams, uranium excavation, cell phone towers, and megadevelopment."

So, has Morales decided on a path of compromise, suggesting that indigenous ways may not yet be sufficiently viable? Or is he heading down a far more familiar national-development path, like most other countries, like Obama, trying to navigate the current crises, and with probably the same grim outcomes? How do these shifts balance with climate change prevention and his devotion to protections for Mother Earth?

In response to previous similarly challenging questions on *Democracy Now*, Morales said this: "Let's be realistic. What is Bolivia going to live on?" Indeed. *That* is certainly at the heart of the central quandaries of our times.

In early September 2011, the quandary blossomed into near catastrophe. Morales okayed construction of a new highway to run directly through the TIPNIS nature preserve, which is the ancestral homeland of fifty thousand natives from three different Amazonian groups, who've lived there for centuries. Morales said the highway was needed for "development," and for creating new economic opportunities in parts of the country that had been long isolated. In approving this project, he was violating a promise he made to the indigenous people concerning prior approval of all projects affecting them.

In a detailed report by human rights watchdog group the Democracy Center, in Cochabamba, director Jim Shultz pointed out that in the name of goals of development, "Morales was willing to ignore the requirements of community consultation and autonomy in the new Bolivian Constitution that he had once championed." Schultz went on to say that Morales "was willing to abandon his own rhetoric to the world about protecting Mother Earth and to ignore studies about the likely destruction of the forest that the new highway would bring. What could have been a moment of authentic and valuable debate in Bolivia about what kind of development the nation really wanted instead became a series of presidential declarations and decrees."

When indigenous groups protested and tried to block the project, they were beaten fiercely by police. These actions came under immediate fire from UN officials and human rights groups. Bolivian defense minister Cecilia Chacon announced she was resigning in protest. In her letter to Morales, Chacon said, "I do not agree with the intervention in the march, and I cannot justify the measure [police action] when other alternatives exist."

Morales attempted to defuse tensions by announcing a referendum on the road project. But indigenous groups began a hunger strike anyway, to protest the "outrage carried out by the government, using police to repress a peaceful march." Meanwhile, Quechua Indians in Cochabamba joined the TIPNIS groups in another hunger strike to support the protestors. Spokesman Reynaldo Flores told Bolivian television, "We are ashamed at what is happening in our country."

On October 21, 2011, Morales reversed course, announcing the road would not go through the TIPNIS national park, or through indigenous territory. This was a dramatic change. Indigenous leaders welcomed the news and said they would speak further with the president and wait for the change to be officially approved by the Plurinational Assembly, considered likely.

There are expected to be further discussions relating to the indigenous peoples' rights to prior consultation, previously promised by Morales, before any development projects could take place in indigenous territories. Meanwhile, Morales said the issue is now resolved and that he is obeying the people.

So, what to make of this? Morales is starting to look a lot like Obama, but let's be fair. He *has* made seriously contradictory moves, of which the dumbest is probably the TIPNIS road project, which violated specific agreements with his people.

But as far as I can tell, he is still the only president of any country in the world who is actually *naming* the global dilemmas clearly and attempting to honestly struggle with the economic, environmental, climate, and resource situations the whole world faces, and the political transformations that are required, while still keeping the boat afloat. The rest of the world's leaders, including Obama and every other G-8 leader, are trying to make believe that there isn't any conundrum at all.

Morales isn't perfect, but he, and the people in Bolivia, are struggling with the right questions. Which way out? Which way forward? How will Bolivia live? Where is sustainability? How will we all live? Should we "develop" further or not? Can capitalism be entrusted with *any* useful role? That's what they are talking about, and that's what we all need to talk about.

PART TWO

The Fatal Flaws of Capitalism

IV.

Intrinsic Amorality &
Corporate Schizophrenia

In the popular movie *Avatar*, directed by James Cameron, a gigantic mining corporation travels to a fictional distant planet where the valuable mineral "unobtanium" has been discovered in large supply. Alas, however, the mineral is located on the traditional lands of the Na'vi people, who live in a magnificent, wild, ancient forest. The corporate armada arrives in spaceships and includes immense military forces, fully equipped to invade and overpower these innocent and remarkable people if they don't agree to move off their lands and yield control of their resources to the corporation.

In the real world today, this scenario is entirely routine and has been played out literally thousands of times on every continent, without big Hollywood movies to illuminate the struggles.

In *Avatar*, the top corporate official on the expedition, a Mr. Selfridge, sends his high-tech private army down from the spaceships to demand that the indigenous people abandon their lands so the corporation can mine them. But the Na'vi make a decision very much like that of thousands of real indigenous peoples on Planet Earth over the last five centuries, and with similar consequences. They will *not* move, even if met with military invasion.

The film then focuses on Selfridge, in his gigantic spaceship headquarters, as he struggles with a monumental choice. Should he unleash his powerful military to kill the people and seize their glorious lands and untapped minerals? Or should he just give up the corporate purpose and go home, leaving the Na'vi and their lands in peace? He is shown in an internal struggle about what to do, whether to act like a human being—with empathy and compassion for these innocent people, and an instinct to do the right thing—or to drop all that empathy and serve the corporate purpose. We have lately come to call this internal executive struggle, a very common one, "corporate schizophrenia."

"Killing the indigenous people will look bad," Selfridge finally says, "but there's one thing shareholders hate more than bad press, and that's a bad quarterly statement." His decision becomes obvious. His personal doubts don't matter. His job is clear. He unleashes the bloody invasion. Corporate purpose trumps human feeling.

In the movie, unlike many similar cases on Earth, the invasion actually does not succeed. This is largely because of the heroic efforts of an individual white turncoat soldier, who was originally sent to influence the Na'vi to surrender. Instead, he falls in love with a Na'vi woman and changes sides. He becomes the brave leader of the native resistance, just as happens in dozens of other Hollywood films, like *Dances with Wolves*, in which a U.S. cavalry officer (played by Kevin Costner) joins the Sioux and leads them into battle. It's a kind of "white messiah" thing in Hollywood films, a highly favored, very unfortunate contrivance meant to attract mainstream audiences and increase the chance for commercial success.

Nonetheless, James Cameron is exquisitely correct with important and original points in this film, particularly on the nature of corporations: *They have split personalities*. Human beings are employed by corporations and usually carry inside themselves some feelings of sympathy, empathy, compassion, regret, loyalty, neighborliness, guilt, and so on. Mr. Selfridge shows some of that.

But then there is the corporation itself, which has no feelings at all, about anything. It is just a legal entity, an idea, a collection of papers in a file drawer someplace, despite that U.S. courts have lately gifted them with legal "personhood." A corporation has no morality, no altruism. Its only actual purpose, built into its operating rules, is to expand its wealth, and then to do it again. And so there is often a serious split between what the human being feels and the expressions of corporate intention and purpose. *Corporate schizophrenia*.

One of the greatest industrial accidents in history happened in Bhopal, India, in 1986. Union Carbide Corporation released chemicals into the wider environment, injuring at least two hundred thousand people—some estimate as many as half a million—and killing upwards of three thousand people.

Soon after the accident, the chairman of the board of Union Carbide, Warren M. Anderson, expressed great personal upset at what happened and tearfully informed the media that he would spend the rest of his life attempting to correct the problems his company had caused. But less than a year later, Mr. Anderson was quoted in *BusinessWeek* as saying that he had "overreacted" and was now prepared to lead the company in a legal fight against paying any damages and reparations. What happened?

Very simply, Mr. Anderson at first reacted as a human being, with feelings of sorrow, compassion, and guilt. Later, he realized (and was surely pressed to realize by corporate attorneys and board members) that his reaction was inappropriate for a chairman of the board of a company whose primary obligations are not to the poor victims of Bhopal, but to shareholders—that is, to its profit picture and stock value. If Anderson had persisted in expressing his personal feelings or acknowledging the company's culpability, he certainly would have been fired.

After more than twenty years, and a vast number of legal actions back and forth among the victims, the corporation, and the Indian government, the case has still not been settled. Mr. Anderson has retired and steadily refuses to return to India to face charges in local courts. Union Carbide has paid out some $40 million to help parties injured in the disaster, but that is considered a pittance by local peoples. The company has been bought by Dow Chemical, which also refuses to respond further. The stock is doing well.

When the *Exxon Valdez* crashed into a reef in 1989 and spilled its oil into the sea and onto the beaches of Alaska, corporate officials at first reacted with apologies and promised to make amends: clean the water, clean the beaches, save the animals, pay for damages. I was surprised at the company's thoughtful stance. It ran directly counter to the way in which corporations usually react. Perhaps in this case the cause and effect were simply indisputable, unlike cases of birth malformations from herbicide spraying or injury to workers in uranium mines, where cause and effect are separated by many years. On the other hand, maybe certain top executives at Exxon *were* truly horrified and felt moved to make things right. But, like Union Carbide's Anderson, they soon came to their senses. The cleanup turned out to be very expensive. Within six months, the company ceased all of its efforts to allay the effects of the spill. In a typical corporate cost-benefit approach, it was reasoned that fighting the lawsuits and making settlements that courts or negotiators might require would be cheaper than cleaning the mess.

These examples from Union Carbide and Exxon are only two of hundreds or thousands that could be cited here: Cigarette companies deliberately mislead buyers about their health effects; pesticide companies do, too; as do asbestos companies, mining companies, and, of course, BP, which made every effort to minimize the effects of its oil spill disaster in the Gulf of Mexico in 2011.

Do you remember the infamous case of the Ford Pinto of the 1980s? That was when Lee Iacocca had become the charismatic chairman of the company and really wanted to show that American companies could take leadership in the growing transition to smaller, lighter, more stripped-down cars that might compete with Japanese imports. The Pinto, however, had a problem. Its gas tank was so poorly designed and placed that it had a tendency to explode in even minor collisions. Such explosions had taken the lives of several owners.

In the legal proceedings following the accidents, Ford was forced to reveal internal memos focused on "cost-benefit analyses." How much would it cost to redesign the car, compared with how many lawsuits the company might have to fight from catastrophic accidents, and at what cost? It was apparently determined that overall, it would be less expensive for the company to allow some cars to explode, and then fight the cases in court, than to have to go back to the drawing board to redesign and retool production. According to the reporter who broke the original story, Mark Dowie, who was then the editor/publisher of *Mother Jones* magazine, such practices are routine in the auto industry and presumably in most heavy industrial contexts—from heavy production to shipping, transport, and mining. Not to mention banking.

The "cost-benefit" approach certainly applied in some form during the 2008 financial crisis. When the crisis exploded, companies like Bank of America, Citigroup, Goldman Sachs, Merrill Lynch, JPMorgan Chase, and Morgan Stanley were all publicly exposed as major contributors to the financial meltdown—first through their relentless lobbying for the deregulation of highly risky maneuvers, then by going on a spree of irresponsible promotion of a variety of financial instruments whose value collapsed, causing millions of Americans to go bankrupt and/or lose their homes. And yet, remarkably, each of these six companies, themselves on the brink of collapse from their shoddy behavior, was offered and accepted U.S. government bailout funds from the Troubled Asset Relief Program (TARP), ranging from $10 billion to $45 billion (the latter amount went to Bank of America and Citigroup), to prevent them from failing. All six were among the "too big to fail" group.

Wouldn't you assume that there would be some degree of shame, guilt, or humility emanating from the top leadership of these companies? Unbelievably, the opposite seems to have been the case. The facts of their irresponsible performance didn't stop the top management of these companies from actually awarding *bonuses* of at least $1 million to each of about five thousand employees. Ten percent of the bonuses were over $10 million each. (This is in addition to very high annual salaries.) Citigroup alone paid out more than $5.3 billion in executive bonuses; members of its Senior Leadership Committee—who brainstormed the entire financial plan of 2008—each got $126 million for their performance.

So, here's the first question: What kind of people are these? Are they different from the rest of us? How do they justify to themselves this astounding public rip-off? Or would anyone put into these positions have done the same thing? Do the needs of the structure overpower all personal choice?

Second question: Within these companies, did anyone ever ask, "Is it really right to take $150 billion in government handouts and then distribute much of it to the people who caused the problem in the first place?" Do you think anyone raised this question? We don't know, but perhaps they had some internal discussion along the lines of "We would be devastated financially without the government money—actually, we would fail—so let's take the money."

Finally, they accepted, made no reductions in salaries or bonuses, and continued to lobby for the laissez-faire government rules that permitted these actions. Most of them are still engaging in the same kinds of financial behavior as they did before and seem to feel chipper about it.

Only rarely does the public ever learn about the behavior of specific individuals within such companies as we've named. Some employees may have held deep concerns about their own corporation's behavior, but had to just shut up about it. In his book *Deadly Spin*, Wendell Potter offers a firsthand report of this kind of internal dichotomy within a company. Potter was a top public relations executive of WellPoint, the medical insurance giant. His book is filled with details of how his job was to help lead the health insurance industry in its campaigns to block President Obama's health plan, using deliberately false claims and accusations, including the infamous "death panels" charge.

"Health insurance companies have used their enormous size to engage in anti-competitive behavior, rig the system to impose unaffordable premium increases, and deliver massive and growing profits for themselves and their shareholders," Potter wrote. "As premiums have skyrocketed, insurers have cut benefits, and shed millions of enrollees who can't afford insurance. Americans have been left to pay more, while getting less and less. For those without enough money for private insurance, and not eligible for government sponsored coverage, there are now only two options: buy coverage that burdens them with soaring out of pocket costs, or go naked."

Potter quotes WellPoint's CEP, Angela Braly, who promised that in the future "'we will not sacrifice profitability for membership.'"

"By necessity and by law," wrote Potter, "the top priority of the officers of these companies is to 'enhance shareholder value.' When that's your top priority, you are motivated more by obligation to meet Wall Street's relentless profit expectations than by obligation to meet the medical needs of your policyholders."

Potter, who is a religious man, tried to reverse these policies, to no avail. He finally quit WellPoint in disgust and wrote his book on the immoral behavior of the company and the health insurance industry, and their fixed focus on profits before health.

Which brings us back to James Cameron. Possibly persuaded by the sentiments of his own film, and certainly persuaded by the plight of thousands of indigenous peoples in the Amazon, Cameron accepted an invitation in August 2010 from the highly effective activist organization Amazon Watch to join the battle against the horrific Belo Monte Dam on the Xingu River in the eastern Amazon. The circumstances are eerily similar to those faced by the fictional Na'vi in *Avatar*, and are typical of many crises around the world.

The Brazilian government and its power authorities, as well as some of the leading international mineral companies working in South America, have been pushing hard to complete work on the dam, which would be the third largest in the world, just smaller than China's Three Gorges project and Egypt's Aswan Dam.

It would dramatically divert 80 percent of the river's flows, creating drought and desert where there was formerly forest. This will all be in the interest of powering new exploration for bauxite (aluminum), copper, nickel, and iron. The mining would be followed by large-scale industrial smelting, logging, and infrastructure development, including the construction of two huge canals, fifty miles long and 1,500 feet wide. The canals will unearth more land than was removed in building the Panama Canal.

According to Amazon Watch, Belo Monte's two reservoirs and canals will flood a total of 400 miles, of which 250 miles is standing forest. All of this activity will bring massive pollution of thousands of square miles of the Amazon basin, including many of the remaining indigenous homelands. It is likely also to bring into the region more than one hundred thousand migrants—though the estimate is that only two thousand or so will get permanent jobs in these projects. Those remaining jobless will likely attempt cattle ranching and illegal logging, further decimating the forests and ecological balance of the region. Megaprojects such as this also typically bring to indigenous communities disease, loss of food and clean-water sources, cultural disintegration, and human rights abuses by illegal loggers, migrant workers, and land speculators.

When Cameron accompanied Amazon Watch into the Paquiçamba and Arara territories of the Juruna and Arara peoples, he brought along two of the stars of *Avatar*, Sigourney Weaver and Joel David Moore. Because of Cameron's celebrity status, he was able to arrange high-level meetings with government and corporate officials, and made use of regional media to appeal to the public to try to help prevent this activity.

So. Should we credit Cameron as the white messiah of the Amazon? Not unlike white messiahs of the movies, he surely managed to stir up considerable new resistance, including formal opposition to the dam from the human rights commission of the Organization of American States. But while it postponed the final decision for more than a year, on June 1, 2011, Brazil's environmental regulatory agency, IBAMA, ultimately approved construction of the Belo Monte dam and an eleven-thousand-megawatt power station to be built along the Xingu River. Xingu tributaries will see reduced water flow, possibly making the river unnavigable and killing off a variety of species of fish and other organisms. Vast areas of virgin forest will be flooded, forcing the removal of at least twenty thousand indigenous people who have lived there for centuries.

Is Greed Good?

A fundamental tenet of the popular ideology of capitalism is that its benefits emerge from its freedoms. It must be left uncontrolled and unregulated, leaving the "invisible hand" of the marketplace to make corrections to suit the needs of the wider society. By this view, it is the very self-interest of the corporations, managers, and owners that ultimately serves the social good. As personal and institutional wealth is permitted to grow freely at the upper levels, it is reinvested in other capitalist enterprise that fulfills human desires and promises that "rising tide that lifts all boats." As profits and growth expand, benefits "trickle down" to all levels of the broader economy. This idea is fundamental to capitalist rhetoric. As Gordon Gekko puts it in Oliver Stone's *Wall Street*: "Greed is good. Greed is right. Greed works. Greed clarifies, cuts through, and captures the essence of the evolutionary spirit."

In other words, no restrictions of any kind should inhibit corporate actions in the marketplace, no matter how potentially devastating to nature or cruel to communities. In the end they are all for the best. The grand quest for personal and/or corporate wealth and economic expansion ultimately benefits everyone by this logic, because as wealth expands its reach and production, jobs and other opportunities are created for many more people. We especially hear this from the Tea Partiers, from the Libertarians, and lately from the mainstream of the Republican Party.

The words of the celebrated eighteenth-century philosopher Adam Smith, often thought of as a kind of godfather of capitalism, are frequently quoted to justify this laissez-faire attitude: "By pursuing his self-interest, [the individual] frequently promotes that of the society more effectually than when he intends to promote it." And in another famous quote, from *Wealth of Nations*, he writes, "It is not from the benevolence of the butcher, the brewer, or the baker that we expect our dinner, but from their regard to their own self-interest. We address ourselves, not to their humanity but to their self-love, never talk to them of our own necessities but of their advantages."

While those two quotes are extremely popular and often repeated, Smith was actually not quite as ardent a free-market capitalism advocate as he has been made out to be. He also argued variously against formation of monopolies and the achievement of excessive financial scale and power. He was against many harmful business practices in the pursuit of profits, and he favored local regulation of business activity, including the export of local resources. He recognized that the size and reach of the enterprise changed its character. In the twenty-first century, we are not talking about butchers and bakers anymore.

Many students of Smith now believe he would have been fiercely opposed to modern economic globalization, as he repeatedly advocated for the greater virtues of smaller-scale enterprises and opposed many forms of corporate and/or capital mobility across borders. He was especially outspoken on the injustices committed against native peoples of the world, who, said Smith, had greeted the first outside resource hunters with "every mark of kindness and hospitality." Nonetheless, the expansionist invaders proceeded to "commit with impunity every sort of injustice in those remote countries."

In a lengthy review of several books about and by Smith in the *New Yorker* (October 18, 2010), Adam Gopnik argued that Smith did not have an unbounded faith in the free market; in fact, Smith distrusted many aspects of it. "He believed that producers tend to band together in order to control prices and eliminate competition, and that historically most of their activity—apprenticeships, guilds, tariffs—had been designed to help them do this. The urge to fair dealing that makes markets happen is always met by the urge to unfair dealing that distorts them.... The laissez faire economy, truly left alone, becomes a conspiracy of producers against consumers, of sellers against buyers." In *The Wealth of Nations*, Smith argued that:

> The interest of manufacturers and merchants is always in some respects different from, and even opposite to, that of the public. To widen the market and to narrow the competition is always the interest of the dealers . . . and can serve only to enable the dealers, by raising their profits above what they naturally would be, to levy, for their own benefit, an absurd tax upon the rest of their fellow-citizens. The proposal of any new law or regulation of commerce which comes from this order ought always be listened to with great precaution, and . . . with the most suspicious attention.

Gopnik goes on to say that "Smith does not think that 'government is the problem,' he thinks that the producers' compact against the consumers is the problem, and that the producers, because they are concentrated and rich, are usually able to make the government take their side. [According to Smith] it is the proper function of the state to prevent the dealers from ganging up on the customers: For Smith, the market moves toward monopoly; it is the job of the philosopher to define, and of the sovereign state to restore, free play."

So Smith was actually a supporter of many of those government regulations of industry that drive the right wing mad. Gopnik continues:

Smith was a firm believer in public goods; he thought that the state has an obligation to build roads and bridges, establish an army, and do all the other things necessary for a sane polity in which the market can function naturally. It would be good, he thought, if these things could be paid for directly, by way of taxes and tolls by the people using them. But when this is neither practical nor desirable, everyone should pay for them, and the rich should pay more than others. 'The rich should contribute to the public expense, not only in proportion to their revenue, but something more than in that proportion,' Smith writes.

In other words, tax the rich *more* than everyone else, not less, as the Republicans argue. "He believed in free markets," says Gopnik; "he just thought that you needed the oversight of the sovereign to make them free."

Ayn Rand, on the other hand, the famous author of *Atlas Shrugged, The Fountainhead*, and *We the Living*, is currently the other most frequently cited guru of free-market magic. She was far less equivocal than Smith and had a vast following among the leading conservative voices in the United States, even the likes of the former chairman of the Federal Reserve, Alan Greenspan, who became her close friend in her later years. Rand argued that individual actors—personal or corporate—should be *entirely* free to pursue higher visions, rather than suffer the inhibitions of social or environmental values invented by lesser, smaller-minded people. Rand was the ultimate advocate for the freedoms of great individuals (and corporations) who expressed "the morality of rational self-interest." Through her great hero John Galt in *Atlas Shrugged*, she said, "the man at the top of the pyramid contributes most to those below him, but gets nothing except his material payment. . . . The man at the bottom who, left to himself, would starve in his hopeless ineptitude, contributes nothing to those above him, but receives the bonus of all their brains." Can we hear current voices in these exclamations?

In an earlier iteration of her philosophy, *We the Living* (1936), Rand put things even more directly. According to *Essays on Ayn Rand's We the Living* (Lexington Books, 2004), editor and Ayn Rand scholar Robert Mayhew, of Seton Hall University, quotes a discussion between two main characters as to whether or not it's okay to sacrifice millions of lives for the sake of "the best people." In the original edition, Rand's main hero argues this way:

> You can! You must. When those few are the best. Deny the best its right to the top—and you have no best left. What are your masses but mud to be ground under foot, fuel to be burned for those who deserve it? What is the people but millions of puny, shriveled, helpless souls that have no thoughts of their own, no dreams of their own, no will of their own, who eat and sleep and chew

helplessly the words others put into their mildewed brains? And for those you would sacrifice the few who know life, who are life? I loathe your ideals because I know no worse injustice than justice for all. Because men are not born equal and I don't see why one should want to make them equal. And because I loathe most of them.

Rand steadily argued for a kind of rational egoism (rational self-interest), as the only abiding moral principle. Man "must exist for his own sake." She advocated the ultimate in laissez-faire capitalism as the only truly moral economic and social system, a viewpoint now widely shared in the United States, particularly among corporate players and the new right wing.

I thought about those statements—and more recent ones from Rand Paul, Paul Ryan, Michele Bachmann, Rick Perry, and Eric Cantor, as well as Greenspan and others, who have incorporated that line of thinking. They tend to apply it in their opposition to government and its agencies, from Social Security to the Environmental Protection Agency to the Department of Education to the Medicare system, all of which they see as serving the undeserving, the non-achievers, and the opponents of corporate freedoms. I especially recalled them when Don Blankenship, the CEO of Massey Mining—the West Virginia surface coal mining company, with a horrific record of environmental and safety violations—addressed the National Press Club in July 2010, three months after twenty-nine Massey workers had died in one of the worst mining accidents in history.

Speaking on the need to increase surface coal mining, Blankenship explained that it is a risky business but that, after all, some eighty million people in the United States depended on the cheap energy it produces. A few accidents are part of the normal equation. He added that "the anti-CO_2 environmental movement is now a big business and is competing with other big businesses," (such as coal and oil companies) and that "green jobs are trumping American jobs," meaning, I suppose, that American jobs should *not* be green?

Blankenship went on to say, "Corporate business is what built America, in my opinion, and we need to let it thrive by, in a sense, leaving it alone." In other words, do you want cheap energy, or do you want worker safety? That is one man who apparently is free of any internal conflicts about great corporate purpose versus the innate values of ordinary human beings. Nonetheless, federal investigations of the disaster finally moved Blankenship to resign his chairmanship in November 2010.

Everyday Life in Advertising

During the 1960s, I was president of an advertising agency in San Francisco: Freeman, Mander & Gossage. It wasn't even one bit like *Mad Men*. My partner in the agency was the great advertising genius Howard Gossage, who nonetheless hated the business and would often say so publicly. He loved to quote his friend James Webb, who said he quit his advertising company because "I woke up one day and realized I didn't give a damn whether we sold more Cream of Wheat than they sold Quaker Oats."

It was also a time of growing environmental awareness and activism. Our agency was especially lucky to have a paid contract with the great environmental leader David Brower, of the Sierra Club. He asked us to help him create an emergency national ad campaign to try and save the Grand Canyon from being destroyed by a series of very large dams that would have submerged the ancient canyons within lakes deeper than the Statue of Liberty is tall. The developers argued that this would benefit tourists in powerboats, who could get a closer view of the glorious canyon walls. One of our newspaper ad headlines was: "Should We Also Flood the Sistine Chapel So Tourists Can Get Nearer the Ceiling?"

That ad also featured a chart developed by Robert Freeman, a very thin line that wound its way back and forth many times across the bottom of the page and that represented the history of Planet Earth, with markers where significant historical moments occurred: the birth of the Grand Canyon, the emergence of fishes and reptiles, the age of the dinosaurs, the first humans. If extended, the line might have been thirty feet long. The presence of humans accounted for only an inch or so. The industrial age was only a tiny fraction of an inch. The goal was to illustrate the level of human hubris expressed by our current activities.

The ad series was very successful and achieved a great victory. It produced tens of thousands of responses to the Department of Interior—no easy matter in pre-Internet days, when people had to cut out coupons, fill them out, and mail them. Plans for the dams were withdrawn and have never been reintroduced. The Sierra Club membership grew by tenfold, and, some, including then–secretary of the interior Stewart Udall, said that the ads were instrumental in launching the modern environmental movement. But that's just the first part of this story.

The second part involves a different client, Rover and Land Rover, North American division. The top executives of that company were wonderful people, highly engaged, for example, in environmental matters. They were active members of their local Sierra Club and worked to keep their community in Westchester County in good condition.

With all that as background, I permitted myself to be interviewed by a *Wall Street Journal* reporter, Henry Weinstein, who wanted to know more about the successful Grand Canyon ads that had caused such a political sensation. And he also wanted to ask me whether, given my apparent dedication to the environment, I had any misgivings about doing commercial work, particularly promoting cars. I felt I had to admit that I did feel qualms, and a bit of schizophrenia about it. Because of that, I told Weinstein, we had recently proposed to our clients at Rover and Land Rover a new kind of corporate campaign, advocating an end to the then popular "annual style change" for cars, certainly a wasteful expression of planned obsolescence. We also proposed a second campaign, on "computer commuting," suggesting that people should use their cars less and engage in computer-arranged carpools instead of commuting by themselves. This would save fuel, which was already showing signs of scarcity, and it might be fun for the participants. We had shown the new campaign ideas to our clients at Rover. However, they had responded negatively. While they agreed with the sentiment of the proposed campaign, they said the ads were "too far ahead of their time." Anyway, they added, they were in business to sell more cars, not fewer, and their shareholders would be very unhappy to see such ads.

The *Journal* published the interview with me the next day on page 1, including the bit about the Rover discussions. By noon that same day, we received a Western Union telegram firing us, cc'd to the newspaper. The day after that, the *Journal* ran a follow-up story with the headline "Ad Man Need Worry No More About Auto Account."

It all turned out okay. Soon after that incident, I gave in to inevitability and decided to quit commercial advertising. I began working with retired commercial ad executive King Harris, plus *Ramparts* magazine art director Dugald Stermer, as well as San Francisco dress designer Alvin Duskin, toward establishing a nonprofit ad company that would work only for other nonprofits— environmental groups, anti-war groups, women's rights groups. Our new operation, Public Interest Communications, was the first such agency, as far as we know, in the world. By the late 1970s, it had morphed into Public Media Center, led brilliantly at that point by Herb Chao Gunther, and continued doing this work until early 2010, when nonprofit funding finally collapsed in the midst of the economic crisis.

About thirty years later, in the mid-1990s, I was invited onto the board of directors of a popular high-end-sportswear manufacturing company. This was and still is a *privately* held company. The stock ownership was in the hands of only five people, the top executives of the company, and was not sold through stock exchanges. That is an important distinction from publicly held companies, because all accountability remained with the five owners, and there was no intrinsic need, as is otherwise the case with publicly traded companies, to try and please thousands of outsiders, stockholders and bankers, and other investors. It gave these few top executives full authority to make decisions, according to their own values and tastes, not necessarily profit—even decisions that might have proven unpopular among stockholders if they had not been not as profitable. They were free from the absolute imperative to grow, grow, grow to satisfy stockholders.

I liked these people very much, and I am still close to several of them. They are avid environmentalists and do great service in many important campaigns, even involving their personal and company resources. The board work was fun, too, and I learned more about the ways decisions are made. Fortunately, I was present when the owner/executives asked the board to okay an immensely important new policy: The company would become the first in the United States to use only organic cotton in all of its sportswear, which would, however, negatively affect costs and profits for at least several years. But, they said, it was the "right thing" to do.

As part of the decision, the company accountants did a full calculation of the changes in costs and profits. The one figure that really stood out for me was that at the end of the year, the net profits of the company would be sharply down. This meant that the five individual shareholders would each experience a personal income loss of (roughly) $5 million by the end of the year. But they decided to do it anyway, defying traditional "corporate purpose." In effect, they each made a personal donation of $5 million to make this innovative, environmentally beneficial move.

The decision to go for 100 percent organic cotton sent a shock wave through the apparel industry, causing other companies to line up with the same policies, which by now have become standard practice. I was very proud of the company for making such an exceptional action, in effect challenging the whole industry to follow suit and to change the business paradigm. Remarkable. But, in another case, I was not so happy.

About a year after the organic-cotton decision, the board was informed that company management was considering moving some of its production operations to China. This would save enormous amounts of production money, due mainly to lower wages and processing costs, thus increasing profitability. The board was asked to vote on the matter. During that period I was already extremely active in the anti-globalization movement and was director of the International Forum on Globalization. I went to great lengths to present the downside of such a decision for the environment—tremendous added use of transoceanic shipping, for example—as well as for American workers. I said it would set a grim example that other companies would emulate. When the vote came, it was unanimous in favor, except for two of us who abstained. I felt I could not vote against my friends, even on principle. But then I resigned from the board, a victim of my own corporate schizophrenia.

For me, the most disturbing contact with corporate schizophrenia occurred in the personal context of a family event during the late 1960s. At the time, I was involved in writing a series of advertisements intended to retard the "Manhatta-nization" of San Francisco. The whole tendency was being aggressively pushed by the vehemently pro-growth then-mayor, Joseph Alioto. He argued loudly that he dreamed of the day when the San Francisco skyline—at that point still characterized by a Mediterranean panorama of rolling hills and small pastel houses, with very few buildings over twenty stories—would instead become just like New York. Alioto promoted the idea with some of the biggest skyscraper developers in the world, including the Rockefeller companies in Chicago.

We were working on these ads together with Alvin Duskin, the fashion indus-try manufacturer turned avid urban environmentalist. Our goal was to ban the construction of any new high-rise office buildings, based on our assertion that they were increasing traffic, noise, crowding, and pollution and destroying the very vistas that had been such a big part of everyday life in that city. Among our points were that high-rise development would cost the city—in services such as police, fire, sewage, expanded electrical power generation, road building and maintenance, and transportation services—far more than could be redeemed even by increases in property taxes. We had many studies that proved this idea. Our first ad had the headline "Skyscrapers Are Economically Necessary, but Only If You Own One."

While I was working on these campaigns, a close friend of my family's—I will call her Melinda—telephoned to say that her father, J. Douglas Butterfield (not his real name), was in town from Chicago for a few days. Melinda wanted to drop by with him and her young children. At that moment we suddenly realized that Melinda's father was actually president of one of the largest of the Chicago-based corporate developers of skyscrapers now being built in San Francisco. Several of his buildings were among the ones we were opposing.

On a bright Sunday morning, Melinda and her family came for brunch in our garden on Russian Hill. Mr. Butterfield turned out to be a most charming, friendly, personable man, and very affectionate with his grandchildren and with our children.

Out of respect for my friendship with Melinda, I did not raise any environ-mental issues on this occasion that might have proven embarrassing. But when Mr. Butterfield remarked on how wonderful it was that we enjoyed such a fine, lush garden in the midst of the crowded city and asked about the vacant lot adjoining our house, things changed. We informed him that only three weeks earlier, a bulldozer had been in the adjoining lot to level a lovely Victorian house and a wonderful formal Italian garden with tomatoes, beans, squash, roses, geraniums, and two small redwood trees. The garden had been tended with immense love by an elderly Italian couple, who had lived in the house for forty years. When the couple died—the husband within three weeks of the wife— the bank sold the property to developers (thankfully, not Mr. Butterfield) who planned to build a twenty-six-unit apartment building. Soon, our views would be totally blocked, and shadows would fall on our garden, as well as our house.

Mr. Butterfield was aghast. "How horrible," he said. "It is amazing they would permit huge apartments on such a lovely, quiet street."

I could no longer restrain myself. Assuming that Mr. Butterfield would easily see the parallels between the destruction of our views and the far larger problems caused by his own appalling complex of thirty-story buildings less than a mile away, I told him of the campaigns to stop such development. He was attentive and concerned. He said he had no idea there was resistance in San Francisco to high-rise development.

This statement, in turn, shocked me. How could he not know of the resistance to his projects? The movement against these new buildings had been going full force for several years and included public protests and considerable media attention, including our own ads. I wondered if he was being truthful with me. I knew that among top corporate executives, who live in a world of spreadsheets and financial manipulations, there is sometimes little awareness of how their actions affect real people. Maybe the protests in San Francisco were not sufficiently threatening that the president of a Chicago corporation would even know about them. If so, it was a humbling reality for anyone seeking to influence corporate actions. I decided to take Mr. Butterfield at his word. In any event, it was a polite way of handling the situation in front of our close friend, his daughter.

The conversation went on. He asked me why people were opposed, and I told him about the studies showing the effects of this kind of development. He seemed fascinated. He handed me his "private" business card and asked me to write to him directly, and to forward the studies and other relevant information. He said he would personally assess the situation and get back to me. He thanked me warmly for the news I brought.

I came away from the exchange convinced the man was in earnest. And probably, while sitting in my garden, he was.

I gathered the material he asked for, wrote him a long explanatory letter, and sent it in a package marked "Personal," as he had suggested. I soon received a reply saying he would study the reports and be back in touch very soon. He never wrote back. A subsequent letter that I sent to him was not acknowledged. Finally, I decided that his polite behavior at brunch was, like my own, out of concern for his daughter. Back at corporate headquarters in Chicago, a different set of rules took priority.

Are Corporations People?

Within corporations, there are human beings who have feelings like love, compassion, joy, sorrow, regret, and guilt, and who live in communities with other people, raise children, and usually have at least some instincts toward altruism. Then there are the strict corporate structures and goals, which have no feelings at all about anything, whether about people, or nature, or community, or any sense of altruism. Their only "values" concern the intrinsic need to expand and profit.

Corporations are just legal creations, ephemeral, with no physicality. In every practical sense, they don't really exist. Though they may operate from big buildings with their names on them, or run advertising campaigns that project a strong "personality" and express opinions about issues relevant to their own future, that is all just public relations imagery meant to create public favor.

Nonetheless, over the last two centuries, the matter of the nature of a corporation has become increasingly confused, as these manufactured entities have been given many of the legal rights of human beings, including what the Supreme Court calls "artificial personhood." They can buy property, can sue in court, and, most controversially, based on the Supreme Court's infamous Citizens United decision of 2010, are granted such constitutional rights as Fourth Amendment protection for "free speech." This includes the right to unlimited advertising spending, even in political campaigns, and without the necessity to reveal whose money is being used.

While enjoying many of the rights of human beings, corporations remain free from many of the obligations, responsibilities, and legal consequences of their actions. Their owners are protected by such legal concepts as "limited liability" of shareholders. Even when a corporation has taken actions that have killed people, the corporation itself cannot be tried for murder, though in rare cases an individual executive may be.

Corporations do not have a moral instinct. Neither do corporations have a normal life span, even though the people who work inside them do. The corporation may outlive those people and indeed may achieve permanent "life," until some unborn generation of new owners decides to dismantle the creature and distribute its assets, at which point it evaporates.

And if circumstances in one community are unfavorable for the corporate "home" or corporate activity, the corporation just dematerializes and rematerializes someplace else, often in another country, as if it has fulfilled human dreams of teleportation. But in the end, corporations are really only pieces of paper with official administrative stamps on them. To project emotional concerns,

or interest in public welfare, onto these fictional entities is absurd. And to permit this technological instrument, which has no living attributes, to operate
on the scale that it does, and to dominate society and governments, and to gain
nearly dictatorial control over electoral processes, acting solely on behalf of its
own built-in self-interest, is suicidal for human societies and murderous to the
natural world.

The Supreme Court's Citizens United case readily cited its interpretation of
the desires of the Founding Fathers and the U.S. Constitution. In that context, it seems entirely relevant to remark that though corporations are now the
primary instrument for economic activity in the modern world, and possibly
the world's single most important geopolitical force, they barely existed in the
United States before the mid-nineteenth century, except as very minor church
entities. In fact, the Founding Fathers were extremely wary of the corporations
that existed in other parts of the world. The Boston Tea Party, after all, was as
much directed at a foreign corporation, the British East India Company, as it
was at the British monarchy; this is something the present-day Tea Partiers,
fighting so hard on behalf of corporate freedoms, would do well to realize.

Even Thomas Jefferson famously warned against the potential powers of
huge corporate entities. When the U.S. Constitution was written and signed
in 1787, there were no corporations in the United States in anything like the
form in which we now know them to exist. It is obvious to any nonideological
reader that the "original intentions" of the Founding Fathers were focused on
protecting the rights of people, not expanding the rights of artificial entities
that might eventually come to exist.

The First Amendment protection for speech, at the time when the Constitution was written, was meant for individual expression and for public access
to freely delivered information. There was barely any advertising at all at the
time of the Constitution and, in fact, very little media of any kind. There were
distributions of handbills, soapbox speeches, one-sheet occasional editorial
papers and wall posters, and some books. That was the mass media that the
Founding Fathers knew. No one could possibly have conceived of the ability
to send powerful electronic imagery instantly into the consciousness of three
hundred million people, fifty times per hour, all day, every day, to convince
an entire population how to live or whom to vote for. The situation has lately
been seriously compounded by the degree of ownership concentration of global
mass media, wherein a handful of giant international corporations own the vast
majority of every kind of media and are easily able to globally amplify their own
views of how we should live.

The corporation did not gain significant primacy in U.S. economic activity until much later in the nineteenth century, concomitant with the rise of industrialism, continent-spanning railroads, and giant banks. Until then, not even Standard Oil or the Rockefeller enterprises were corporations; they operated as partnerships or trusts. But by now, of course, these fictional entities called corporations have become *the* most powerful and ubiquitous players in *every* aspect of modern life. They advance their domination through a nonstop intense effort to influence the rules by which business is done, the geopolitical process, global and domestic governance, the way elections are held, and who is elected. They make considerable effort to drown out opposing noncorporate human speech with tidal waves of billions of dollars of corporate speech. This significantly distorts the U.S. political process in a direction that is favorable and profitable to the corporations. This is certainly *opposite* to the Founding Fathers' intention, which was to protect the rights of speech for individuals.

Corporations Are Machines

Earlier, we spoke about the tendency of corporate critics to believe that the solution to negative corporate behaviors will be in persuading them toward more socially and ecologically useful activity. The effort is to change "greed to green."

We continue to think of corporate executives as being in charge of corporate behaviors, but the truth is not so clear. Not even the highest executives can easily alter the fundamentals of corporate purpose, any more than the foot soldier or lieutenant can resist the orders of the commander, or than an army can win wars without shooting. Now, let's *not* let anyone totally off the hook. Ordinary employees and even high executives are ofttimes willing to do the job exactly as asked. But the point is this: Whatever the personal feelings and inclinations of employees who work for it, the priorities of the corporate entity are always the same, focused like a laser on profit, growth, self-interest, economic domination, accumulation of capital, and shareholder benefits. Without achieving those, the corporations go bankrupt and dissolve.

If it were true that the root problems with corporate performance were the *people* who work in corporations, then all that would be necessary would be to replace the people with a new, more idealistic set of people, and everything would be okay. But it isn't. Whatever their personal morals and feelings, employees are routinely required to abandon their own standards in favor of the corporate purpose. Like assembly-line workers who operate at the speed of the machine, corporate employees, even top executives, are strapped onto the apparatus of the corporation and operate by its rules. A corporation is itself essentially a machine, a technological structure, an organization that follows its own built-in narrow drives, in which human morality is anomalous.

The problem is not the people in the corporation. It is the capitalist form itself, as expressed in the corporation. If anyone working within it doesn't like it, they are free to leave, or they are likely to be released. Then another person is strapped onto the machine, and nothing changes. The schism between these contradictory drives—human vs. structural—is *corporate schizophrenia.*

V.

Intrinsic Inequities of
Corporate Structure

Neither capitalism nor any of its structures was created to produce equity, internally or externally. Nor, to be fair, has it ever promised that. The job of capital, and its owners and managers, is to grow, expand, profit, and produce as much wealth as possible for executives and investors. That's it. There are no other goals.

Corporate capitalism *does* produce jobs. And companies are required to pay a wage sufficient enough that people are willing to work there, instead of at some other company. That is surely beneficial. And, at least until the Tea Party takes over, there *is* a minimum wage that employers have to pay. Michele Bachmann is the first presidential candidate who has publicly advocated *against* any minimum wage at all. Let's give her credit for not hiding it. She said that eliminating the minimum wage would help businesses grow. She might someday advocate slavery again, which might help businesses grow even more.

Corporations also make things and provide services, which the public uses. That's an apparently good thing, too, though often the benefits of these products and services are overhyped and fantasized, and have produced what some call a national commodity addiction.

Of course, corporations always retain the option to altruistically sacrifice profits for some higher cause. At least the smaller corporations retain that option, those that are privately owned, and not displayed on the stock market. They may want to pay some beloved long-term employee wages higher than the going rate. Or they may occasionally engage in some kind of public service work. Sometimes they even pay their own corporate staff to do public interest work. However, the larger the corporation, the less likely that becomes, because there is such tremendous pressure within publicly held concerns to satisfy the needs of shareholders, *this* quarter. In terms of the corporate future, it is a life-and-death matter.

All of their activity is touted by corporate capitalists as the nuts and bolts of our way of life. As the homily goes, "Capitalism has produced the world we live in." And it's true, at least if we ignore nature and the planet. Everyone has daily contact with corporations, whether they work in one or not. Some people argue that corporations are the key operative component of our society. And I think they are, without question.

But they do not produce equity; every aspect of their structure, and their place in society, leads toward the opposite: inequity. Neither are corporations interested in social or environmental values, except to the extent they may need to counter criticism for negative behavior toward the community or the environment; then they use their advertisements to tell us about how much they care when actually they do not. Corporations are only one thing: Technologies for the purpose of creating profits for their owner, whether it is an individual, or a group of shareholders. *Period*. If any benefits come from that, they are an incidental benefit of self-interest. Form determines content.

I first began thinking about these matters—the intrinsic inequities of corporate form—in the early 1960s because of prodding from my partner in the advertising business. Howard Gossage was deeply bored by advertising, constantly searching for a way out. He became well known for hosting seminars in our offices, inviting relatively unknown but seminal thinkers and exposing them to people who could help launch their ideas. Gossage famously did that for Marshall McLuhan while McLuhan was still a relatively obscure Toronto professor. The McLuhan seminar in our offices in 1963 was where Tom Wolfe, who later wrote extensively about McLuhan, actually met him for the first time.

During this series of events, Gossage also hosted Louis Kelso, the late corporate economist, scholar, lawyer, and author of an important book for the time, *Two-Factor Theory*, a work dissecting some principal inequities of the modern corporate structure. Kelso was already known at the time for his pioneering work on behalf of *worker ownership* and *co-op* structures for corporate enterprises as the best—and, he argued, the only—practical chance our society had to move toward a higher degree of equitability.

The fundamental point made by Kelso and other critics is that corporate hierarchical structure was far more extreme and consequential for society than it would appear based on its friendly superficial veneers. He pointed out that owners and top executives of corporations enjoy an amazing *multiplicity* of pathways within corporate structure, toward personal financial benefit. We should think of these as *multipliers*, well in addition to their very high salaries and shares in the distribution of profits.

Meanwhile, lower-level executives—office staff and subordinates, and production-line workers—get only one kind of benefit: *salary*, itself already far lower than salaries paid at the top. Kelso acknowledged that these were obvious points, if you delved into them, but that they are not taken seriously enough, given the kind of society they inevitably produce. If you explore the structural aspects of corporations, the impacts and scale of the distortions are far more profound and extreme than we generally notice.

So, I think it will be useful to list a few of the more important aspects of corporate structure, however commonly known some of them may already be. When we get a single clear picture of the complete structure—how bound it is to serve hierarchical values, how powerful it is, and the degree to which government serves it—we can see a composite structure far more ominous than its parts.

Eight Intrinsic Inequities of Corporate Structure

1. Profits from Business Operation

This is the most obvious. As indicated, profits equal the operational surplus of corporate revenue over all expenses of operations. So there is immense pressure to increase income and lower expenses to accelerate profits for the owners/investors of the corporation. Those profits can then be reinvested in the company to try to create even more profits in subsequent years. Or the profits can be distributed among the shareholders. Profits in one year can multiply, and they compound their effects in the next year.

In small, privately held corporations that are not listed on the stock market—for example, the furniture store in this book's introduction—there is often only one or very few shareholders. With publicly traded stocks, there may be millions, though typically there are a few dominant individual shareholders. The dominant shareholders are often also members of the board and/or the top operating officers of the company. They are the people who determine how profits get used, whether they are reinvested or distributed.

In some instances a high percentage of nonemployee stockholders are actually *speculators*, people from outside the company, who have no operational hand in the corporation's success or failure. They just buy stocks and sell them based on their calculations as to whether and how fast their value will rise or fall. It's gambling. These people have less real influence on the success of the company performance than any secretary or production worker does—except they have invested money, which can multiply. Their degree of influence parallels the scale of their investment. Nonetheless, they share in the full bounty.

End-of-year profits do not generally benefit anyone but shareholders and top executives, who make the final choices about how to use that money. Lower-level staff or production workers are not involved in these decisions and rarely receive any benefits at all from profits, other than job preservation and occasional wage increases in the future. Lately, profits don't even assure job preservation, as some of the most profitable companies in the world are actually *reducing* their workforces, often by substituting machines.

2. Profits from Capitalization of the Public Commons

Income over expenses from normal business operations is only one way to generate profit. There are many other, more complex and subtle *profit-creating* possibilities that have nothing whatever to do with service- or product-oriented operations. These are not sufficiently recognized or credited for their contributions to profit and wealth creation. But, in certain ways, they are *direct subsidies* from government and taxpayers for the welfare of corporations, their owners and managers. Ultimately, these features benefit only the highest echelons of corporations and add significantly to wealth disparities.

The most obvious and superficial among these are the various aspects of government largess in the form of special tax breaks for corporations in certain industries, enabling them to distribute greater profits to shareholders than they rightfully ought to. In addition, a variety of tax breaks are available for top-echelon executives in certain industries, especially finance. Often these special favors are the result of corporate campaign contributions. We will come back to that part in chapter IX.

But there are also other, far more subtle contributions routinely made to corporate profit by the government and the public. Three of the most important are these:

COST EXTERNALIZATION

This term describes various corporate activities that cause problems in the wider society, like pollution, climate change, public-health crises, or depletion of common resources, such as forests, water, air, or genetic diversity. Most of these negative effects, and many others we could list, are usually not paid for by the corporation; they are *externalized*. So in the end, they have to be paid for by the rest of us. The environmental impacts—let's say, polluted rivers—may eventually be cleaned up, but not usually by the corporation; most commonly the cleanup is done by local, state, or national government, using citizens' tax monies. The amounts thus saved by the corporation immediately transfer into improving its profit picture and are eventually distributed to private shareholders. It all amounts to an indirect transfer of public (or taxpayer) funds to private corporations and the pockets of investors. It is possible that without such an externalization subsidy—especially in highly polluting industries like oil, autos, chemicals, pharmaceuticals, and industrial agriculture—the corporate activity would not be profitable at all. On the other hand, if a company really had to pay for all the harmful externalized costs it created, there might be considerable incentive to avoid doing the harmful activity at all. This is why so many companies lobby so hard for deregulation, to avoid rules controlling their pollutions or any necessity to reimburse society for them.

Limited Legal Liability

Another insufficiently discussed factor in the ability of corporations to so freely do harm is that most forms of corporate structure are "limited liability corporations." That is, if the company commits some public harm that the local or state or national government is able to sue about, it can sue only the corporation itself, not its owners, the shareholders. In most cases the government cannot even hold liable the high-level executives who may have personally initiated or managed the dangerous performances. Corporate structure is actually an insulation protecting its primary actors, and its owners, from the consequences of most negative acts they may commit. Without such insulation, many harmful acts might never be initiated in the first place, so the legal structure effectively helps create the harms, while also assisting profits and causing an additional effective transfer of wealth from ordinary taxpayers to corporate coffers.

Exploitation of the Intellectual Commons

Canada native/New Zealand–based business executive Jack Santa Barbara has written that most businesses and corporations and their top executives make extensive use of what we might call the "appropriated intellectual commons," the c...ections of innovative ideas and practices from prior years. In an internal report for IFG, Santa Barbara argued that, "Humanity has a vast store of knowledge that is in the public domain—an intellectual commons—that is a shared heritage. To significantly reward only the marginal improvement that any one person or team makes to a technological invention or innovation totally ignores this common heritage, and the critical role it plays in the production of any good or service."

Public contributions inherent in this are hard to define or put a value on at varied levels, but the case is clearest among tech entrepreneurs. Bill Gates, for example, made tens of billions of dollars for "inventing" important computer processes. But his inventions and innovations were actually dependent on the many platforms of knowledge that had been generated long before his time and passed on to him and his colleagues through education and media, often in addition to government-paid scientific research, prior business applications, etc.

"Bill Gates did not invent the personal computer, nor did he make a significant contribution to software for operating systems," according to Santa Barbara. "He did make a contribution, of course, but it was marginal compared to the vast store of common knowledge that preceded his involvement. . . . There were literally hundreds, if not thousands, of small steps that brought personal computers to the point where they are today."

This is not to say that Gates does not deserve considerable reward for putting something original and very spectacular together—but should the reward be $40 billion? Isn't that a bit ridiculous? Would that be the right reward for anyone? Isn't he just another human being who breathes and eats and then dies? And since he was partly building on the works of others, some of it financed by our taxes, shouldn't the benefits be shared, at least to some extent?

In our society we tend to exalt the wealthiest among us, and project all sorts of special qualities onto them to explain their great performance. But great ideas, talents, and hard work are not confined to the super-rich; often they are not rewarded at all. What Bill Gates put together is significant, but not as original or glorious as our response to it has made it seem. His achievements partially represent a capture of *collective* wisdom, built up by prior generations of inventors who may have received no recognition from it and little compensation.

The corporate attitude about such matters, and the obligations corporations might face if the contributions made by the wider society to their wealth were fully acknowledged, were well captured in a 2011 meeting between President Obama, Steve Jobs, and other executives from Apple. Obama was reportedly complaining to the high-tech executives that too many jobs had moved to China. He wondered if corporations feel any obligations to the United States: "Why can't that work come home?" he asked.

According to one report on this confrontational incident in the *Nation* (February 20, 2012), Alexander Cockburn describes Steve Jobs's reply as "unambiguous: 'Those jobs aren't coming back.'" Cockburn quotes another Apple executive as saying, "We don't have any obligation to solve America's problems." Cockburn then quotes Clyde Prestowitz, a top U.S. trade negotiator, who wrote in *Foreign Policy* that "virtually everything Apple had for sale, from the memory chips to the cute pointer mouse, had had its origins in some program wholly or partially supported by U.S. government money. . . . The heart of the computer is the microprocessor. Apple's derived from Motorola's 680X0, which was developed with much assistance, direct and indirect, from the Defense Department, as were the DRAM memory chips. The pointer mouse came from Xerox's PARC center near Stanford (which also enjoyed government funding). In addition, most computer software at that time derived from work with government backing."

According to Cockburn, "Prestowitz also points out that Apple assumes the U.S. government is obligated to stop foreign pirating of Apple's intellectual property and, should supply chains in the Far East be disrupted, to offer the comforting support of the Seventh Fleet." In other words, says Coburn, Apple does not feel any obligation to the United States, but the U.S. should be willing to send in our navy if some country disrupts its supply lines.

In fact, exactly this latter turn of events occurred in late 2011 when China threatened to reduce exports of scarce rare earth minerals that are crucial to computer production. The U.S. responded as if it were nearly an act of war, with Bill Gates and Hillary Clinton making sudden direct threats. We don't know if Apple felt any gratitude to the administration for supporting it that way, or even for the long history of services the U.S. government provides for intellectual property itself, and for copyrights and other legal protections. Obviously, most corporations feel that their job is to serve their own interests only, and for government to do that, too. It's a one-way street.

While it would be very hard to put a specific number on the value of the intellectual commons, some effort should be made to reflect the reality of this. Inventors should be asked to acknowledge the debt to prior generations, with at least some tax on profits that might be used to help future generations of innovators. Let's call it a Gratefulness Tax on Excessive Profit (GTEP).

Opponents of Santa Barbara's ideas say that the intellectual commons, which is available to all, should be free to anyone able to make good use of it. But my own opinion is that once a certain application of the commons has been taken, it is then usually privatized (sometimes making use of patent or copyright protections) and becomes more difficult for any others to use. This is as true of pharmaceuticals taken from the natural commons as it is of technical innovation and ideas, such as the Internet and its offshoots.

Whoever has the luck and brilliance to apply the intellectual commons to commercial advantage owes a debt, in my view, to the unpaid contributors to that commons. Though it obviously cannot go directly to those earlier contributors, it could certainly go to today's generation of idea explorers. The principle, I think, is the same as would favor the right to tax the wealthiest elements of society a bit more than everyone else. Since they have profited greatly from many earlier elements of society, they owe part of their achievement to the larger society. A 5 percent "commons use" tax, say, or even a 1 percent tax, would leave them as wealthy as before and give the rest of us a better chance, too.

Of course, this discussion of issues surrounding the "intellectual commons" is really part of a much larger discussion concerning the corporate appropriation, privatization, and depletion of what was for centuries more widely thought to be the common property of all people in a society, the *natural commons*—i.e., nature: water, forests, land, rivers, biodiversity, the pharmaceutical properties of plants. Over the last few hundred years, much of this has slowly become "enclosed," or, as we now call it, "privatized." Even fresh water—there is no more important common property than that—has been largely privatized. You can buy a plastic bottle of water for a dollar at any grocery. Meanwhile, a whole lot of public water is still provided, free, to keep industrial ag corporations operative and computer chips properly clean for production, a very important factor. We should call those *public subsidies* to those industries. And what of the freighters filled with Lake Superior water that head for China every day for use in that country's high-tech production systems, often on behalf of U.S. companies? There's another theft of the commons for private corporate use.

The Tomales Bay Institute is a nonprofit organization in California directed by business entrepreneur Peter Barnes, former CEO of Working Assets. The organization argues that many kinds of private corporate activity cause direct harms to the *common* property of all peoples, which instead ought to be officially recognized and protected as a "commons." Air pollution, for example, impacts what Barnes has labeled the "Sky Commons." More than six billion people all use this same atmosphere to breathe in and out of our lungs thousands of time every day, as if we were all actually one giant breathing planetwide organism, the Earth Creature.

Barnes advocates that polluting industries should be charged specific amounts, relative to the level of their pollution, to partly compensate citizens for this potentially dangerous intrusion. Annual payments could be sent directly to every individual in the country, and conceivably the world. It's more or less the way the state of Alaska pays all of its citizens annually for their percentage of the oil that has been extracted from Alaska by corporations—an appreciation that oil in the ground should be thought of as a commons. This is called the Alaska Permanent Fund. (*How did Gov. Sarah Palin manage to support such a progressive idea?*) Barnes is now proposing an American Permanent Fund to similarly distribute a portion of the proceeds from the use of a variety of public resources.

More broadly implemented, a policy like this would surely have some negative effect on individual corporations and shareholders and private-wealth accumulation, as well as on corporate profits at public expense. However, to a small degree, it would help promote equity and slow down the level of pollution a little bit. But there's also an important downside to doing this. As with carbon trading ideas, it would allow polluting and exploitative industries to *commoditize* nature even more than it already is, and might grant them new permission to keep doing what they are doing and to diminish the natural commons, simply by paying for it.

And then, finally, there is the domain we have come to call the *public commons*: government services like education, healthcare, military, security, transportation—all the things that we take for granted but that ultimately make all private economic activity possible. Many in the Tea Party movement advocate that whole government agencies should be privatized, certainly including Medicare and Social Security, and should operate on the principle that profit comes first. Actually, that's pretty much what our private health insurance offers us now: If your injury or disease will be too unprofitable to cure, then you are rejected as unprofitable. (At least until 2014, if the Obama health program survives the many assaults against it.)

3. CEO Megasalaries & Bonuses

Let's turn back directly to corporate operations. Another obvious well-known inequity within corporations concerns the salary scale of the average corporation. According to the Institute for Policy Studies, among the average S & P 500 American companies, top executives' pay is now roughly 325 times greater than that of lower-level executive staff and production-line workers. That is a disparity that has been steadily growing in recent years. Similar large inequities are found in every capitalist country, but nowhere is it greater than in the United States.

According to a study by *Mother Jones* (March/April 2011), during the two years between 2007 and 2009, the average salary of CEOs of American companies increased 185 times more than the average line or staff employee salary.

William Domhoff of the University of California, Santa Cruz, put "the median annual compensation for a CEO in *all* industries as of early 2010 at $3.9 million; it's $10.6 million for the companies listed in Standard and Poor's 500, and $19.8 million for the companies listed in the Dow Jones industrial average. The median worker's annual income is about $36,000."

The usual excuse for giving salaries in the megamillions to normal people who work as CEOs is that it is necessary to retain "competitiveness," to attract the "best" people, and to get the highest possible performance. But is that really true? Would a Dow Jones CEO paid, say, a mere $5 million a year, rather than $19 million, really give a worse performance? Would he be so put off by such a pathetically low salary that he would decline to perform at his best? But anyway, is any CEO really worth three hundred times more than any other worker? Is he three hundred times smarter or more creative than the average person? I don't think so. The logic is flawed, if not absurd. And isn't there any role anywhere in this for "intrinsic rewards"? Doesn't it feel good to do a good job and get paid fairly?

One little-noted factor may help explain this peculiar situation: In most companies the board of directors sets or at least approves the pay level for the CEO and other top-management figures. But meanwhile, it's usually the CEO who sets the pay level for boards of directors. Often, in Fortune 500 companies, board members make about $1 million per year for their part-time duties, involving only a few meetings per year. Doubtless this puts them in a good mood to pay back the favor with high CEO salaries, and bonuses. In any case, the salaries of all these people reduce distributed profits that could otherwise go to shareholders or workers—yet another case of wealth transfer from workers to CEOs.

As if already large executive salaries weren't sufficient, bonus payments are often many times larger. According to a *New York Times* report (April 10, 2011) on top CEO salaries:

- In 2010, the CEO of Viacom, Philippe P. Dauman, received a total pay package of $84.5 million. His base salary was a mere $2,625,000; his bonus was $11,250,000 (about four times more than his pay); and his stock and options totaled $69 million.
- At Occidental Petroleum, CEO Ray Irani received $76.1 million as total compensation, but only $1,192,000 as salary; $33 million was a bonus, about thirty times larger than his pay.
- Robert Iger of Walt Disney made $2 million in salary and $13 million in bonus pay.

The *Times* calculated that the median value for all two hundred CEOs was about $1,150,000 as salary, $2,471,000 as bonus, and $5,150,000 in stock and options. Together with a few other variable things, like "perks"—those might be personal use of a company airplane or a paid vacation retreat or the like—the median pay was about $9,644,000, a 12 percent rise from 2009.

Keep in mind that giant bonuses were often granted despite the fact that a company showed a loss during 2010. This self-determined generosity at the top did not trickle down to lower-level employees. In the banking and finance industry, especially in the past few years, bonuses were routinely in the millions of dollars, occasionally as high as $150 million. Several of these finance

companies received government bailouts during the same period, after suffering losses, but that seemed to have little effect on the granting of high-level
bonuses. For example:

- Despite having received a TARP bailout of $35 billion, JPMorgan Chase
  paid out $8.7 billion in bonuses, including 626 bonuses of at least $1
  million.
- Merrill Lynch, which lost $27 billion in 2008, accepted a TARP bailout
  of $10 billion but still managed to pay 696 bonuses of at least $1 million,
  and $3.6 billion in bonuses overall. *Bonuses for what?* one might ask.
- Goldman Sachs paid out 953 bonuses of at least $1 million, and six
  bonuses at $10 million, while still accepting a 2009 government TARP
  bailout of $10 billion. The *New York Times* (January 18, 2011) reported that
  some Goldman Sachs bonuses in 2008 were as high as $150 million. This
  was at the same time the company was steering many of its clients into
  bankruptcy.
- And Citigroup, which lost $27 billion in 2008, nonetheless paid $5.3 billion in bonuses that year, with 738 people getting more than $1 million.
  Forty-four received more than $5 million, while the "senior leadership
  committee" got $126 million. "And Citigroup paid these bonuses even
  though it accepted support of $45 billion from TARP."

It seems appropriate to ask, what on earth were the top executives of these
companies thinking? Has there ever been a clearer example of blind, passionate
self-interest in history? Or *dis*interest in the public welfare? These people just
did this because they could.

4. Stock Payments & Dividends

The stock and options with which many executives are partly paid—sometimes
at a much higher level than salary—can potentially bring them huge benefits
from dividends and rising stock values, as a result of short-term growth. Even
when values start to decline, they are often able to sell high and rebuy lower.

But there is a tricky element built into this kind of compensation, as it reveals
the degree to which top executives of corporations are actually in partial competition with their own shareholders—technically their "owners"—for the
bigger pieces of the pie. The corporation needs the shareholders, of course,
who capitalize the company; but the shareholders, in turn, must see benefits
in terms of rising values and/or higher dividends. And yet the decisions about
whether to pay dividends at all, and at what level, reside with the top executives
(in contrivance with the corporate board). Top management often feel justified
in sweeping up as much of the available profits for themselves—in terms of

salaries, bonuses, and further stock options—since they are the ones who show up every day and do the hard slogging.

Mitigating the executives' power over them, and threatening it, is the awareness that shareholders' great love for any corporation can be notoriously fickle, switching quickly to the next cute-looking corporation sashaying down the street. If too many shareholders choose to drop out, it can create a trend in the market, and the whole company can find itself in trouble. So, it's a balancing act. One very popular response to this problem is to put the squeeze on lower-level employees, especially production workers, for salary and benefit cuts. That idea is attractive to both executives and shareholders. In the end, the whole institution is like a three-legged stool. There are the top executives, the employees, and the shareholders, all in constant struggle with each other to determine whose interests will prevail. It is *never* the workers.

5. Invested Earnings: The Multiplier Effect

Executives who are already paid very large salaries and/or bonuses and/or stocks and dividends are of course also able to then *invest* the money they have earned (from those items), either in interest-bearing bank accounts or other business activity, or else in financial speculations, or new houses, or yachts or Pacific islands, for that matter. Any and all of these properties have the potential to multiply their value, and their eventual earnings from them, many times. People at lower levels, paid just a straight salary, get none of this added action.

At a certain point, top-level executives and owners may face another common problem of their ilk, which is to somehow find profitable opportunities, every year, for their own "surplus capital." Line workers have no such worries, as surplus capital is never a problem for them.

6. Wage Repression of Employees

Up to now, we have been describing a few of the many ways in which shareholders and high executives are able to *multiply* their earnings—the built-in opportunities to take base pay and benefits and amplify them. However, increasingly important to profit margins these days is that higher echelons of corporations can also benefit greatly by finding means to actively suppress lower-level wages, thereby increasing profit margins—the ratio between income and expenses—often by the exact amount of reduced wages. In effect, this is yet another simple transfer of funds from workers to executives and owners. It is also the easiest and most efficient path toward profits for any corporation.

In Marxist terms, this simple effort to cut wages in order to expand profits is an exacerbation of an already intolerable situation, in which workers are routinely underpaid for the actual "value" of their contribution.

Here's the crux of the matter: As workers perform their tasks, they are constantly "adding value" to the products they work on. Products become more salable at higher prices because of the work performed by the laborer. The products are then sold to the public at a price that includes the value the workers have added, but the worker receives no extra income share from that.

In other words, there is a major difference between what workers are actually paid for their time and the ultimate value of their efforts to the sales and profits of the company. So workers are, in effect, subsidizing corporations. Meanwhile, even the relatively trivial amount they are paid—hundreds of times less than their executive superiors—is under pressure from management to be further reduced or eliminated. If that happens, the executives can use that money to increase their bloated salaries or distribute the money to shareholders.

This built-in corporate tendency to continually seek ways and means to cut wages has always been a prime concern of labor. But it was partly alleviated during the years following World War II, when collective bargaining through unions became increasingly popular. But since the financial crisis of 2008, and the surge of corporate-backed right-wing movements, efforts at wage repressions have increased spectacularly, as we have seen in Wisconsin, Ohio, Indiana, New Jersey, and elsewhere.

Even when wages are not repressed, there is often pressure for "give-backs" in other costly areas, such as healthcare or retirement benefits, even at times when corporate profits are very high.

Corporate executives have many tools to express pressures on workers, including constant threats, often acted upon, to move company operations to lower-wage countries. (The WTO rules of free trade encourage companies to freely move among countries. Capital may also freely move. But labor may *not* move. If they try to do so, they often gain the status of "illegal immigrants" and become the subject of tremendous political battles and threats in many countries; some of these migrating workers find themselves in jail or deported.) Or the company can simply *threaten* to move unless workers and unions grant major concessions as to wages and/or benefits.

One could argue that this is not an intrinsic quality of capitalism. Many companies that are privately owned do not seek give-backs and lower wages for workers, at least not in profitable times. However, among publicly held companies, profits *must* be achieved, stock value *must* go up, and dividends *must* be paid as often as possible. All of those goals benefit greatly from cost savings at every level of operation, including employee pay.

Mother Jones blogger Andy Kroll does a good job of relating the rise of the plutocracy in the United States over the last three decades to the enormous success of the right-wing anti-union movements. "As late as 1970," says Kroll, "private-sector union density was still more than 25%, and the absolute number of all union members was at its highest point in history." Now, private-sector union membership is down to about 7 percent. And, according to the *Wall Street Journal* (June 22, 2011), among all unions in 2010—private and public—only 11.9 percent of workers were union members. In 1983, unions represented 20.1 percent of all workers.

This slide in union membership was accompanied by vast downward pressures on wages during that same period, thus increasing the marginal profits of companies, the salaries of top management, the dividend payments to shareholders, and usually the value of the stock. The Economic Policy Institute has reported that median hourly wages are down by 10 percent in real wages over the last twenty-five years, although executive salaries continue to rise. It's one more shift of wealth from the bottom to the top.

Another contributing factor in these shifts, says Kroll, has been the gradual withdrawal of the Democratic Party to the political center, away from its formerly strong support for unions. He also cites the media's overall wholesale abandonment of the union cause. "About a year ago, the Pew Research Center looked at the sources reporters used for stories on the economy. The White House and members of Congress were often quoted, of course. Business leaders. Academics. Ordinary citizens. Who's missing? 'Representatives of organized labor unions,' Pew found, 'were sources in a mere 2% of all the economy stories studied.'"

The 2011 union protests against Wisconsin governor Scott Walker's efforts to destroy collective bargaining in that state, and the huge protest movement demanding the governor's recall, represented the first time in decades that any union action received significant media coverage. But will it last? By the time you read this, the vote on Walker will probably have happened. One way or another, however, some believe that the movement that began in that Wisconsin battle directly sparked the Occupy movement and brought about a far greater media focus on and public awareness of equity issues. We will see if it sustains.

7. The "Worker Productivity" Scam

We are used to seeing financial pages publish monthly figures on "American worker productivity," i.e., the measure of whether the average individual worker in the United States is producing more "product" more efficiently this month than the last. Everyone gets very excited when the figures go up, and it is duly reported in the mainstream media's financial pages and in news shows.

The implication of that "productivity" measurement—or the way it has been made to sound—is that workers are somehow working "harder" or faster than they did before, or are more skillful, or else the manufacturing plant has been made more technically "efficient." While these may be factors, a large percent of the complicated calculations for "productivity" has to do with workers' being replaced by machines or new technological processes.

The next time you hear President Obama celebrating the fabulous productivity of the American worker, "the greatest working people in the world" (a phrase every president uses over and over again), remember this: What Obama means is that we have either replaced a percentage of workers with machines or achieved an increased output with the same number of workers, because of revisions in production processes. So the ratio of output to workers increases, but the number of workers may actually decline. Obama should be ashamed of making such misleading statements.

Meanwhile, the machines and industrial processes that replace the workers don't take vacations, don't require salaries or sick leave, or pensions or health plans, and aren't in unions, either. So, profitability is directly enhanced, which is the only value for corporations. That's a dimension of the "jobless recovery" phenomenon that our country is currently experiencing. Profits soar, but employee salaries and jobs nosedive.

But, of course, as ex-president George W. Bush argued in Michael Moore's film *Capitalism: A Love Story*, ours is an economically mobile society. Workers can always just move on to their next opportunity. "Capitalism is the best system ever devised," said Bush. "Everyone has the opportunity to pick the kind of work they want to do . . . the freedom to choose where they work, or what they do . . . the opportunity to buy or sell products they want, get the opportunity they want. . . . If you seek social justice and human dignity, the free-market system is the way to go." That wisdom comes straight from a third-generation multimillionaire-family scion. Maybe those laid-off workers should just invest a couple of million and start a new business hiring other workers—unless, of course, machines get the job done more productively.

8. Cashing Out: The Sale of Company Assets

Finally, of course, company management always has the right to propose the outright sale of the company as a whole, or a portion of the company's assets— perhaps a subdivision, or another company or two that it owns. This kind of action can obviously produce the greatest net profit of all, including gigantic cash windfalls for all shareholders, though, regrettably, nothing for anyone else in the company. The largest shareholders are often the CEO and other top executives, who reap the greatest gains. Sometimes, however, the executive management does not want to actually sell the company to the buyer on offer and becomes the victim of a "hostile takeover" from elsewhere. Either way, they get the benefits of the cash received, and they can just go out and buy something else, exactly as Mr. Bush suggested.

The Illusion of Corporate "Efficiency"

There is one more example of the distorted privileges of corporations that also needs amplification, though it is marginally different in form from those we have discussed so far. This inequity is not so much expressed as internal form as it is based on a false understanding of corporate processes, as promoted for many decades by corporations and their advocates. The inequity is between the corporation and the interests of the wider society. To explain:

We are forever hearing from corporations and their supporters about how "efficient" private corporations are, as compared with far more inefficient and wasteful government-run public activities. Public acceptance of this allegation has arguably advanced corporate interests and profits over many years more than any other factor. In the United States, it has been a prime reason why private enterprise has been granted such advanced access to the public commons and has also been highly favored for contract work in areas of major national interest, such as for military production and services, health services, transportation, security, energy, mass media, and many others. In other countries, these kinds of services are not usually privatized to the same degree; since they involve crucial public services, they are normally government operated.

It is amazing to me that the prevailing homily about corporate efficiency is generally accepted, because it is very far from true. As the story goes, the profit motive acts like an engine that drives executives and their corporations to hone their enterprises and eliminate fat and excess expense (which usually means workers), so as to seek constant efficiencies that will add to their profits. Theoretically, this enables the corporation to increase the quality of services or goods and reduce prices, thus benefiting the wider society. But that is not how things actually work.

In practice, corporations increase their service or reduce their prices only if management concludes that better service or lower prices will also increase total sales and profits. Depending on the activities of competitors in the market, they may not. In many product lines and public services—for example, offering gasoline at the pump—public demand for the product or service is what economists call highly "inelastic." That is, it doesn't really matter (within limits) what the company charges for a gallon of gas. If people need to fill their tanks, they will do it, unless the price is so high they cannot actually pay. So, the oil company increases its charges to a level that is "as high as the market will bear." This is why oil companies are the most profitable companies in the world. Simultaneously, they also try, wherever possible, to *reduce* their services. Do you remember the good old days, when gasoline station service attendants used to fill your tank for you, at no extra charge? That service has been nearly totally dropped. But you have to fill your tank anyway, even if you may spill some gas on your hands or clothes. So you, in effect, become the substitute for the salary of the worker who used to do that service. Of course, if the price rises sufficiently and stays high for a period of time, people might finally decide to quit driving altogether and ride the bus or train—if, that is, that trains or bus services are available. So oil companies do try not to raise prices all the way to that turning point, unless they can lobby the government to let them privatize and operate the train service, too. They will argue, as usual, that they can run the train more efficiently. Then prices for both will go up.

Here's the point. For corporations, profit drives the process, and profit consists of the total amount of income above the actual costs. In the end, consumers have to pay the actual costs *plus* profits. So, if profits are 20 percent above costs, we all pay 20 percent extra, which goes directly to shareholders and/or top-executive salaries.

On the other hand, let's say governments ran the service. Governments do *not* really need to charge above actual costs, since they do not have shareholders to satisfy, nor could they pay the kinds of salaries private enterprise allows. Without a profit motive, governments don't really need or want to make every possible dime they could—and so they have at least the opportunity to actually deliver the service more cheaply (*efficiently?*) than an institution that needs to profit, or to pay huge salaries or dividends to stockholders. So, that 20 percent the consumer paid above costs, to pay for corporate profits, would be unnecessary. Or, if it were paid, those same extra monies would likely recycle back to taxpayers for additional services—let's say, to public schools. *That* would be real *efficiency*. It would not go to $10 million salaries. From a systemic point of view, profits are actually a waste of resources and money, and they deprive society of alternative uses for those funds, which are now privatized.

When private owners perform the service or provide the product, doing privately what could have been done publicly, retaining all income above actual costs, what is finally revealed is the exact amount that the service is costing beyond what it actually needed to cost. That is the precise amount of wealth transfer—or let's call it subsidy—from the public to the corporation to get them to perform the service. Without such profits, they wouldn't do the service. So inefficiency—that is, unnecessary surplus cost—is a structural component of the corporate version of the identical service.

But there is one more key question: If profits and high salaries are the motive for private corporations to provide a service, what then would be a *government's* motive for providing a good service or product? Do we really have to accept the idea that the *only* motive for providing good service is profit?

I traveled enough in communist countries in the 1960s and 1970s to remember the experience of going into government-run stores to try to buy something. This was often a negative experience. I found many employees who were totally unmotivated and passive, if not rude. But, on the other hand, I also found some who served me very nicely.

I think I have to say the same about private corporations. In a well-run company, the people try to tune in and be helpful, especially if it's a personal service of some kind. But, I could offer plenty of examples of private corporations' acting rudely or stupidly and utterly failing to provide the service promised— or, worse, cheating me out of a few extra dollars. Private insurance companies provide lots of good examples of that behavior, at least in my experience. On the other hand, among government agency employees, I could describe examples where government employees act on behalf of the public with engagement, pride, or altruism as their motive—the idea of good service.

My experiences dealing with the Social Security Administration and Medicare have been especially positive. I have found the employees invariably well trained, knowledgeable, and fast-thinking. They tune in and get it right. But, admittedly, it's not universal.

I have come to view all this as mainly a personal variable. Some people care and some don't, whether they're corporate or government, capitalist or socialist. But the overarching argument that privatization of public services automatically increases performance and efficiency and lowers costs—even aside from such considerations as quality of service to all people—is not true. Corporations continue to unabashedly hawk the argument that they are more efficient in producing a service. But their motive is not really to do a better job than the government. Their only motive is to advance profits and pay high salaries, which, from a systemic viewpoint, is highly inefficient. And without those, they would simply quit the assignment.

There are, in fact, people who view taxes for public services as a kind of "confiscation of wealth," and worse. In U.S. Senate testimony (May 11, 2011), Sen. Rand Paul, who is otherwise a doctor, described passage of any tax-financed government healthcare program as putting him into the position of a "slave" by forcing him to serve patients against his will. I sometimes think that such people might actually prefer that we aim for some kind of *benevolent* monarchy, or a new feudalism, where superwealthy charismatic individuals take over the reins of "democratic" governments, locally, regionally, or nationally. But, of course, one problem with giving power to a few individuals is that if some of them may be wonderful people, others will not be; it will be hard to discern the differences simply through their campaign advertising. We are left to pray for the benevolence of the king.

The reality is that capitalism has many intrinsic aspects that work toward rigid hierarchy, centralized power, and inequity at every level of structure and performance. If you are going to have a capitalist system, you are going to have a society with gigantic economic disparities in income, wealth, and power.

This is not new news. Most of us, if we have thought about that at all, take it for granted. There is plenty of evidence to support the point. The only question is whether there is anything we can do to change it.

VI.

Endless Growth on a Finite Planet

Capitalism can be understood as a kind of global, system-wide Ponzi scheme. In order to profit and thrive, or even merely survive, the macro system must *never* stop feeding itself new resources, developing new markets, creating wealth surpluses, and reinvesting in itself. Expansion is the juice that drives the system and the individual practitioner, and gives it all a creative urge. *Got to find something new to invest in. Got to create a new product. Got to get a better interest rate. Got to add a new feature so they'll buy a new one.*

Growth is the primary measure of overall well-being for industrial, capitalist societies. This is why captains of industry, bankers, politicians, and media from every country—in all their public utterances, convenings, and campaigning—never stop talking about it. It is the basis for corporate stock value, shareholder satisfaction, the ability to attract and sustain investments and loans and to offer competitively high executive pay and bonuses, and the opportunity for continued capital expansion and wealth accumulation.

Growth is primary whether we are describing the *real* economy—where capital is used to find and process resources from nature, to transform them into commodities, or where direct services are provided to people—*or* the *virtual* economy, where money is invested in financial instruments that may have little or no connection to real production or services. *Money investing in money.* In all cases, growth is the essential lifeblood of the system. Either the system grows, with a constant stream of new income and investment, or it fails.

Every politician running for office knows all this very well. Whether on the federal, state, or local level, each of them will claim to be the person who can best restimulate system-wide growth, when actually none of them can anymore. The same may be said of politicians in other countries, and all corporate leaders of publicly held companies worried about the values of their stocks. Even liberal media economic gurus like Paul Krugman agonize over growth rates if they fall to a mere 1.5 percent, when they *must* become about 2.5 percent for adequate profit distribution, and 3.5 percent for new-job creation. In capitalist economies, growth is what it's all about.

To achieve constant growth in the *real* economy, capitalism requires constant expansion of three primary ingredients *that are, alas, impossible to sustain*:

(1) An always expanding and varied cheap-resources base and its continuous transformation into commodities that people or industry will buy.

(2) Always expanding consumer or industrial markets, and a generalized philosophy of life that equates constant consumption with happiness and success.

(3) Always expanding availability of cheap (or slave) labor.

Resources, markets, labor. None of these conditions can possibly continue forever on a finite planet, where the limits of nature are now apparent. Global resources are shrinking rapidly and becoming more costly as a result. The various techniques of boosting supply have run into intractable limits.

Neither are markets forever expandable. They are prone to saturation. Even highly addicted consumers can buy only so many refrigerators, cars, and computers. This will be especially so if population growth levels off, which it is likely to do, by either individual or community choice, or public policy, or starvation, if global food supplies continue to diminish and prices continue to rise. That is the reality, despite the steady onslaught of consumption stimulants such as mass consumer advertising, the constant promotion of new technologies and new product features, the advance of globalization, the growth of new, formerly "third world" markets, and the spectacular increase of the war economy.

Meanwhile, labor doesn't really want to be cheap anymore. In an era of globalized media imagery showing the joys of excess wealth and indulgence, workers in many places no longer accept that they should be the footstools of global prosperity. Especially not if their work is performed in unhealthy conditions, or their wages remain below levels of economic sufficiency—the level where basic needs are covered: food, shelter, clothing, education, health, security, and community. Labor increasingly finds itself in conflict with another fundamental drive of capitalist growth—to suppress wages, as we have seen in Wisconsin, Ohio, New Jersey, and elsewhere. Economic downturns offer corporations windfall opportunities to challenge unions and demand give-backs.

Even when corporate profits are high, workers are intimidated with threats that their jobs could be moved to lower-wage countries, or they could be replaced by machines, a growing trend. The issue is even playing out dramatically in China, where a countrywide resistance has emerged among industrial workers traditionally subject to poor working and living conditions and low wages. Their protests have begun to influence national labor policies and have brought about some increases in wages.

Our current economic model *did* achieve significant growth throughout most of the nineteenth and twentieth centuries. At that time we still lived on a planet blessed with an abundant resource base and a more-than-ample supply of cheap (and/or slave) labor. Nearly everyone who grew up in the twentieth century believed that this could be sustained forever. But, as with the Ponzi schemes that eventually run out of new investors, never-ending growth in a capitalist system has proven to be impossible. Given the glaring resource crises of our time, and the costs of resources rapidly rising, and with nature in great revolt, failure is already visible and tangible.

The modern capitalist system is actually very fragile. During the recent economic crisis, the failure of the U.S. economy to grow for several quarters brought the entire system to the edge of collapse. Even when economic growth curves decline by only a tiny amount, like from 1.5 percent a year to 0.5 percent, as they recently did—because of oil shortages, or prices, or market saturations, or value "bubbles," or mortgage failures, or commodity purchasing slowdowns—what a mess that creates! The entire system starts to break down. Financial, corporate, industrial, and banking classes all begin to panic. So does the political process. New investment slows down, old investment gets sold off, consumption slows down further, "value" disappears, jobs are lost, Tea Partiers take to the streets, people go bankrupt, banks start to fail, and, despite our so-called "free market" system, the biggest of them have to be bailed out by government, further eroding our economic foundations and stimulating the downward spiral.

All this negative reaction is generated by the most minor drop in the growth curve. Imagine the consequences when the curve stays low for several years—or forever. The whole apparatus is a house of cards, capable of collapsing from the next foul wind. Growth is the only prop it has. Without growth, it cannot sustain itself. To have believed in this system's viability and its efficacy required extremes of hubris and denial.

As the planet's remaining resources become ever more scarce, they become more difficult to find and recover. They're far more expensive and dangerous to extract, they're of lower quality, and they're more inefficient to use. Such problems are repeatedly exposed by highly destructive methods, such as oil recovery in the tar sands of Canada and Utah, the infamous BP deep-water oil-drilling catastrophe in the Gulf of Mexico, and the horrendous mountaintop coal-removal process in Appalachia, among hundreds of other, similar events.

In thousands of places on the planet, the ecological and financial costs of recovery of fuels and minerals have risen to be nearly equal to the net value of the recovery itself. With a diminishing resource base on a finite planet, and a limit to planetary carrying capacities, systemic capital growth cannot possibly be sustained forever as if it were disconnected from all that, nor can profits, stock values, investment levels, or large-scale capitalism itself. What may have worked in 1890 and 1950 is absurd in 2012.

Ecosystem Into Economy

Environmental author and activist Derrick Jensen reduces the discussion of industrial growth to its fundamentals in *Truthout* (July 16, 2011): "What is production? It is the conversion of the living into the dead; the conversion of living forests into two-by-fours, living rivers into stagnant pools for generating hydroelectricity, living fish into fish sticks, and ultimately all of these into money. And really, what is gross national product? It's a measure of this conversion of the living to the dead."

University of Maryland economist Herman Daly, author of the great ecological classic *For the Common Good*, takes a view similar to Jensen's, describing the process this way in the *Daly News* (August 15, 2010): "[It is] a transformation of ecosystem into economy in physical terms. Trees are physically transformed into tables and chairs; soil, rain, and sunlight are physically transformed into crops and food, and then into people; petroleum is physically transformed into motive force, plastics, and carbon dioxide." He describes the process as a "takeover" of the ecosystem by the "physical growth of the macro-economy. . . . The more matter and energy are appropriated by the economy, the less remains to build the services of the ecosystems that sustain the economy. . . . These are the basic facts about how the world works. They could plausibly be ignored by economists only as long as the macro-economy was tiny relative to the ecosystem." That is no longer the case.

Jensen and Daly might have added that when government financial reports are published in the financial pages, they tend to be broken into categories like "output from manufacturing" or "services" or "new housing starts" or "new car sales," with little effort to illuminate the exact exchanges involved in those abstract categories. "New housing starts," for example, masks the reality of how much of nature is being sacrificed to build beams and floors and fabrics for the house; how many pipelines—built out of minerals like iron, steel, and copper—have to be put through the soil to move water, gas, and electricity (copper/rubber) lines to the house; how much formerly pristine land, open space, or farmland gets converted to suburbs and roads. If such factors were amplified in the reports, possibly we would better see the virtues of older houses.

Similarly, "new car sales" doesn't indicate the volume of minerals, plant-based fabrics, and other materials that were likely extracted in South America, Africa, Indonesia, etc., and then shipped around the world to be processed into cars and then sold. How much more concrete gets put down on the land? How much oil has to come from the bottom of the ocean or from tar sands to power the things? If we could picture all these implications and interactions, perhaps we would conclude a used car would do well enough. On the other hand, if enough of us did decide that, what of the harms to the capitalist system that has been our sustenance? It's a dilemma.

All of the above is ignored by currently dominant economic measures, which avoid the material realities of our economic exchanges. But even more abstracted are society's official *megameasures* of growth.

Gross Domestic Product (GDP)

As far as most mainstream economists are concerned, the rate of transforming nature into commodities is not a visible part of the calculation. Economic "growth" is simply a measure of the advance (or decline) of total economic activity, from "resource" to store to home. This is usually expressed systemically as gross domestic product (GDP) or gross national product (GNP). GDP and GNP are very similar compilations of every transaction involving a payment for a resource, commodity, or service over a period of time, whether by companies, consumers, or government. Economists can make this calculation very complex, but for our purposes I think it's sufficient to say this: When you hear in the news that "U.S. economic growth is stagnant," it simply means that roughly the same amount of money changed hands this year as last within a national economic framework (GDP), and that the rate of transformation—nature into commodities—was stable. If the figure includes activities of American corporations and banks operating outside of our country, that is more likely to appear as part of GNP.

Downturns in either measurement are bad news for capitalism because investors depend on an expansion of their investment value. Most large investors are using *surplus* or *excess* funds (that is, the money they have available beyond what it costs to run their business, and that their family spends to live, or that they personally spend on entertainment, travel, new yachts, or second or third houses around the world).

Very few investors will deliberately put excess funds into any normal bank account, or into any projects that produce zero or nominal growth. Owners of excess wealth are normally seeking much higher rates of return than, for example, banks will *ever* pay for personal savings. Among investors trying to park excess capital, 10 percent is the lowest approximate standard of acceptable return. Short of that, they may be inclined toward more daring gambling opportunities in virtual economy markets, offering derivative products, hedge funds, arbitrage, and the like.

As Jensen and Daly suggest, in the real economy of material goods and services, "growth" of the system is measured as the total financial output of all the steps required to transform nature into commodities, and then to transport the commodities across continents and oceans to markets. These steps may include everything from the mining of the minerals that make the product to the felling of the trees that build the house—from, say, the jungles of South America—to the shipping of these raw materials across oceans to some other country to be processed, shaped, and transformed into usable production components. These new product components may then be shipped again to yet another country to be assembled into final form—a car or a missile or a steel beam, or a computer, or a toaster or hair dryer, or a pair of sunglasses, or a book or a Kindle. In the case of consumer products, they are finally transported to retail outlets in cities and towns. Hopefully, consumers then jump into their cars (or buses) and go buy the things and transport them to their homes or offices. Eventually most of it gets carted away to dump sites or landfills, tossed into the ocean, or dropped by the side of a road somewhere. According to the *Story of Stuff*, by Ann Leonard, of the Global Alliance for Incinerator Alternatives (GAIA), more than 99 percent of new commodities are thrown away within one year of their purchase.

All the above steps get included in the GDP of the United States or some other country. GDP also incorporates the "value added" from every step of the process. "Value added" is the increase in value at each stage, toward the eventual selling price of the commodity. (A raw log or boards is worth less, of course, than a piece of wood that has been sawed into appropriate pieces, ready to be made into furniture.) However, there is no recognition at any point, when reporting such activities as GDP, that there has been any rate of "depletion" of nature from any of these processes.

The overall measurements of economic activity also include payments to the people who do the physical labor, as well as the operating costs of the vehicles they use (or buy during the year), and the meals they eat, and the clothes they wear, and all the communications gear and office equipment needed to arrange things and package them and then sell them, and the cost of the office buildings where all this is managed, including its furniture and carpets and windows and upkeep.

Each one of these steps adds to GDP and is considered a "good thing" by economists and politicians, as it demonstrates growth. But from the point of view of nature and long-term planetary viability, it is not a good thing; it might be a bad thing.

There are, of course, hundreds of other steps and processes that we are leaving out. For example, we could go through a similar chain with energy/electricity as it gets from coal in the ground, or oil at the bottom of the sea, to your wall socket. At every stage the process involves an economic exchange. Hopefully, the final sales value for the material or commodity amounts to somewhat more than the total combined costs. That then would represent profit.

But even when a string of activities is *not* profitable, every bit of it contributes to the measure of our national economic performance, or GDP and GNP. If a foreign company did, for example, all the mining, it may be included in some other country's GDP. The measurement of all countries' GDPs combined would (approximately) suggest the rate of *global* economic growth, or decline. But one might also use it to express the approximate rate of the *depletion of nature*.

Meanwhile, at a corporate level, if your company were able to be involved in a part of these activities, and did more of them this year than in a previous year, and was able to do so at a total cost per unit that is below what it received in the final economic exchange (at retail), then your company probably made a profit. If so, its stock value might go up, and new people might invest in hopes that next year you will be even *more* profitable than this year. GDP will have been increased by the amount of your company's expenditures, and you will have helped the system achieve systemic "growth." If most other companies in the country, as well as consumers and governments, also expanded their total spending, that will be reported in all media in a celebratory manner, as it expands the national GDP measurement. Economists would be happy, and politicians from both parties will take credit for it in their reelection campaigns.

What's Left Out of GDP?

Because the GDP does not identify any rates of depletion of resources or the transformation rate of nature into commodities involved in any of these activities, the average citizen is left unaware that such a negative exchange has even taken place, or that there is any negative long-term effect from growth. It's also important to note that GDP measurements do not make any mention of or distinction as to what *purpose* is being served by all this economic activity.

All the expenses of war, for example, add directly to the GDP and in that sense are considered "good." So is prison construction, and the care and control of inmates. Even accidents and pollution can boost GDP. When the *Exxon Valdez* spilled eleven million gallons of oil into Alaska's Prince William Sound, it appeared on economic ledgers as a positive event. The cleanup created jobs and restoration contracts that moved millions of federal "disaster dollars" to local businesses and corporate coffers. However, the loss of seabirds and marine life did not enter on the tote sheets of the economists.

Repair from hurricane devastation, tidal waves, or viral-disease epidemics or bridges washed away also add to GDP. So does "redevelopment" or "gentrification," though they often destroy perfectly good communities or buildings that could still be useful for many decades more. These are all "positive" expressions, as far as GDP is concerned, and count for as much as building schools or hospitals or private cars or public transport or computers. The whole measurement system is without any moral or environmental value components, except to measure individual and institutional gains in wealth.

Meanwhile, many activities certainly do add "value" of another kind to society at large—let's say, in-home personal care of the elderly, or domestic work at home, where a wife takes care of the kids and makes the meals and keeps up the house so the husband can go to the office, or vice versa. Or by communities of indigenous people who have *not* cut down all their forests over millennia, or farmers who let lands lay fallow for a recovery period. These are not valued as contributing to the economy, though they certainly bring real benefit to human well-being, the lives of families, and the condition of the natural world. Since such activities are unpaid, they do not contribute to GDP and are not among the standards by which modern capitalist societies today measure success.

For example, a farmer who grows food for his family, who then enjoys the food without additionally paying cash for it, contributes nothing to the measure of economic wealth or growth of the country under the lens of the capitalist system. This is especially true if the farmer gathers and conserves seeds from year to year, rather than buying new seeds annually. But the industrial corporate farmer—Cargill or Monsanto—that grows hundreds of square miles of industrial monocrops, using pesticides and giant oil-guzzling machinery, or maybe biotechnology, and ships them by boat to overseas markets, using refrigeration, is adding a lot of "value" at every stage to the economy, from the mechanized growing to the long-distance shipping. From the capitalist point of view, the self-sufficient farmer is useless, but the corporate farmer is to be subsidized and assisted in every way possible. In fact, the self-sufficient farmer is a negative to capitalism. He is essentially "wasting" what could be profit-producing land, and the opportunities of supporting shipping companies and retail markets. So is the indigenous group that does *not* cut down its trees.

A very high percentage of economic growth also consists of the creation of thousands of products that could be classified, if anyone wanted to bother, as "trivial." That is, they may add economic value to GDP measures, but they arguably don't add much to the quality of life. Everyone has an opinion about what they consider essential, but my list of extraneous *products* includes automatic hand-drying machines and toilet flushing; electric can openers; annual style changes for cars; GPS systems, iPads and cell phones; annual "spring" and "fall" fashions; and those ubiquitous, huge flat-screen TVs; all of which accelerate the sacrifice of nature for short-term, highly dubious pleasures. And while we're at it, can we get rid of those drone aircraft?

Minneapolis economist David Morris loves to use the illustration of plastic-wrapped toothpicks. Many of these are manufactured in Japan, but Japan has no oil reserves to make the plastics, and insufficient forests for the wood or the cardboard boxes that the toothpicks are packaged in. The wood gets cut down mainly in Indonesia or Borneo, and the plastic is made from oil from the Middle

East. All of that goes to Japan on ships that typically run on "bunker C" motor oil, the most polluting kind of petroleum, and gets unloaded and then processed into toothpicks and plastic for the individual toothpick wrappers. Then they are put into a paper box and shipped eight thousand miles to your grocery store.

All of this adds to the GDP of Japan, and of some other nations, too, and adds to economic growth, profits, and investor gains. You then buy the toothpicks, tear off and throw away the plastic, pick your teeth, and throw away the wood. Then it all winds up in the landfill. Every one of those acts adds to GDP, here in the United States, in Japan, in Indonesia, in Dubai, and for the shipping company, perhaps from Korea.

If GDP had increased lately from 1 to 2 percent, it would mean we'd converted nature into commodities, i.e., eliminated parts of nature, at a rate that was twice as fast as the prior year's. You can understand why some people might view economic growth as a *negative* measure, not a positive one.

Dave Gardner, director of the film *GrowthBusters*, prefers to read reports of *declining* growth rates: "I would guess that 99.9 percent of the world considers this bad news," Gardner says about the dismal economic performance. "It's characterized in the *New York Times* as a 'snail's pace.' Journalists and commentators around the world are typing out words like *weak, anemic, malaise, gloomy, bleak*. . . . So why would I celebrate? Do I get morbid pleasure at seeing fellow humans unemployed? I do not. The fallout of the recession is real, it's painful, and it's sad. But declining GDP is not bad news. These are the pains of adjusting to a new reality: the end of growth. They are a necessary part of a temporary phase. We might call it the cocoon phase, as we metamorphose into something new."

Gardner lists some recent good news from declining growth rates: After thirty years of ever-increasing square footage, home sizes are now decreasing; oil consumption has declined; the human reproductive rate has slowed down; "new home" construction has declined; coal use has slowed; Home Depot is not expanding; GM stopped production of the Hummer; bottled water consumption has declined; airlines have reduced flights; and bicycle sales have increased.

Gardner might also have added that during the recent recessions there were reports that the level of CO_2 emissions significantly declined, as did the rates of biodiversity decline and wildlife extinction.

Virtual Growth

A different kind of "growth" is represented by *virtual economy* investing. This kind of activity is designed to appeal to those elements of society—the upper 1–2 percent—with enormous unemployed *surplus capital*, hungry for someplace

in which to invest that will produce more excess capital. Growth in this category is even more tenuous than in the real economy and is based mainly on
perceptions of the value of investment products that are many stages removed
from any concrete source of value, like land or manufactured products—virtual
investing requires the attitude of a gambler. This is the ultimate Ponzi expression. The iconic figure here is Bernie Madoff.

Virtual investments remain viable only as long as their perceived "value"
steadily rises, thus justifying investors' faith and continued support for the
vague distant "products" (for example, a collection of packaged-together, quite
fragile securities-backed home mortgages). It is a roll of the dice.

The continued growth and success of these activities are dependent, as well,
upon continued laissez-faire government policies on financial institutions,
including banks and hedge funds, that allow largely unregulated investment
practices. These include very high leverage rates for banks, allowing them to
make loans on as much as 90 percent of the general public's deposits that they
are supposedly protecting, as well as permission to invest funds for their own
benefit in highly risky made-to-trade "derivative" products, such as "credit
default swaps," "exchange traded derivative contracts," "credit-linked notes,"
and "total return swaps." Laissez-faire also seems to apply when it comes to tax-
ing these people. Fund managers are allowed shamefully low tax rates and the
prospect of generous bailouts if they fail. Those special tax breaks are achieved
by armies of lobbyists and hundreds of millions of dollars of campaign donations to government officials.

Meanwhile, none of this activity actually produces anything of material
value to society. These virtual instruments provide the possibility of spectacular growth, even if the growth in value exists nowhere except within computer
programs, which can evaporate very quickly.

Right-wing rhetoric justifies lower taxes and various other tax breaks for the
ultra-wealthy investors who engage in the virtual economy, and for the super-
rich financial managers they work with—often as low as 15 percent—arguing
that as these people get richer, they will reinvest their new wealth in job-creating
productive activity. All evidence suggests the opposite, that the ultra-wealthy
rarely use their virtual funds' growth to reinvest in the real economy, which
would be far more time-consuming and difficult. Do they really want to have to
deal again with more labor unions and pesky environmentalists? It's easier to
stick with financial instruments, but only as long as they're growing. The idea
that there is economic or social benefit from tax breaks for the rich is preposter-
ous. When you hear a congressman like Paul Ryan make such a claim as to the
job-creating benefits of lower tax rates, you can be sure of his need for more
campaign donations.

While growth in the virtual sector is duly reported, it is categorically different from the measurements within GDP, and most of these transactions are not incorporated into GDP. This investing has more to do with Las Vegas gambling activity than with much of anything real in the economy. It is just rich people trying to get richer. Unfortunately, however, the outcomes can have actual consequences in the real world. Failure of some of these virtual products can produce failures down the investment line, including banks eating into their available leverage allowances.

At some point, as with any Ponzi scheme, the gamblers' assumptions may prove wrong, or the bubble gets too bloated and bursts; markets collapse, jobs are lost, homes are foreclosed on, fortunes evaporate, and the government is called in to bail out many of the billionaires who started it.

On the other hand, some virtual-investment money does sometimes find its way into hedge funds and arbitrage systems that, for example, may buy vast acreage of agricultural lands, or mineral deposits in Africa, only to be resold to Russia or China or corporations in the United States. In many cases, such sales lead to the removal from the traditional lands of formerly self-sufficient farmers or local communities. That certainly has real impact on people's lives and food supply and prices in the real world, as we will discuss.

"Planetary Boundaries"

In a series of articles in *Monthly Review Press* (2009 and 2010), Fred Magdoff, University of Vermont professor emeritus of soil science, is joined by John Bellamy Foster, University of Oregon professor of sociology, reporting on the environmental consequences of capitalism and its obsession with growth. In "What Every Environmentalist Needs to Know About Capitalism," they focus on the variety of catastrophic potentials of key resource-related issues, from climate change to food shortages. They do not pull any punches in placing blame for the environmental and social disasters they are reporting upon.

> Capitalism's basic driving force and its whole reason for existence is the amassing of profits and wealth through the accumulation (savings and investments) process. It recognizes no limits to its own self-expansion—not in the economy as a whole; not in the profits desired by the wealthy; and not in the increasing consumption that people are cajoled into desiring in order to generate greater profits for corporations. The environment exists, not as a place with inherent boundaries within which beings must live together with earth's other species, but as a realm to be exploited in a process of growing economic expansion.

Indeed, businesses, according to the inner logic of capital, which is enforced by competition, must either grow or die—as must the system itself. . . . It is precisely the fact that ecological destruction is built into the inner nature and logic of our present system of production that makes it so difficult to solve.

Magdoff and Foster illustrate their report with numerous examples of the system exceeding "planetary boundaries/thresholds of the earth's systems." These include the advancing acidification of the oceans; ozone depletion; biodiversity loss and species extinctions; atmospheric aerosol loading; and hundreds of kinds of chemical pollution, sickening natural systems.

The authors discuss such grim consequences of climate change as the rapidly diminishing Greenland and Antarctic ice sheets, and the melting of the planet's glaciers. "Even a sea level rise of 1–2 meters would be disastrous for hundreds of millions of people in low lying countries, and various island states. . . . At present, more than 400 million people live less than five meters above sea level." And once glaciers are gone, so will be the rivers that have irrigated farmlands throughout Asia and elsewhere.

Devastating droughts from climate change will potentially affect 70 percent of the planet's land surface within the next several decades, say the authors, and are already evident in parts of India, Africa, and Australia. These droughts will decimate food supplies, increase prices, and bring extinctions of certain crops and animals. The oceans, meanwhile, are impacted by miles and miles of trash, much of it plastics. "A recent survey estimated," according to Magdoff and Foster, "that over 17,000 animals and plants are at risk of extinction . . . more than one in five of all known mammals, over a quarter of reptiles, and 70 percent of plants are under threat."

Resource Shrinkage on a Finite Planet

Richard Heinberg, of the Post Carbon Institute, is one of the world's leading researchers, thinkers, and authors on the phenomenon of "peak oil"—that global oil reserves are now in sharp decline. Those reserves that remain are far more difficult, expensive, and ecologically dangerous to extract. In his book *Peak Everything*, Heinberg expands his reporting to include a very long list of other global resources that are in a similar irreversible state of decline, and concludes, "We are at the end of the period of the greatest material abundance in human history."

Heinberg points out that cheap, highly efficient oil was the main driver in the spectacular performance of industrial capitalist society over the last two centuries. Particularly during the latter half of the twentieth century, we gorged ourselves on all these nonrenewable resources, without any thought of limits.

In his most recent book, *The End of Growth*, he calls *no growth* "the new normal," and goes on to say, "Economic growth as we have known it is over and done with. . . . There are now fundamental barriers to ongoing economic expansion, and the world is colliding with those barriers."

It's not that there will be no short-term spurts of growth, or growth in certain well-positioned industries or even country economies—in alternative-energy industries, for example—but "from now on," says Heinberg, "only relative growth is possible: The global economy is playing a zero-sum game, with an ever-shrinking pot to be divided among the winners."

Heinberg gives additional evidence that we are beginning to run out of hundreds of resources crucial to the industrial economy. They include not only oil, gas, fresh water, and food grains, but forests, biodiversity and genetic diversity, wild-fish stocks, coral reefs, many kinds of crucial elements and minerals, including coltan and lithium (for cell phones and electronic purposes), zinc, phosphorous, iron ore, copper, tin, platinum, cobalt, and critical "rare earth" elements needed for electronics, 95 percent of which are now confined to China. This is only a highly reduced partial list.

Some geologists, says Heinberg, believe we even face near-term shortages in high-quality coal and uranium, usually thought of as our post-oil "fallback" fuels. As with other scarce resources, when the supplies of each diminish, the quality deteriorates and the costs inevitably increase. Remaining supplies are in more remote places, or are more expensive and environmentally devastating to mine.

Many countries are already deeply concerned about the economic effects of disappearing resources. In March 2010, the Institute for Sustainable Futures (ISF) of the University of Technology in Sydney, Australia, issued a report, "Peak Minerals in Australia," documenting future physical and economic constraints in the country's domestic production of coal, iron ore, steel, bauxite, aluminium, gold, lead, zinc, silver, copper, rutiel, ilmenite, zircon, diamonds, manganese, nickel, tin, uranium, lithium, tantalum. These represent about 8 percent of the county's GDP, and 56 percent of exports.

The study cited decreasing accessibility of supply, declining quality of resources, and rising energy prices (making extraction much more expensive) as all conspiring to make the future look grim for Australia. The report might have added the problem of water supply, a major factor in mining; Australia has been suffering from a raging drought over the past few years. Similar packages of problems could be applied to dozens of other mineral-dependent countries at this time.

Meanwhile, a few countries are at the opposite end of the cycle. Siberia and Mongolia, for example, once considered too remote for corporate resource accessing, are finding themselves very popular, especially for their lithium supplies. And the northwest coast of Greenland has suddenly been discovered by resource corporations, including Alcoa, looking for untapped bauxite deposits under the disappearing ice sheet. The company hopes to build giant aluminium smelters near the tiny fishing village of Maniitsoq. Some villagers are aghast. A National Public Radio report on *Morning Edition* (August 18, 2011) quotes Aqqaluk Lynge, of the Inuit Circumpolar Council, who worries about social and environmental impacts: "I think it's way out of touch if we are helping a multinational company like Alcoa gain their foothold in Greenland."

Financial Speculation in Food Supplies

Of all oncoming shortages, a global food shortage is possibly the most frightening and imminent. As with many resources, peak food has unleashed a massive burst of capitalist financial speculation. Food-growing lands, especially in Africa, are attracting capital from every direction, *not* to grow food, but to "buy low and sell high," as with any other real estate investment. But this one brings with it a whole new level of tragedy.

In the *New York Times* (December 22, 2010), Neil MacFarquhar reported, "Across Africa and the developing world, a new global land rush is gobbling up large expanses of arable land. Despite their ageless traditions, stunned villagers are discovering that African governments typically own [the villagers'] lands and have been leasing them, often at bargain prices, to private investors and foreign governments for decades to come."

The World Bank is supporting the practice, which has thrown thousands of small farmers off their lands and created "a volatile mass of landless poor. Making matters worse," the article continues, "much of the food is bound for wealthier nations." The World Bank said that during 2009 alone, the land purchase deals covered "at least 110 million acres—the size of California and West Virginia combined." More than 70 percent of the deals were for lands in Africa, "with Sudan, Mozambique, and Ethiopia among those nations transferring millions of acres to investors."

In some cases, certain countries (China and Libya were cited) are trying to acquire good agricultural lands beyond their borders to protect themselves against predicted global food crises. But "many investments appear to be pure speculation that leaves land fallow," the report found. "Farmers have been displaced without compensation, land has been leased well below value, those evicted end up encroaching on parkland, and the new ventures have created fewer jobs than promised."

In June 2011 an even more blistering study was published by the Oakland Institute in California ("Understanding Land Investment Deals in Africa"), reporting that "land grabbing" in Africa was frequently initiated by giant hedge funds and bankers in the United States and England. Other major investors turned out to include prestigious universities like Vanderbilt and Harvard.

Reporting on the Oakland study, the British *Guardian* newspaper stated that "much of the money is channelled through London-based Emergent asset management," which finances "one of Africa's largest land acquisition funds, run by former JP Morgan and Goldman Sachs currency dealers." The Oakland Institute report says that $500 million has been invested in some of the Third World's most fertile lands, with expectations of harvesting 25 percent returns. Emergent confirmed, "Yes, university endowment funds and pension funds are long-term investors . . . we are investing in African agriculture and setting up businesses and employing people," said the *Guardian* story. "We are doing this in a responsible way. . . . The amounts are large. They can be hundreds of millions of dollars. This is not land-grabbing. We want to make the land more valuable." In other words, Emergent and the other investors are "do-gooders."

The way they make the land "more valuable," apparently, is by buying it from African governments, who have *expropriated* it from the people whose ancestors have lived there for centuries. Then investors like Emergent resell the property to land-hungry investors in other countries, a process known as arbitrage. Sometimes the land is left fallow and remains an arbitrage commodity. Other times the lands, which once supported local farmers, go into industrial-style export agriculture, producing biofuels or such high-value export crops as exotic flowers or luxury food items for wealthy countries. Very few people get jobs in these newly mechanized and chemical-intensive farmlands, and no one local gets food. The land does become more valuable, but only for the wealthy investors.

In Tanzania, the central government has an agreement with AgriSol Energy, in collaboration with Iowa University, for a $700 million project on land that previously supported 162,000 people who had farmed there for more than forty years. Similar deals were made in Mozambique and South Sudan. In the latter case, a former U.S. ambassador, Howard Eugene Douglas, who now heads a Texas-based company, Nile Trading and Development (a partner in the deal), will obtain a forty-nine-year lease of four hundred thousand hectares for about $25,000. According to the *Guardian*, this will allow "the company to exploit all natural resources, including oil and timber." In most of these deals, the people who had been small farmers, supporting themselves for generations on the land, are suddenly viewed as "squatters" and are removed.

"No one should believe that these investors are there to feed starving Africans, create jobs, or improve food security," said Obang Metho, of the Solidarity Movement for a New Ethiopia. "These agreements—some of which may be in place for 99 years—do not mean progress for local people, and will not lead to food in their stomachs. These deals lead only to dollars in the pockets of corrupt leaders and foreign investors."

Anuradha Mittal, the executive director of the Oakland Institute, elaborates: "The same financial firms that drove us into a global recession by inflating the real estate bubble through risky financial maneuvers are now doing the same speculations with the world food supply. The result is displacement of small farmers, environmental devastation, water loss, and further political instability." Mittal warns that the conversion of Africa's small farms and forests into high-value investment assets "drives up food prices everywhere, and increases the risks of climate change."

At several points during her research, Mittal herself went to Africa, posing as a wealthy potential land buyer. She inquired with the big landowners as to good farm workers in the region—at that time they were still claiming it was all about giving people jobs—but the owners advised her "confidentially" that the best thing would be for her to import white farm workers from South Africa.

Another wide-ranging report, by Lester Brown of Earth Policy Institute in *Scientific American* (May 2009), titled "Could Food Shortages Bring Down Civilization?" says that "the biggest threat to global stability is the potential for food crises in poor countries bringing on government collapse.

"As demand for food rises [partly from population growth] faster than supplies are growing, the resulting food-price inflation puts severe stress on the government of countries already teetering on the edge of chaos. Unable to buy grain or grow their own, hungry people take to the streets . . . if the food situation continues to deteriorate, entire nations will break down at an ever-increasing rate, and we have entered a new era in geopolitics. . . . "

Brown cites global population growth of seventy-plus million per year, as well as the growing number of people wanting to move up the food chain to consume grain-intensive livestock products.

Meanwhile, about a quarter of the U.S. grain harvest will go to fuel cars; that's enough grain to otherwise feed about 125 million Americans—or half a billion Indians—at current consumption levels. Much of the Amazon rain forest is being sacrificed to sugarcane production of biofuels for automobiles.

Brown continues: "Topsoils are eroding faster than new soil forms on perhaps a third of the world's croplands. This thin layer of essential plant nutrient, the very foundation of civilization, took long stretches of geological time to build up, yet it is typically only about six inches deep. Its loss from wind and water erosion doomed earlier civilizations."

But the *most* pervasive environmental threat to food security, says Brown, is rising surface temperature from climate change, which affects crop yields everywhere. "In many countries crops are grown at or near their thermal optimum, so even a minor temperature rise during the growing season can shrink the harvest.... For every rise of one degree Celsius (1.8 degrees Fahrenheit) above the norm, wheat, rice, and corn yields fall by 10 percent. No country is immune to this."

Privatization of Water

An arguably even worse situation is emerging vis-à-vis the world's water supplies. The amount of fresh water on Earth represents only 0.5 percent of total water supply, but its consumption is doubling every twenty years. United Nations reports indicate that more than one billion people on Earth already lack access to clean drinking water.

Population growth is one cause of this crisis, but the increase in water use is twice the rate of population growth. Irrigation wells for food production are pumping water faster than it can be replenished by rainfall. Water tables are falling in countries housing more than half the world population. According to Lester Brown, because of water shortages, "China's wheat crop, the world's largest, has declined by 8 percent.... China's rice production dropped by 4 percent."

Nations dependent on runoff from mountain glaciers are taking an even worse hit, as glaciers are rapidly melting from climate change. The first consequence is massive flooding. That's followed soon after by water shortages. Particularly affected are India, Bangladesh, and Pakistan, which have historically survived from annual glacier melt within the Himalayas. But now such countries as Bolivia, Ecuador, and Peru are being effected by melting in the Andes.

Human beings use only about 15 percent of the global fresh water supply. Industrial agriculture takes 65 percent, using water at a much higher rate than do small farmers. A high percentage also goes to high-tech manufacturing, especially for computer chips, which require absolutely pure water. High-tech production is increasingly moving to low-wage Asian countries like China, whose own water supply is nearly exhausted.

The matter is so serious that quite a few nations are near the brink of war over water. Turkey is already at war with its Kurdish population, which seeks independence; the Kurds live in the mountain region that supplies much of southern Turkey's water. Water scarcity is also an issue among quite a few African nations, between Israel and Palestinians, and even among the U.S., Mexico, and Canada. The World Bank has gone so far as to predict, "The next World War will be about water," though oil certainly remains another candidate.

As the water crisis gets worse, one would expect governments and global bureaucracies to advocate conservation. Instead, what are under way are the privatization, commodification, and globalization of the planet's remaining fresh water—its lakes, rivers, streams—to sell exploitation rights to corporations and let the global market decide who gets to drink it or use it.

NAFTA and the WTO already have provisions that define water as a "commodity" and "a tradeable good"—no longer protected as part of the natural commons—with rules requiring that governments permit foreign investment in local fresh water supplies, and even allowing foreign companies to export the water under certain trigger conditions. One WTO condition is that if any locality anywhere in the country—a city or a province—privatizes any part of its fresh water resources or delivery operations and opens it to bidding by foreign investors, then the entire country is obliged to follow suit. In other words, if British Columbia proceeds with plans to allow a foreign investor to take over its water delivery system, then all of Canada's lakes and rivers are open to exploitation and export.

Resource corporations are excited by this. Water, after all, may soon be arguably more valuable than oil. Among the brilliant corporate schemes to profit from this situation is one that would ship North American lake, river, and stream water across the Pacific Ocean to Asia, where the need is growing, due to industrialization of agriculture and investment in the region's high-tech industries.

So picture this: gigantic supertankers, bigger than any present oil tankers, filled with fresh water, steaming across oceans, while towing humongous floating plastic water-filled balloons the size of a baseball stadium, carrying a big part of Lake Superior to China. Such plans are being discussed now. Just as with the ag industry, which likes to say it is feeding a hungry world, the new emerging water industry likes to say it is bringing water to a thirsty world. But not only will most of the water go to industrial users—once water systems are fully privatized and globalized, most of the people on the planet who are actually thirsty will not be able to pay for it.

Peak Species & Peak Beauty

On June 21, 2011, the International Union for Conservation of Nature (IUCN) reported to the United Nations that a joint study undertaken with the International Programme on the State of the Oceans (IPSO) had made the most dire conclusions of any till now. It predicted an unprecedented mass extinction of life in the oceans, caused by a combination of factors including global warming, dead zones from farm pesticide runoff, increased acidity from carbon dioxide, habitat destruction, melting sea ice, chemicals and plastics in the oceans, and overfishing. Carl Lundin, director of global marine programs for IUCN, said "things seem to be going wrong on several levels simultaneously . . . faster than the worst case scenarios that were predicted just a few years ago."

From the IUCN report: "There's a brewing die-off of species that would rival past mass extinctions. . . . We now face losing marine species and entire marine ecosystems, such as coral reefs, within a single generation. . . . Multiple high-intensity factors also led to the previous five mass extinction events in the past 600 million years."

A World Resources Institute report concurs, saying that all coral reefs could be gone by 2050 if no action is taken to protect them, while a 2011 study published in *BioScience* declares oysters "functionally extinct." Their populations have been decimated by overharvesting, disease, and pesticide runoff from farms.

In a separate report in the *Independent* (U.K.) (July 12, 2011), science editor Steve Conner states, our planet is currently experiencing the "sixth great mass extinction in the history of life on earth." He also reports that the National Academy of Science (U.K.) concluded "that around 10 percent of species alive today could be facing extinction by 2100."

The IPSO report calls for immediate changes in several key areas: immediate reduction of CO_2 emissions, coordinated efforts to restore marine ecosystems, and universal implementation of the precautionary principle, so "activities proceed only if they are shown not to harm the ocean singly or in combination with other activities."

Doug Tompkins is founder and president of the Foundation for Deep Ecology. He is profoundly concerned about the exploding extinction crisis. "There's no worse expression of our dire situation than species extinction. And there's no clearer way to assess the failure of the Human Project. What could be worse than removing elements of the web of life? Once we lose species as a result of our actions, they disappear forever from the pool of biodiversity. The absolute finality of extinction is chilling enough, but there are secondary effects: the dislocations caused within the ecological web when you kill off part of it. It's the fabric of life unraveling."

There is another extinction that Tompkins brings up on every occasion he can, as it's rarely referenced in scientific discussions of these issues: "the extinction of beauty." Tompkins says this is every bit as important as the rest of it—and directly connected. "If it was possible for humans to continue to live in a world emptied of wildness, and biodiversity, and the beauty of nature, would we want to?" Tompkins invokes the words of authors Sandra Lubarsky and William Blake (from *Carnal Knowledge and the World's Beauty*): "If the word 'sustainability' means something more than mere survival and perseverance, then we must speak of beauty. . . . And yet our rhetoric of advocacy shuns the language of beauty. . . . Though we aim at the noble goal of keeping the earth and its diverse populations abundant and thriving, our language is almost exclusively a language of economics . . . a rational language, a language of accounting and ordering."

The U.K.'s Dark Mountain Project summarizes the situation as "ecocide":

> We are the first generation born into a new and unprecedented age—the age of ecocide. . . . We are already responsible for denuding the world of much of its richness, magnificence, beauty, color, and magic, and we show no sign of slowing down. For a very long time, we imagined that "nature" was something that happened elsewhere. The damage we did to it might be regrettable, but needed to be weighed against the benefits here and now. And in the worst-case scenario, there would always be some kind of plan B. Perhaps we would make for the moon, where we could survive in lunar colonies under giant bubbles as we planned our expansion across the galaxy. But there is no plan B, and the bubble, it turns out, is where we have been living all the while. . . . Of all of humanity's delusions of its separation from and superiority to the living world which surrounds it, one distinction holds up better than most: We may well be the first species capable of effectively eliminating life on Earth.

Earth Island

While writing this chapter, I thought very often of David Brower. In the mid-1950s, Brower was already speaking from his leadership perch at the Sierra Club of the urgency of limiting economic growth. This was long before the brilliant efforts of Rachel Carson in *Silent Spring* (1962) to help awaken an environmental movement, and the famous Club of Rome report, *The Limits to Growth* (1972). But the world was on a spending spree in the late 1950s through the 1960s and wasn't ready to hear any of it.

One of the concepts Brower repeated over and over was that "Earth is an island in space," our only home, and that each of us needs to develop "island consciousness." We are *all* island dwellers, he said. On an island, you are aware of limits—just so much land, just so much fresh water, just so many fish in the ocean, and that's it, at least until you can ship food in from Africa, and energy from the Middle East. You learn to sustain your communities on what is given. After Brower left the Sierra Club, he founded Friends of the Earth. And a few years before his death in 2000, he founded Earth Island Institute, to celebrate the concept. The organization remains very active today.

I think of Dave's admonitions especially when visiting two of my favorite places in the world: the island of Majorca, off the east coast of Spain, and the island of Kauai, Hawaii. Both are now suffering greatly from the failure to appreciate their "islandness," and they will be saved only if they do. Both islands are awesomely beautiful. They were both, until relatively recently, virtually self-sufficient in all fundamental resources: food production on land, fishing in the sea, water, energy needs, renewability. Both had great soils and thriving traditional agriculture production, ample water and rainfall to keep their farmers and people nourished, and little need for much energy in ideal climates. And, they are both windy and sunny.

Since World War II, however, both islands have given in to the ubiquitous "myth of progress" and to the demands of their business and governing communities to accelerate development and to achieve greater "growth and prosperity." In both cases that has meant encouraging massive tourist resort developments—let's call it commodifying the "beauty commons"—expanded highway systems, new airports, increased development of huge private real estate tracts (often owned by movie stars, billionaires, and other celebrities seeking peace and tranquility at the expense of everyone else), and the import of their food and energy supplies, in which they were formerly self-sufficient, to meet the needs of a burgeoning transient population.

In Majorca, I was told by Guillem Ferrer, of the New Sustainable Majorca Movement, that the traditional agriculture systems—which had fed the island for many centuries—have now been abandoned to tourist developments. About 95 percent of food, water, and energy on the island is currently imported—at greatly increased cost. The powers that be also built a gigantic airport on this tiny island with a capacity as big as Frankfurt's, which famously handles thousands of flights per day. Majorca's absurdly huge airport is not nearly as busy as Frankfurt's—and will probably never be—as the costs of travel are zooming and economies based on long-distance tourism are dying. Hotels are half full. Walking through Majorca's airport has a post-apocalyptic feeling. Huge, slick, beautiful, empty, as if the population has been carried away by a terrible disease. And it was. Capitalism.

Of course you needn't literally live on an island to have what Brower called "island consciousness." Hundreds of societies on our planet are still functioning quite well without employing economic principles predicated on growth beyond the capacities of their local resource base.

It's a highly important (though little appreciated fact), for example, that of the planet's remaining natural resource reserves, a very high percentage are found on the lands of indigenous peoples. Some estimate that these reserves may run as high as 50–60 percent of total global reserves, especially in the case of forests, water, biodiversity, and genetic diversity. This is especially so among the peoples of the Amazon, the Andes, and the forests of Indonesia, Southeast Asia, and in the northernmost regions of the world.

That's the good news. The bad news is that this has made these indigenous communities even greater targets than in the past for global resource industries and national governments, who would like to shove the indigenous peoples off their lands and out of the way, by whatever means necessary.

There is such tragic irony in this. The very ability of indigenous societies to successfully live for millennia by economic, political, and cultural philosophies and values that do not require them to use up all the resources of their regions has made these same peoples a primary target in the desperate corporate search for the last resources on Earth. The ongoing attempted theft of indigenous resources themselves is only one of the problems; there are also the intrusive infrastructures that are introduced by developers onto still pristine lands: the roads, the pipelines, the electrical grids, ports, airfields, dams, all on indigenous land. Many times, this has led to massive resistance, most recently in Bolivia.

In late 2007, after two decades of effort, the indigenous peoples of the world succeeded in passing the highly important, and very radical, United Nations Declaration on the Rights of Indigenous Peoples (UNDRIP). Comparable to the UN Declaration on Human Rights, forty years earlier, this newer declaration confirms indigenous sovereignty over most of their traditional lands and resources, and it further confirms their rights to their own traditional forms of governance.

UNDRIP also articulated indigenous peoples' explicit right of "free, prior, and informed consent" for any resource development forays by global corporations and nation-states, and confirmed their right to maintain traditional indigenous "subsistence" economic practices. The General Assembly vote was 144 to 4, with the only negative votes coming from four of the most resource-exploitative countries: the United States, Canada, Australia, and New Zealand. These four countries did not see how it could possibly be beneficial to their own resource hunts if native peoples had any legal instruments to sustain control of their traditional lands and resources.

Over the following two years, however, Canada, Australia, and New Zealand changed their positions to support UNDRIP. It was not until the very end of 2010 that Barack Obama announced that the United States, the world's last holdout, was also changing its vote to favor the UN declaration. The only problem that remains is how to apply the principles of the declaration in actual policy and practice, and how to persuade nation-states to live within the carrying capacities of the planet.

Fundamental Questions

Given the inescapable consequences of capitalist growth, economist Herman Daly offers some direct economic questions that are at the heart of the matter:

"Are the extra benefits of physically transforming more of the ecosystem into the economy worth the extra opportunity costs of the ecosystem services being lost in the transformation? Surely economists have thought about such simple and basic questions as: 'Can the economy be too big in its physical dimensions relative to the ecosystem? And are the marginal costs of growth now larger than the marginal benefits?' Surely economists have good answers to these obvious questions!"

But have they? Maybe not. Few mainstream economic pundits, government economists, media economists, or IMF or WTO economists will admit (at least publicly) that they've even noticed this problem. They remain mute in the face of the rapid, suicidal depletion of nature—the basis of all life—while continuing their futile search for long-term acceleration of systemic growth and profit. *Except* there has lately been the merest inkling that Paul Krugman, the Princeton economist and Nobel Prize winner, who writes for the *New York Times*, may be getting the point. In the past he repeatedly said growth has to be above 3.5 percent to meet our society's needs. But then, on December 27, 2010—in the most tentative voice, and in only a small part of his column—Krugman used the "f"-word. He suggested that the world's resources just may be "finite." There just may be "limits" to resources, he said, especially oil, and this may be affecting prices and growth. *Wow.* It was only a few sentences, but somebody finally got through to him. Maybe it was Daly. How many years more will it take to get him to use the "c"-word?

Under present circumstances, you might expect that any responsible society would be loudly promoting "conservation consciousness" strategies. It would be mobilizing to convince people that current crises demand that we consume far *less* energy and *fewer* materials, not more, and that we rearrange our economic strategies so that our activities remain within the carrying capacities of the planet.

However, if governments actually tried to do that, it would quickly lead us to the same conflicts we discussed in chapter III. If nations did take a conservationist path, businesses based on growth, already in trouble, would be in still more trouble. So governments do *not* finally propose the kind of radical change that, someday soon, will certainly be mandatory. In fact, nothing happens at all, while months roll by without anyone in positions of national or international leadership proposing any kind of transition plan.

Quite the opposite. It remains the urgent cause of the capitalist system—

including all its players in government, industry, and economics—to *deny* all of the above. The simple recognition of such *intrinsic* aspects of a fatally flawed economic model would send panic through communities whose lives are dedicated to and dependent on constant growth. Any call for a truly "ecological economy" would negatively affect stock prices instantly and dramatically.

So, for most of industry, and for most governments, (particularly the U.S. government), the goal remains *avoiding* conservationist solutions. Conservation offers zero "value added." Instead, the goal of businesses and governments is to somehow turn these grim crises into new business opportunities.

VII.
Searching for Growth:
Desperate Measures

So, the problem comes down to this: To sustain capitalist society into the future, we need to find ways to lift economic growth to a minimum of 3.5 percent annually, domestically and globally, and keep it there. If we cannot do that, everything we understand about our economy is moot, and we may be looking at imminent ecological, economic, social, and political collapse. However, if we *do* try to achieve that growth, as every elected official in national, state, and local governments in the United States and every other country is desperately trying to do, along with every corporation, bank, and mainstream media outlet, that will *also* lead to ecological, economic, social, and political collapse. It's another conundrum.

Exploitation of global resources has already collided with its limits. Rates of species extinction are far greater than they have been in six million years. Climate change. Rising waters. Disappearing fresh water and food supply. As we have said. We are walking on coals, but even the coals are running out. For the most part, however, none of this is admitted by public officials or in the mainstream media.

There *are* some promising theoretical solutions being discussed for possible long-term planetary survival, some of which we will report in chapter XII. For the moment they can be summarized with such words as these: *Less. Local. Equitable. Cooperative. Community-Based, Eco-Centric, Steady-State. Antiglobal, Powered-Down, Conservationist.*

Sustained systemic economic growth is not included in the list and is no longer a realistic long-term option. But the people who manage the system cannot accept that. They constantly try to defy reality by seeking new ways to grow. Currently, much of their effort falls into seven broad categories. The first two, we discussed earlier, and I will review them only briefly in the present context. The third, expansion of the military economy, will be covered in the next chapter, and I give only a short summary here. The others in the list (4–7) are discussed in greater detail.

Seven Explorations in Growing Growth

1. Shifting from Real Growth to Virtual

The underlying drive of capitalists is to find ways for the wealth they have already accumulated to be used to generate *more* wealth. For most of the history of capitalism, investments were concentrated on tangible commercial activity: manufacturing products or selling them, or generating and marketing services of some kind.

The last two decades have seen a spectacular shift. Now, most investments of "surplus capital"—that is, available funds that are not being used for personal or family lifestyle activity, or for already ongoing business activity—are not going toward *real* production but are invested in financial instruments of some kind: money investing in money, the *virtual* economy.

Stocks are the most respectable of those options; international currency purchases are another. But, we have lately seen the powerful lure of the *speculative* economy, economic gambling in the world of subprime financial instruments, derivatives, and the like.

The net outcome of this shift in investment strategies, aside from its contribution to economic collapse, is that it deprives the real economy of investment monies and diminishes real growth. It creates no jobs and narrows wealth distribution, ultimately broadening economic inequity.

2. Creating "New Resources"—Privatizing the Commons

Another popular alternative to normal business investment is to put large amounts of surplus capital toward investing in Congress and other public officials, i.e., lobbying and campaign donations. The potential payoff from this is huge, including a whole array of government largesse, such as no-bid contracts and many kinds of tax benefits. The most important push is for the privatization of government services and agencies, and the conversion of public and natural "commons" to private corporate control. These privatization schemes amount to the transfer of "public property" toward the creation of *new resource pools*, which effectively expands the exploitable supply of *raw materials* for profitable development and economic growth. These can include natural resources like water, forests, or genetic materials, or they can be government agencies like TSA, the military, prisons, or the Department of Education. Lately, even such sacrosanct public commons as Medicare, Medicaid, and Social Security are being proposed for privatization and profit. In some locales, the Tea Party has been advocating for privatization of government itself.

3. Expanding the Military Economy

From an economic-continuity point of view, war has much to recommend it. Preparation for war involves many years of industrial innovation and production, and lots of jobs are involved, to help absorb any surplus labor. Then comes what may be several years of raging destruction, then more years of rebuilding what was destroyed. Then a new round of weapons production to replenish supplies; redesigning, modernizing, and maintaining new weaponry; and also deploying bases and troops around the world to maintain the peace. And military preparation and action can become reliably permanent. Very economically stabilizing.

The United States currently has only four ongoing wars, but it is always looking for others. North Korea, Iran, and Venezuela are on the short list of promising growth prospects, including maybe Pakistan. And there is always China, though that is still in phase one—preparation. Businesses can't really depend on that happening in the short run, as there are still too many overlapping, coinciding interests, including China's vast investments in U.S. Treasury bills.

4. Green Capitalism

On April 12, 2011, I attended a seminar on "Climate Capitalism" at the Commonwealth Club of California, featuring four green-business pioneers. The discussion was on how to reform capitalism to face the age of climate change while finding expanded business opportunity in it. The panelists included Hunter Lovins, president and founder of Natural Capitalism Solutions and the author of *Climate Capitalism: Capitalism in the Age of Climate Change*; David Chen, CEO and founder of the Equilibrium Capital Group; and Bruce Klafter, managing director for Environmental, Health, and Safety at Applied Materials Inc. Joel Makower, chairman and executive editor of GreenBiz Group Inc., was the moderator.

Lovins said that the "climate crisis is very real . . . and we have to rethink the way our whole system operates." She said she hoped to discuss "capitalism the way that capitalism should be done." She pointed out that current subsidies for nonrenewable-energy companies amount to about $500 billion annually, while renewables get only $25 billion. She suggested that clean-tech companies are now so perfectly attuned to the moment, they would gladly accept cutting of "all government subsidies, because we would win any competition strictly on our merits. The reality is," she said, "if you are a regular profit-maximizing capitalist, you will do better with renewables."

"This is just smart investing" said Chen, who specializes in green investment consulting, "not a lower rate of return. We formerly saw it as a sacrifice to do the right thing—but now doing the right thing may give you a much better return. . . . Green buildings are not only green in themselves, but they benefit the community, they excite the community, they set a standard and a fashion, they are easier to rent out, and they have lower vacancy rates."

Bruce Klafter said that "what's needed now is corporate and global consciousness change," though he admitted that not every business can ever really become green. "Take fast-food outlets like Burger King or McDonald's," he said. "They cannot really become green, because their basic model is distorted. Nor can they really change their basic model. They can have efficient lighting and electricity use, but can they really buy local foods? Can they get enough meat locally, and is it sustainably raised? Can they really plan for nutritional foods?" So, consciousness change would not work for them.

After the panel, the participants joined the audience in the lobby, and we were able to ask questions. One woman asked Chen, "Are you all really saying we can have more and more consumerism, etc., as long as it's of a certain kind? What about resources that are used in these businesses, and impacts between industry and nature? Can we have expanding consumerism without threatening resources and still sustain the natural world? Aren't you leaving something out here? How can we be sure companies do the right thing?"

Chen gave a thoughtful and revealing answer: "Every business, green or otherwise, operates for a profit, but at some point they come face-to-face with an 'ethical dilemma.' If they proceed further in certain directions, they may become less sustainable. So, when that moment comes, we hope they will make their decisions on an ethical basis. But there is certainly no assurance of that."

Indeed. I thought to myself that must be a problem that Chen frequently faces in dealing with investment clients. In the end, he was saying that the capitalist system—otherwise demanding of profits—leaves it as a question of individual ethics. At a certain point, capitalists may need to back off one set of values—the focus on ever-expanding capital and profit—and apply another set of values: the common good. Do they ever really do that? Perhaps, but not often.

In any case, is it really going to be sufficient in an age of climate change to hope for businesses to make the right move when faced with their ethical dilemma? Can we afford to allow the future to be determined by the individual choices and values of businessmen? What if you are what Lovins called "a profit-maximizing capitalist" and you *don't* "do better with renewables"? What do we do about Burger King? What if you're an oil company? What if you're an airline?

What if you make a much bigger profit by doing the *wrong* thing? What if, in one of those "ethical moments" that David Chen mentioned, you realize that doing the right thing means your business should really close its doors?

ECO-PORNOGRAPHY

There is scarcely one Fortune 500 company in the United States that is not currently running expensive advertising campaigns citing the amazing breakthroughs it is achieving in fighting climate change, saving energy, creating jobs, expanding growth, helping small business, and protecting resources. My favorite green ads—which some call "greenwashing" and others call "eco-pornography"—are from oil companies. ExxonMobil, ever eager to provide jobs, says it is devoted to developing the tar sands of Canada. It's "good for our energy security, and our economy. . . . This resource has the ability to create hundreds of thousands of jobs right here at home." It is also arguably the dirtiest form of energy (next to nuclear) and has a negative "net energy" ratio. That means it may actually cost more in terms of energy use to extract that oil, process it, ship it down a pipeline a thousand miles to Texas, and process it again than it will finally produce in new energy. More energy invested than produced.

It is a general rule of thumb about all corporate *institutional* advertising that the things being advertised are the opposite of what is actually true. Banks like Goldman Sachs are now advertising their great personal service and their dedication to small businesses' financial needs precisely because they have no dedication to small businesses—they recently destroyed many of them. Airlines like to advertise the enormous legroom they provide in economy class, and insurance companies of all kinds like to advertise how quickly and fully they respond to your claims and provide you with lifetime security.

Chevron's ads say the company is all about serving communities, small businesses, and jobs. "Oil companies should put their profits to good use," says the ad. In fact, Chevron is one of the worst oil companies in the world in terms of damage to communities. It has single-handedly devastated the homelands of the *Achuar* people of Ecuador with oil in their waters, destroyed forests, and devastating health impacts on the local communities. As for putting their profits to good use, they have been a leader in distributing their profits to their billionaire CEOs and shareholders, with infinitesimal percentages going to anything useful.

Cell phone companies are also working to save the planet. Verizon advertises its "smaller footprint," and how it is "making the best of precious resources" by recycling "millions of feet of cable and thousands of PCs. . . . And last year, we started offering carbon-free smartphones." What, exactly, is a "carbon-free" smartphone? Is it coltan and lithium free?

Sprint is also going green, saying, "Let's make green thumbs happy with the eco-friendly android phone . . . built partly with recyclable materials" and a solar charging accessory. What parts are built with recyclable materials? This will help "earn Mother Nature's approval," says Sprint. Neither of these green companies mentions that the most urgent ingredients in the phones are the coltan that is mined in parts of Africa, against the fervent protests of native communities being wiped out from the mining, using some of the dirtiest processes in the world. They also depend on the similarly destructive lithium mines in Bolivia and elsewhere, not to mention the plastic used in every phone.

I also love Monsanto's ads about how it is dedicated to "feeding a hungry world" via biotechnology and biofuels. They don't mention that the United Nations has officially reported that biofuels are directly implicated in the increase of global hunger (by pushing farmers off their lands, converting food production to fuel production, and raising prices for diminishing food supply). Biofuels production also is highly energy intensive, creates enormous pollution problems, and does *not* provide as many jobs as they destroy.

GREEN SHOPPING

Everybody is "going green" to save the world. We all have to do our part *now* to save the planet, and one good way is to *shop green*. The slogan for the website ClimateCooler.com is "the smarter you shop, the cooler it gets." Here's the idea: You use the site to buy new jeans or dozens of other products, and some of your money goes to fund groups that plant trees to offset greenhouse gases. It's a kind of carbon trading through shopping.

Another popular YouTube video names the current trend "greensumption," satirically suggesting that the best way to save the polar bears is to go shopping and "shop green." Or, says the video, we can always focus your planet-saving zeal on buying a Toyota Prius hybrid. Lots of ecology-conscious families are buying Priuses, says the video; some people have bought three and four "so that every member of the family can help save the planet."

Hybrids *do* use less fuel; that's true. But, says the "Greensumption" video, fuel use is not the only way to judge a hybrid or any other car. Better fuel mileage is undeniably good, but isn't the Prius built out of something? Where did all that material come from? What are the social and environmental consequences of those mines? Nickel mining, for example, to build Prius batteries, is responsible for the devastation of a huge area of Ontario. Many of the other scarce materials come from Africa, South America, and Asia. Lithium is very crucial, mined mainly from Africa and Bolivia. Rare earth minerals for batteries come mostly from China.

How much energy is used to mine, process, ship back and forth across oceans, and build all the parts of the car and to assemble it? In environmental terms, a far better choice would be to *not* buy a new hybrid or any new car at all. Find a low-mileage used car that has relatively low fuel consumption, if you need to have a car. From a systemic point of view, that is a better ecological choice.

The apex of green-consumerist celebration are the various Green Festivals that showcase low-carbon-tourism ideas, green gadgets, fashionable clothes made of indigenous fabrics, et al., continuing to promote the idea that what you buy is more important than how much you buy, and whether you buy, and the degree to which you are focused on consuming things. The shows imply that "conscious capitalism" will solve all problems, when the problems caused by capitalism have nothing to do with consciousness. They have mainly to do with the absolute necessities of consumption, growth, and profit. Without consumption, growth, and profit, there is no capitalism. Promoting more consumption, green or otherwise, is not good for the rights of nature, though it may prove helpful in the short term for the salvation of capitalism.

And then there's the Jevons Paradox. First cited in the nineteenth century by William S. Jevons, the paradox consists of the little-noted phenomenon that once technological efficiency is achieved, increased *usage* often results, leaving the total problems of resource supply and waste disposal little different than beforehand. A more popular, if more efficient, car like a Prius encourages more driving and more sales and leads to more material production and consumption; more mining of materials from the earth; more shipping, shaping, and distribution; and more use of these newly efficient treasures. No net gain.

5. Search for Green Energy

With increased recognition of the environmental impacts of fossil fuels, a great deal of discussion now focuses on renewable energy resources that can fuel a future dependent on continuing growth. Alternative systems, such as wind, solar, hydro, biomass, and wave, promise to improve matters ecologically. But it is unrealistic to expect them to serve as a substitute for fossil fuels, to keep industrial society performing at its present scale or growing at acceptable rates.

Most governments, including the U.S., still cling to the idea that fossil fuels, or nuclear energy, represent good possibilities for renewal. Some of the grandest techno-utopian predictions are focused on "clean coal," via carbon sequestration, and "clean nuclear," via a new, "safe fourth generation of reactor design." Both of these have already been revealed as little more than the wild fantasies of energy-industry executives as they peddle their talking points to politicians—from local congressmen all the way up to Obama. Thousands of lobbyists work every day to persuade congressmen to subsidize such projects. On other days, the same lobbyists hand out the campaign cash.

Unfortunately, after a decade of talk about "carbon sequestration" and clean coal, there is still no evidence that any progress has been made anywhere except in the realm of science fiction. Even if it were attainable, it will surely not come in the next four to five decades, when it will be most needed. The quest is actually just an excuse to continue to subsidize big corporations for doing make-work research.

In any case, the entire argument for clean coal, however absurd, still ignores what happens to the places from which coal comes. Appalachia is nearly desertified from mountaintop removal. Calling such a process "clean" only reveals the degree of desperation on this whole topic.

As for so-called "clean nuclear," it offers similar anomalies and worse. No currently contemplated solution for radioactive-waste disposal is anywhere near practical—even if uranium supplies were not running out nearly as quickly as oil. Anyway, to speak of nuclear as "clean" or "safe," after Fukushima, is delusional. And yet it is still promoted by some as the best noncarbon "clean energy" alternative. This is without even considering its overwhelming costs, inefficiencies, and dangers. The transformative challenge is overwhelming. And the radioactivity issue is permanently unsolvable.

The nuclear industry continues to assert that the deadly radioactive waste from nuclear energy can be sequestered from human beings and the rest of nature for the roughly 250,000 years that it remains dangerous to all life. The costs and risks of this lie far beyond the horizon of our calculations and imaginations. Few civilizations have lasted even a couple of hundred years. The Romans lasted seven hundred years, did very well for a while, and made some assumptions about their permanence that are similar to our own. But *250,000* years? The situation would be comical if it weren't so deadly.

No waste-containment system has been invented to package this stuff successfully beyond a very short period. Right now, much of the waste storage in the United States is in open, highly vulnerable *aboveground* pools of water, just as in Fukushima. Everywhere, efforts to store the wastes underground have been resisted by local communities, and with every good reason.

And yet, in an expression of official desperation, subsidies for nuclear continue to be viewed as viable. As of February 2012, the Obama administration still advocated a $35 billion subsidy for nuclear development, with hints it might go higher. If spent on new railroads instead, that money could revitalize local economies, create a lot more jobs, and save a lot more lives.

NET ENERGY LIMITS

What about the promise of alternative energy systems? In 2009, the International Forum on Globalization, in collaboration with the Post Carbon Institute, published a landmark report, *Searching for a Miracle*, which for the first time applied the newly emerging techniques of "life cycle technology assessment," and in particular "net energy" analyses, to make in-depth comparisons among *all* presently touted "alternative" energy schemes. These included all the major renewable systems currently being advocated. For the first time, we were able to fully realize the degree to which our future energy options are far more limited than optimists have been asserting.

The term "net energy" refers to the amount of energy that must be invested in an energy system, as compared with the amount of energy that is produced— energy in versus energy out. This includes all energy used in the *full life cycle*, from mining of raw materials to transportation, construction, operation, generation, storage, distribution, and eventual dismantling.

Searching for a Miracle reports on the unique advantages of fossil fuel systems, which in their heyday were able to produce enormous quantities of cheap energy *outputs*, with relatively little investment of energy *inputs*. Dr. Charles Hall, of Syracuse University, puts the ratio for oil production during most of the twentieth century at about 100 to 1. *One unit of input produced per one hundred units of energy output.* It was truly liquid gold and made our consumer society viable. Natural gas was close behind. Coal hovered in the area of 50 to 1. Our entire industrial system and its great rate of growth during that century were made possible by this fantastic abundance of oil and other fossil fuels, operating at very high-net-energy ratios.

Today, the grim reality is that no current energy systems, and no systems even remotely contemplated, can begin to approach such ratio numbers, *including* those same fossil fuels. The difficulty and expense of retrieving and processing remaining supplies has reduced net energy for oil down to an estimated 20 to 1, and that ratio is sinking fast. The terrible ecological and financial costs of tar sands are a clear example. Natural gas is little better now; it hovers near 10 to 1. Coal remains higher than either of those, but with staggering external costs to the environment.

Meanwhile, all those celebrated *alternative* energy systems, which in most respects are surely *far* cleaner in environmental terms than fossil fuels, cannot yield net-energy ratios that are anywhere near what was possible with fossil fuels. Their output per unit of input is very modest by comparison—too modest to be considered a sufficient substitute for fast-disappearing fossil fuels. Among these, wind power has the highest net-energy ratio, roughly 18 to 1 on average at press time, though it is steadily improving. On the other hand, a fevered opposition to wind has developed because of its unsightly high-tech displays on otherwise pristine lands and waters, not to mention that many kinds of windmill blades kill thousands of birds.

Among solar energies, solar photovoltaics come in at about 10 to 1. Meanwhile, biofuels are actually a *negative* figure—that means it costs more energy to produce most kinds of biofuels now in use than the amount of energy that results. This is aside from the impacts of biofuels, especially corn ethanol, on food-growing capacity for the planet, as they are rapidly replacing food-growing lands with fuel-growing.

As for nuclear, its net-energy ratio hovers just slightly above zero, even if you don't add in the thousands of years of costly damages to land, air, oceans, and communities from even one expression like Fukushima. There will be more.

There are additional relevant factors included in the overall assessments from *Searching for a Miracle*. The primary author of the report, Richard Heinberg, also assessed such aspects as these: *cost* (How expensive is each system per unit of output? Nuclear was by far the worst); *"scaleability"* (Will its benefits apply at a meaningful volume over time?); *location* (How difficult is it to work on, and how far and how costly to transport?); *density* (How compact is the source per unit?); *reliability* (Unfortunately, the wind doesn't blow, nor does the sun always shine, all the time), *et al*.

Without going into every detail, the conclusion of all this is exquisitely clear. *All* of these alternative systems—notably solar, wind, wave, small-scale hydro, and even certain small-scale biofuels and possibly certain kinds of biomass—represent improvements over fossil fuels and nuclear, and we should be investing in all of them now. They are far more amenable to local and domestic control and are not as subject to geopolitical trauma, including wars, as are oil, gas, and nuclear. However, even a full array of alternative renewable systems could never sustain the current industrial growth model at its present scale. Scientists on all sides of these issues confirm that if renewable systems such as wind and solar were deployed on a very large industrial scale, the energy and material used to produce those facilities, and the relatively low-net-energy return, as compared with oil, would make it impossible for renewals to duplicate the performance of oil.

Alternative energy systems should not be thought as instruments to resurrect the wasteful industrial growth economy. Renewables should be expected to only *partly* replace a highly destructive carbon and nuclear system and must be used in combination with increased efficiency, conservation, lower consumption levels, and lower material throughputs to bring society back within the limits of nature.

6. Creative Destruction

Natural disasters, though not as predictable or controllable as war, have similarly positive aspects where capitalism is concerned, as Naomi Klein described in her book *The Shock Doctrine: The Rise of Disaster Capitalism*. Huge land areas and/or giant cities may suddenly be destroyed by tornadoes or hurricanes or tidal waves, or by giant oil spills, chemical releases, or nuclear releases, all of which bring the urgent need to provide emergency services, cleanup, and temporary or new housing, and to rebuild cities and redevelop landscapes. All of these are excellent business opportunities and often bring greater profit opportunities for cities than what was available prior to the disaster.

An article titled "Creative Destruction?" by James Surowiecki in the *New Yorker* (March 28, 2011) described how many areas that are hit with terrible natural disasters, or even corporate-created disasters (such as the BP oil spill), become the subject of immense government interventions and spending. In the modern world, this kind of spending does not take on the job directly, as, say, Franklin Roosevelt did during the Depression. Now, the spending must always be directed toward the private sector, for rebuilding and to boost private profits and campaign donations.

> The quintessential example comes from Japan: In 1995, an earthquake leveled the port city of Kobe, which at the time was a manufacturing hub, and the world's sixth largest trading port. The quake killed sixty-four hundred people, and left more than three hundred thousand homeless. . . . Yet twelve months after the disaster, trade at the port had already returned almost to normal, and within fifteen months manufacturing was at ninety-eight percent of where it would have been had the quake never happened. On the national level, Japan's industrial production rose in the months after the quake, and its GDP growth in the following two years was above expectations.

Surowiecki offers similar reports following the devastation of Hurricane Hugo in 1989, Charleston, South Carolina, and the 2008 Sichuan earthquake in China. He calls the phenomenon "the Jacuzzi effect," like homeowners desire to upgrade. Or we could call it natural "planned obsolescence," like trading in the old car for a new one. In *The Enigma of Capital*, David Harvey also uses the term "creative destruction" but applies it to a much wider variety of capitalist expressions, from remaking urban contexts to remaking nature—nanotechnology, biotechnology, geo-engineering. He calls it "the creation of 2nd Nature" (to substitute for the one we are killing).

Harvey's "creative destruction" relates particularly to capitalism's periodic need to deal with accumulated "surplus capital," and surplus underemployed labor, part of the *boom-bust cycle* intrinsic to capitalism. Wealth sees a new opportunity, and the money comes pouring in to exploit the moment; workers are hired; the wealth accumulates and accumulates, until the opportunity is saturated and becomes no longer productive—hence the "bubble." Then the industry begins to deflate, until it slows and stops. Now, then, what to do with the surplus capital that has been generated?

Harvey uses the example of Paris during the 1850s. A "Europe-wide economic crisis in 1848 was one of the first clear expressions of unemployed surplus capital and surplus labor existing side by side with seemingly no way to put them back together again."

When Napoleon took power in 1852, he realized he had to find new investment opportunities. Harvey describes how Bonaparte brought Baron Haussmann to Paris to take charge of public works, and to build a new infrastructure turning Paris into a "centre of consumption, tourism, and pleasure."

The reconstruction that Harvey described in Paris, we would now call "redevelopment." Paris is one of few positive examples of that instinct. Some prefer to call the process "gentrification," and one wonders, what became of the people who lived there before?

Very few redevelopment projects turn into Paris. But the roots of the instinct may be the same: finding new profit-making uses for surplus capital and labor through redeveloping cities or parts of cities, arbitrarily deciding they are obsolete, like a two-year-old car. The capital expansion opportunity comes from tearing down what is already there, even if it is actually still highly functional, to build something new all over again. Thus, the system can generate another round of profits in the same locale as before, and then perhaps still another one.

Harvey also describes the much less heralded work of Robert Moses in the New York area after World War II. Moses laid out a new conceptual framework for development, encompassing a whole city and region. It did not produce another Paris; it produced a world of capitalist consumerism.

Moses gets credit—or, I would say, blame—for the invention of large-scale, mass-produced suburbs, which ultimately led to the explosion of a lifestyle that swept the United States, and then much of the rest of the developed world. Mass suburbanization was a tremendously profitable and financially stimulating concept for capitalism, as it required that every family duplicate the purchases of every other family. Each suburbanized family lives in a separate house, with front and back yards, and their own washing machine, dryer, lawn mowers, TV, two cars—a model consumer paradise at a time when there seemed to be no limits. Only a half century later did anyone grasp the ecological effect of all this duplicative buying, and single-family isolation, with its built-in dependence on private auto ownership and transport.

Roman Polanski's movie triumph *Chinatown* was set in 1930s Los Angeles and closely describes actual events of that period, focused on development schemes for the Central Valley. Jack Nicholson plays a private detective asked to solve the murder of a public water-systems engineer named Hollis Mulwray, who was trying to bring water to small communities and farmers in the valley, still essentially a desert. The detective figures out the reality: Mulwray's plan for a public water supply defied the wishes of one supremely wealthy oligarchical character, Noah Cross, played with great spirit by the film's director, John Huston. Cross wants to destroy Mulwray's *public* water scheme. He wants to divert that water to irrigate his own huge agriculture project in the Central Valley, and to suburbanize vast desert lands that he secretly bought at very low prices. With a new water supply, these lands would be worth billions.

The key moment of realization for Nicholson's detective in the movie comes during a lunch with Noah Cross. He confronts the billionaire with evidence that Cross killed Mulwray because he was in the way of Cross's schemes. With great confidence, the billionaire responds by suggesting that the detective accept a friendly buyout from him and join the new team. Nicholson's character is stunned, and then asks Cross why he is doing this: "You're a very very rich man. And you're old; you don't need this money, or this whole scheme," which would deny sustenance to small residents and farmers and benefit only one giant project. "Why are you doing this?"

The answer is great: "I do it for the future," Cross says. It's a visionary thing. And you can see the outcome today, from Bakersfield to Sherman Oaks.

I had the chance to personally observe a series of redevelopment schemes in action. When I first moved to San Francisco in 1959, it was remarkable for its scale—small buildings clinging to a landscape of many small rolling hills, small neighborhoods—pastel colors, great light, open views in all directions of a magnificent bay, with mountains on the other side, ocean breezes. And *quiet*. It was wonderful. But for developers, it reeked of opportunity.

Over the next thirty years, San Francisco offered dozens of chances to see these redevelopment/gentrification processes in action. In each project, somebody—either government or developers or both—decided that some area of the city should be torn down, modernized, and replaced with more commercially positive opportunities. Most often, it would require that some group of longtime local residents—nearly always in poor or immigrant neighborhoods—be moved out, sometimes strongly against their will, and their homes torn down and replaced with new, upscale versions, usually appealing to white, upper-income populations. "Gentrification." It was all an expression of excess capital agitating to tear down whatever was there—even if it worked perfectly well and usefully—to rebuild new, more, "better" housing for wealthier people, accompanied by commercial developments, theaters, etc.

Already under way by the 1960s was the vast redevelopment of the Fillmore district, the "Jazz District," pushing out thousands of black and other poor minorities in favor of upscale residence projects. In chapter IV, I briefly mentioned the rapid acceleration of these tendencies in San Francisco in the late 1960s and early '70s under then-mayor Joseph Alioto. He argued that these projects would provide great construction jobs, though studies showed that would be true only while the construction was ongoing. One study showed it would have been far less expensive for the city to just give checks to all the workers for what they would have been paid, and then not do the projects.

One of Alioto's earliest big ideas was to suggest the redevelopment of Alcatraz Island. He persuaded the board of supervisors to approve a proposal by Texas billionaire H. L. Hunt to develop a space museum complex where the old prison stood. I was directly involved in the movement opposing this initiative, again working with local dress designer Alvin Duskin to produce an advertisement titled "A Little Bit of Texas in San Francisco Bay?" The ad produced such an outpouring of public anger—more than ten thousand pieces of mail within a week—that the board of supervisors reversed its approval. Five days later, the Indians of the Bay Area got the idea, invaded the island, and occupied it for eighteen months. The space museum was dead. But the larger battle over the future of the city did not have such a favorable outcome.

Alioto ignored that defeat and proceeded with great speed to tear down the small private commercial enterprises that had thrived in the city and replace them with sixty-story office buildings, sort of a San Francisco Wall Street. It did make the city resemble Manhattan and destroyed a series of small neighborhoods. Each building was named after some giant transnational financial corporation: Bank of America, Transamerica, Alcoa, etc. We fought back with more ads in the local newspaper, but we lost.

At about the same time, a local wealthy developer named Jeremy Ets-Hokin, a friend of mine, actually, decided that he wanted to tear down the most wonderful old small amusement park that covered four to five square blocks by Ocean Beach in San Francisco. This was a magical place, filled with weird dioramas, photo machines, talking figures (Laughing Sal), and the requisite fun houses, merry-go-rounds, loop-the-loops, and roller coasters. It was surrounded by a lively middle-class neighborhood and was jammed on weekends. Kids loved it, and I did, too.

But Jeremy had a lot of excess capital looking for a home, and he bought the whole place. He decided he could make a lot of money by ripping down Playland and redeveloping it into fancy housing, across from the beach. After many struggles with local activists, he did. Now, forty years later, the area is covered by deteriorating condos for a few hundred people living with a view of the sea. Some argue it's time for a new, fancier redevelopment there, facing the ocean. Meanwhile, Laughing Sal and a fair array of the other machines from Playland were saved and can be found in a small storefront in El Cerrito, California, also filled with pinball machines and other games, with the name *Not* Playland at the Beach. I take my grandchildren there. *Creative destruction.*

One more example. In the late 1970s, there was the horrific International

Hotel battle. A developer wanted to evict, with the city's support, several hundred very poor Filipino residents in order to "upgrade" the neighborhood. Some had lived there for thirty years and had nowhere to go. This was in North Beach, the same neighborhood where City Lights Bookstore was the intellectual center, and where the likes of Allen Ginsberg, Lawrence Ferlinghetti, Gary Snyder, and beatnik celebrities like Jack Kerouac and Gregory Corso used to hang out in local cafés and bars.

A huge "Save the International Hotel" protest movement developed to stop the eviction of its residents. Giant demonstrations ensued; hundreds of people were dragged to jail, including the former sheriff turned protestor Richard Hongisto. Just the year before, he had been the one doing the arresting. Sadly, that battle was also lost, and the hotel was eventually torn down. But then, because the developer couldn't raise sufficient development capital at a good rate to rebuild his upscale new housing project, the site remained an awful gaping hole in the ground for the next twenty years, reminding us daily of what had happened. What finally replaced it was an anonymous-looking set of stores that were no urban improvement at all. But our own city of light had taken another step toward gentrification, and toward becoming one of the most expensive cities in the world, just like Paris.

7. Techno-Utopianism & New Nature

When push comes to shove in our society, we place our faith in technology to save the day. Americans share a nearly religious faith that technology can solve whatever intransigent problems emerge; human technical ingenuity, creativity, and innovation can surmount any problems including problems caused by nature's boundaries. If necessary, we can always redesign nature into a form far more compatible with continued rapid growth and industrial expansion. Failure is not an option.

Techno-optimism has been greatly encouraged by the fact that in capitalist societies, most descriptions of new technology come from the corporations and other institutions that are developing the technologies. Their descriptions—especially in advertising—are invariably optimistic, even utopian. Negative potentials are left out of the description. This has been the practice since the Industrial Revolution.

At the turn of the twentieth century, the automobile was introduced by Henry Ford as clean, safe, convenient, private, fast, and nonpolluting (unlike horses). No mention of pavement eventually covering the landscape, air pollution, noise, death on the highways, or oil wars. Perhaps the inventors themselves didn't foresee all that, but they probably had their suspicions, as big companies spend a lot of time studying the downside potentials of their inventions—though they may not publicly report those. In any case, the invention of the automobile turned out to be arguably the most impactful event in modern history, and arguably the most destructive.

Midcentury, pesticides were launched. They were going to save our crops and "feed a hungry world." No mention of poisoned food, land, wildlife, water, or growing rates of cancer. Something went wrong with the arrangement, because there are more starving people now than ever before.

Television was going to "democratize information," educate the poor, and promote world peace. No mention of mind-numbing commercialization, global homogenization of consciousness and culture, or the dire fact that control of this powerful instrument—which plants imagery in billions of minds around the world—is by a small number of corporate interests who have their own intentions for it, which do not include saving nature or the public good.

Nuclear power was promoted by the energy industry as a "clean, safe, infinite" source of energy, with no mention of negatives. However, unlike other technologies, nuclear power had a much rougher time sweeping its problems under the rug, since the first time we ever heard of nuclear energy was after the bombing of Hiroshima, followed by the most terrifying images of destruction. We understood its *worst-case* potential instantly, slowing down its growth until recent decades. Then came Fukushima, which, hopefully, may slow it down again.

The chemical industry had similar early setbacks in the 1960s, especially at Love Canal, when horrible toxic materials bubbled up onto people's lawns, bringing illnesses and birth deformities. The industry denied responsibility for years.

The unfortunate fact is that despite the oftentimes negative impacts of their inventions, corporations have no legal requirement to disclose, and no financial stake in disclosing, worst-case scenarios, unless government requires it. It rarely does, except for certain medicines and cigarettes, and then only after decades of battling corporate power to issue its warnings. The public is routinely deprived of the information we need about the pros and cons of technical evolution.

REINVENTING NATURE

It is clear that technology is deeply implicated in what is becoming the most important question of our time: Will we finally recognize that the natural world has been so negatively impacted that it may no longer be able to sustain us?

The good news is that, for once, society has clearly identified the causes of the problem. In the case of climate change, for example, the prime cause is obviously the continuous, concentrated, and expanding impacts by certain technologies, notable among them energy systems based on fossil fuels, which are dedicated to maintaining our hunger for growth. A rational society would try to solve the climate problem by eliminating fossil fuels, as well as by diminishing the use of *all* energy systems, since they all conspire to further overdevelopment and the depletion of nature. The rational society would also reassess its commitment to constant expansion in a finite system.

But that is not what is happening. Most governments, including the U.S., have chosen to view the matter as just a new business challenge and opportunity. Government programs, financial subsidies, and pronouncements focus on ways we can try to develop and profit from new green-energy industries on the one hand, as well as from something radically new: the redesign and reconstruction of nature. The central principle is this: *If the old nature can't properly serve our growing economy anymore, why not make a new nature that's more compatible with our needs?*

Many expressions of this idea are well under way. Some of the better-known ones include:

- *Biotechnology*: the science of rearranging the genetic structures of living creatures so that they will be better positioned to be useful to people. The process has already produced everything from gigantic salmon, to birth-control corn, and plants with pesticides built into them, etc.
- *Nanotechnology*: the science of re-engineering the molecular structures of all living things to create new, better animals, trees, plants, and microbes that can thrive in utterly remade conditions. Nanotech is already used in hundreds of military applications, including development of stealth weaponry, commercial applications in everything from skin cream to "easy-wipe" surfaces, and many medical contexts, but there are profound concerns over its safety. Bill Joy, founder of Sun Microsystems, an early advocate of nanotechnology, now advises that we outlaw the technology. His concerns have to do with the self-replication and autonomy of some nanotech structures, which could create entirely unpredictable outcomes. He fears an upcoming "arms race between negative uses and positive."
- *Synthetic Genomics*: the recent creation of "new synthetic life forms." The first of these has been produced and named Synthia. It was announced in 2011 by corporate inventor Craig Ventnor, who synthesized a DNA code, injecting it into a single bacteria cell, which then grew and divided on its own, producing a new self-reproducing life form. Industrial techno-celebrants instantly proclaimed it would lead to such benefits as carbon dioxide–eating bacteria and new do-gooder viruses. According to Ventner, speaking on KQED radio's *City Arts & Lectures* (March 22, 2012), they are also hard at work on an entirely new, remade synthetic-food supply that could be manufactured in factories by rearranging genetic codes—no need for soil anymore, or any of what we have called nature—and that

would feature invented "plants that would taste exactly like meat." Ventner didn't indicate any downside potential. Others, including Pat Mooney of the Etc. Group (the leading Canadian technology/science watchdog), called this a "Pandora's box moment—like the splitting of the atom, or the cloning of Dolly the sheep." We may all eventually have to deal with the consequences of new out-of-control life forms bursting onto the scene, doing their thing. Meanwhile, we can look forward to some growth bubbles in synthetic-life-form industries.

- *Other Planets*: We now hear of renewed interest in the old science fiction plan for mining other planets for their resources, or for moving the population of the earth to other planets, when ours gets finally destroyed by our lifestyle experiment. That would certainly be a responsive solution. But will the spaceships take all eight billion of us? Even the poor people? Even the birds and dogs? With the end of the U.S. space shuttle flights in 2011, the terrain is now wide open for private mega-entrepreneurs to fill the breech. Privatization of space. Several are interested, including Richard Branson and Bill Gates.

ATMOSPHERIC ENGINEERING

The techno-utopian idea that has the greatest commercial potential and is most touted right now, and is also the most terrifying to me, is geo-engineering. This is the science of redesigning the physical properties of the earth, oceans, lands, and atmospheres to make our heavenly sphere immune to climate change.

Geo-engineers do *not* deny the realities of the moment. These realities are what motivate them. They assume that our political and industrial leaders, and the public as well, really cannot or will not do anything to mitigate the climate problem. This group of scientists *does* want to do something about the problem, but without changing anybody's lifestyle or threatening global business growth. They view themselves as do-gooders, just like the perpetrators of economic globalization who met at Bretton Woods a half century before and wound up accelerating the very problems we now face.

The geo-engineers propose relatively simple adjustments in the way the planet works—its chemical and biological structures, including the level of the planet's "albedo," or the degree of the reflectivity of the planet's surface. Such changes might enable scientists to cool things down or warm them up virtually at will, thus changing the climate, species selection, plant life, and ocean ecology. This might involve some adjusting of the varieties of life in the seas and of prevailing atmospheric conditions. It is also likely to change the color of the sky from blue to white, among other irritants.

For the scientists, managing these changes will be as simple as pushing different buttons on your convection oven at home. For the rest of us, it will mean submitting the entire human population and the natural world itself into a first-of-its-kind global experiment to change all current planetary balances into a more acceptable form to accommodate continued economic growth. Admittedly, it might seem odd at the outset to see a world with a permanent, ubiquitous white sky. But geo-engineers think we'd all get past that little problem in the interest of a cooler planet.

Many governments of the world are already busy researching the grand possibilities, albeit very quietly, so the public will not be unduly alarmed. But there have been some cracks in the silence. Back in 1965, a U.S. presidential advisory committee predicted the oncoming problem of climate change. But rather than proposing we reduce fossil fuel use, they recommended secret work on geo-engineering solutions. By June 2008, then–speaker of the House of Representatives Newt Gingrich was ready to say, "Geo-engineering holds forth the promise of addressing global warming concerns for just a few billion dollars a year. . . . Instead of penalizing ordinary Americans [by having to drive less], we would have an option to address global warming by rewarding scientific innovation. . . . Bring on American ingenuity. Stop the green pig."

By April 8, 2009, President Obama's chief science advisor, John Holdren, was reported by the Associated Press as saying that geo-engineering was being "vigorously discussed" as an "emergency" option by the White House. But once the story hit the wires, Holdren backed off, saying this was only his personal view. The following month, however, U.S. energy secretary Steven Chu, speaking in London, indicated his support for "benign" geo-engineering schemes. So, the idea is not new to the U.S. government.

There are also suspicions that geo-engineering is already being tested by the military and is showing up as those persistent *contrails* across the sky. Maybe those vapor trails across the sky, which some people worry are from another planet, are just creations of our own homegrown mad scientists.

The Swedish Society for Nature Conservation (SSNC), in a blistering 2009 report, "Retooling the Planet," prepared in partnership with the Etc. Group, offered a detailed history of geo-engineering. They gave substantial credit to Dr. Edward Teller, the Nobel Laureate responsible for the hydrogen bomb, who joined two other scientists, Lowell Wood and Roderick Hyde, to publish a 1997 paper strongly endorsing geo-engineering, "Global Warming and Ice Ages: Prospects for Physics-Based Modulation of Global Climate Change." The three men combined for another paper in 2002, arguing "that geo-engineering, not reduction, of Greenhouse Gas Emissions," was the best way to fulfill the mandate of the UN Framework Convention on Climate Change, as it would not require much in the way of lifestyle changes.

Outside the United States, a 2006 editorial by the highly influential German atmospheric chemist Paul Crutzen, who also won the 1995 Nobel Prize (for chemistry), stated that cutting emissions is "by far the preferred way" to respond to global warming, but he supported the "usefulness of artificially enhancing Earth's albedo, and thereby cooling the climate by adding sunlight-reflecting aerosol in the stratosphere." That might be an emergency "escape route," he said, if global warming gets really out of control. SSNC took the opposite position, warning of grave "unintended consequences" of such experiments with the chemical and biological structures of the planet.

One group that *loves* bio-engineering unequivocably is industry, as bio-engineering represents the ideal type of response to environmental threats. Rather than acknowledging the limits of the earth's natural resources, they can change the earth itself. Instead of adapting to planetary limits, they can change the planet to adapt to economic growth! Great new profit opportunities are clearly possible. Not surprisingly, many of America's leading right-wing politicians and think tanks who were formerly adamant climate change *deniers*—including the American Enterprise Institute, the Club for Growth, the Competitive Enterprise Institute, and the Heartland Institute—are now enthusiastic about geo-engineering to stop climate change. There seem to be two reasons for this: (1) It will be very good for business, and (2) it celebrates human dominion over nature, just like God wants.

If these advocates get their way, here is a short list of some of the hundreds of geo-engineering ideas that government and industry are seriously promoting:

- Fertilizing the ocean with iron filings to promote growth of tiny marine plants, phytoplankton, that absorb carbon dioxide and eventually sink to the ocean floor. The Swedish report suggests this might create huge "dead zones," as well as oxygen depletion (anoxia) in the deep sea; disruptions in food-chain balances; increased release of other greenhouse gases, such as nitrous oxide and methane, that could further alter weather patterns; potential toxicological impacts, such as dinoflagellates; and worsening ocean acidification; not to mention impacts on the livelihoods of fisher-people and others who depend on life in the deep ocean and among coral reefs.

- Installation of a vast number of floating giant "funnels" in the ocean, which can draw nutrient-rich cold water from the ocean depths to the surface, encouraging algae blooms on the surface to suck more carbon dioxide from the air, eventually sequestering it permanently in the oceans' depths.

- Building thousands of devices called "sodium trees" that would extract carbon dioxide directly from the air and turn it into sodium bicarbonate, from which carbon dioxide could be separated before being safely stored.

- Shooting some sixteen trillion free-flying spacecraft into space, toward the sun, to form a cylindrical cloud sixty thousand miles long, aligned with the sun's orbit. These teeny ships would carry lots of one million sixty-centimeter "sunshades," or reflective discs, every minute for thirty years, to a point in space known as L1, about a million miles from Earth. This cloud of sunshades would prevent sunlight from hitting our planet— a kind of permanent partial eclipse.
- Cloud whitening, by spraying seawater aerosols directly into clouds from aircraft. Also proposed is the launching in the oceans of five thousand to thirty thousand unmanned ships with powerful turbines that plow the seas, creating giant plumes of saltwater vapor that whiten clouds and thus deflect sunlight. (There is a concern that reducing sunlight reaching the earth "could also change global weather circulation, storm tracks, and precipitation patterns throughout the world. This could seriously affect marine ecosystems, bird and plant life, and rainfall patterns everywhere on Earth.)
- Mandating the whitening of city rooftops all over the planet—a requirement already for many houses in California (and in Santorini, Greece). However, scientists say that shining white cities would not offset warming by much.
- Genetically engineering thousands of species of crops to grow new bio-leaves that can better reflect sunlight.
- Covering entire deserts with huge reflective sheets to keep sunlight off the earth.
- Covering the Arctic snowpack and glaciers with a nano-film to reflect sunlight and prevent melting.
- Putting vast arrays of superfine reflective mesh of aluminium threads, space mirrors, up in space between Earth and the sun.
- Re-engineering the flow of rivers on the planet in order to provoke new kinds of cloud formations to reflect sunlight.

ARTIFICIAL VOLCANOES

According to the celebrated Australian ecological economist Clive Hamilton, who helped put together the above list for the Swedish report, "The option that is taken most seriously proposes nothing less than the transformation of the chemical composition of the Earth's atmosphere so that humans can constantly adjust the temperature of the planet."

The scheme involves injecting sulfur dioxide gas into the stratosphere, up to thirty miles above Earth's surface, to create sulphate aerosols to reflect solar radiation. The idea, says Hamilton, is to create artificial volcanoes and mimic the effects of volcanic eruptions, such as the 1991 explosion of Mount Pinatubo in the Philippines, to increase Earth's reflectivity.

Currently, the atmosphere reflects about 23 percent of solar radiation back into space. Scientists believe they can do better. "It's estimated that the injection of enough sulphate aerosols to reflect an additional two percent would offset the warming effect of a doubling of atmospheric carbon dioxide. In the stratosphere, sulphate particles remain in place for one or two years, unlike aerosol pollution in the lower atmosphere that may last only a week."

Mega-rich economic adventurers, like Richard Branson and Bill Gates, are gearing up. They have each expressed interest in doing something useful via geo-engineering, and might at any time decide to save the world all by themselves, as the costs may not be beyond them. There are no international laws that prevent any of the national or private actions described above, so individual players or countries could easily produce a global *fait accompli* and bring us white skies forevermore, whether we vote on it or not.

According to Clive Hamilton, "not all influential advocates of climate engineering adopt a cautious approach; some are gung-ho. When the potentially severe side effects of geo-engineering are pointed out, the more cavalier climate engineers say they can be managed with other techniques, such as spreading lime in the oceans to counter acidification. Some concede that liming the seas would not be feasible as a generalized response, but maintain that it could still be deployed to protect highly valued zones. One idea is to offset ocean acidification [advanced by geo-engineering projects] by installing a network of undersea pipes that inject alkalis around sites such as the Great Barrier Reef."

This might help protect them as some kind of underwater nature preserve while the rest of the ocean continues to be redesigned. "For some, turning the (parts of the) planet into a museum of natural artifacts while the rest goes to ruin seems easier than phasing out coal."

DEBATE: INTELLECT OR WISDOM?

On July 21, 2011, the Earth Island Institute and the Nation Institute jointly hosted a debate between American Indian activist Winona LaDuke (Ashinabe) and Stewart Brand, the founder of the Whole Earth Catalog. Brand's most recent book, *The Eco-pragmatist Manifesto*, had caused considerable outrage in the environmental community, to the extent that some people suggested that he should not be invited to display his views at Earth Island, thus delaying the event by nearly a year. In his book, Brand favors nuclear power, urbanization, genetic engineering, and bioengineering.

The moderator of the event was Mark Hertsgaard of the Nation Institute, also the author of a book about the problems of climate change, *Hot*. He quoted from Brand's opening lines in his new book: "We are now as gods, and better get good at it."

Brand said he favors technological solutions, albeit carefully thought-out and efficient. He advocates rapid expansion of nuclear power because it does not add much to climate change, while still providing reliable energy needed to sustain an industrial growth society. He acknowledged some safety hazards with nuclear energy but said they are fewer than the hazards of climate change, which he believes is the major problem of our time. He said that no one actually died from the nuclear mess of Fukushima; they died from the earthquake and tidal wave. He went so far as to say that no one has *ever* died from nuclear energy.

As for biotechnology, Brand doesn't see why humans should not rearrange genetic structures, even if it means assuming authority over the structures of nature. He argued that human beings have been "terraforming" the earth for thousands of years. He strenuously supports geo-engineering to deal with climate change. He acknowledged that corporations and scientists don't always do the right thing, but says we should give them the benefit of the doubt, since they are the most effective players we have.

Winona LaDuke argued that Brand's perspective was confined within an anthropocentric acceptance of the dominant system's goals and practices. She said the indigenous worldview sees these problems entirely differently, operating from a much longer view of nature's processes and with an "intergenerational" perspective. "We are not living in a petroleum age," she said, in answer to one of Brand's framing statements, "we are living in a petroleum bubble. You can't know about the earth unless you can touch it every day" and grasp it. "I want people to quit shopping and start growing. Happiness does not come from things."

LaDuke accused Brand of being misleading about nuclear energy, pointing out that thousands of indigenous uranium miners have died from exposure to it, and thousands more people have died from radiation sickness over time from the various accidents the world has experienced. Fukushima is the latest acceleration of the problem. Brand was camouflaging reality, LaDuke said, by speaking only of immediate deaths from explosions and the like, rather than of long term-degradation to humans and the viability of nature from the spread of radiation over eons.

When the audience was invited to ask questions, many criticized Brand for his pro-nuclear stance, but one member said that we were not talking about the most important issue: whether it will ever be possible for capitalism to adjust to the realities of these times. Hertsgaard reacted quickly by saying, "We are not going to get anywhere if we try to talk about eliminating capitalism; Americans love capitalism."

When Hertsgaard called for one final question or comment from the audience, the questioner turned out to be the actor Peter Coyote, who, aside from his film career, has been deeply engaged in environmental causes. He directed his comments to Brand. "Stewart, we are not as gods; we are idiot savants." This debate, said Coyote, has shown two very different ways of speaking about these issues: "One of you is using intellect and intelligence, and the other is using wisdom. But if *you* are going to use the American style of consumption and production as the standard for what must be sustained into the future, then we are going to need a whole lot more than nuclear; we will need hydrogen plants to sustain this system. I'm afraid that I hear you suffering from a serious absence of doubt, even as you continue to advocate profound violations of the commons we all depend on. The only reason you do that is to support this culture. The better solution would be to change it."

VIII.
Propensity Toward War

Wars were not invented by capitalism. Historically, plenty of other motives have triggered war —from theology to ideology to avenging insults, recovering land previously taken, resource capture, monarchical or imperial ego and madness, romantic love (Helen of Troy!), and the search for slaves, among others. But if capitalism didn't invent war, it has frequently chosen it to great benefit. The United States is a good example of this tendency.

In modern times, war and the steady drumbeat for military "preparedness" have had important short- and medium-term benefits for capitalist economies, particularly in hard economic times. Here are a few:

- Maintaining high levels of spending for military production, thus helping to sustain growth, corporate profits, and jobs—economic stimulus programs in themselves.
- Projecting national economic interests—i.e., *corporate* interests—into distant regions, to secure resources against competitors.
- Providing intimidation of potential economic and military adversaries— aided by hundreds of military bases on foreign soils and in faraway places. These in turn require networks of profitable commercial services to maintain the bases, from McDonald's restaurants to garden-furniture sales in PX stores.
- Arousing and uniting a domestic public toward common external enemies, thus gaining political support at home in hard times.
- Finding opportunities to usefully deploy old military stockpiles, which then have to be replenished. Keeping the inventory moving.

All of these activities, on the battleground, in forward base locations, and on the home front, can be viewed as an alternative form of economic development. The "war economy" has advantages over more routine development models, in that its benefits usually come free of normal marketplace rules and procedures, including competitive bidding on contracts and regulations to prevent cost overruns.

While weapons development programs are usually launched by government officials, the details of the decisions are likely to have been made in tandem with the interests of large industries and corporations. Many contracts for warplanes, ships, weapons, and other military-related activity take place outside the "free market," as government is essentially the only market. Competitive bidding for large contracts is more the exception than the rule.

The "war economy" offers important political advantages to corporate players. Typically, in the United States, there is a minimum of partisan political wrangling over military budgets and deployments—especially if production contracts are widely spread across political constituencies in many different states, though there may be significant competition among states and regions for government largesse. "When it comes to national security, we all speak with one voice"—so goes the political homily from Democrats and Republicans alike, and lately even from most so-called Libertarians. That's not to say that sticky issues don't pop up.

But in a book about capitalism, how do we characterize government-initiated military contracts made jointly with giant private corporations? Is this really capitalism? Or is it a bit more like *state* capitalism, as in China or Russia or Venezuela, where state interests are often merged with corporate interests? In a prior context, Italy and Germany in the 1930s, a similar degree of state-corporate-military merger was called fascism.

Chalmers Johnson, the great military critic, former U.S. intelligence officer, and author of *Blowback*, labels the whole military-economic merger as "military Keynesianism"—just military versions of corporate stimulus programs during stressful times.

War as Economic Strategy

There is little arguing the point that massive military spending was the main factor that lifted us out of the 1930s Great Depression, firing up our shuttered factories and creating millions of new jobs—while other, flailing capitalist mechanisms were getting us nowhere. The war effort massively expanded industrial production and innovation in the 1940s, it provided jobs to women as well as men—whether as military or factory workers—and it motivated public spirit as nothing has since. It was paid for by common sacrifice, from the soldiers sent abroad to consumers suffering rationing. Even the wealthiest Americans contributed greatly back then, enduring substantial tax increases without forming Tea Parties. Increased military spending, even in the absence of war, has since advanced to become a more formal economic strategy.

When World War II ended in 1945, it didn't end our mid-century economic traumas. There was great worry that we would backslide into a postwar depression, with the loss of military production and jobs, especially for the women who had "manned" the industrial production lines during World War II. Would there be *another* war, this time with Russia and the other communist countries?

At the end of the war, the world quickly found itself in a new global economic and geopolitical crisis, a realignment that split the countries of the world into communist and noncommunist blocs and produced a dangerous Cold War that would last for nearly a half century. A new, modernized form of economic globalization was quickly created and began to be deployed among noncommunist countries. It sought to homogenize and integrate all "free world," capitalist economies in the cause of expanding and revitalizing markets through reconstruction, development, free movement of capital, and free trade, per the Bretton Woods initiatives, as described earlier. But there were also some major accompanying shifts in U.S. domestic policy.

By 1950 in the United States, the efforts at economic revival were proceeding. And yet there remained a clear awareness that the world had been forever changed by the traumas of the preceding decades. In the United States in particular, now officially the "leader of the free [capitalist, noncommunist] world," there was major emphasis on military and security structures—the beginnings of a transition to "a permanent war economy." With the Depression still in mind, and with the new challenges of militant communism, and its potential to stimulate constant skirmishes, many felt that high spending on military preparedness should be the new normal, *especially* since it was a great economic fallback strategy. The two factors combined—a military economy integrated with an expanding consumer economy—seemed to be a good way to resist the advancing threats of communist competition while also continuing to support the post-Depression recovery.

On April 14, 1950, five years after the end of World War II, the National Security Council under Paul Nitze issued its infamous report, NSC-68, advocating the formal merger of military policy with economic policy. Within a few months, President Truman accepted and signed the report. The United States immediately began drafting its basic strategy for the Cold War and beyond, putting our country on what has become a virtually permanent war footing. Military spending in the United States has now advanced to become roughly equal to the combined spending of all other countries in the world. But even now, a half century later, there is very little awareness of or debate in the U.S. on the fact that our defense strategies have merged with our economic strategies.

The new Truman policy had corollary benefits. It propelled a burst of new technological explorations, achieving the advancement of "peaceful" nuclear technology, at the same time as we developed bigger and more powerful nuclear weapons, and nuclear submarines. The policy also enabled major innovations in space-age propulsion technology; the invention of advanced computation technologies; intercontinental ballistic missiles (ICBMs); new surveillance and communications satellites; new chemicals and pesticides; and 32,000 nuclear bombs.

Eleven years into this new policy, in 1961, an apparently worried President Eisenhower, a former general, didn't like what he was seeing, and in his farewell address delivered his remarkable warning against the whole trend. Eisenhower famously spoke of the dangers of a growing "military-industrial complex," adding that "the conjunction of an immense military establishment and a large arms industry is new in the American experience."

Of course, as president, Eisenhower himself actually contributed to the problem. His "Atoms for Peace" initiative aggressively promoted, among many other things, a push to persuade Japan that its fears of atomic energy were unfounded. Japan was asked to accept boat-loads of new nuclear power technology from General Electric, which was, at that time, the corporate prince of the military-industrial complex. Atoms for Peace really amounted to yet another bailout strategy for military industries that had no big war to fight anymore. GE obtained many of the postwar construction contracts for nuclear energy in Japan, helping to give birth to the mess at Fukushima.

By the 1960s the whole industrial-military-merger trend was too advanced, and too profitable, to reverse. Giant corporations have been making good livings from military contracts ever since. For some of them, the contracts have represented the great majority of their businesses. This hyper-readiness stance, begun in the 1950s, has always been justified as necessary, as much now as it was then, as we arguably continue to live in a dangerous world.

But one wonders: *How did our leaders in the White House and in Congress ever manage to justify building 32,000 nuclear bombs?* As a practical matter, these could never possibly be used. You need only a handful of those bombs to blow up the world. Even now, we have about 8,500 of them, several thousand of which are "live."

Similarly, we must also ask if the overall threats we face justify spending at least $700 billion on military, or possibly more than $1 trillion (depending on whose figures you believe) per year. Does it really require that we spend more than all other countries in the world combined? Are we that scared?

But in the modern world, wars, and preparation for wars, are only sometimes in response to direct geopolitical threats. Just as often, they are about political and economic hegemony—control of competitors, their populations, and resources. Military preparedness is also about keeping giant industrial enterprises alive and profitable.

Since World War II there has been constant pressure to be alert to new enemies in order to justify military production at a high level. First, we had the Soviets to keep us focused during the Cold War, and then came the Chinese Maoists and the defense against potential threats to Formosa. Soon after came invasions of Cuba, Korea, and Vietnam. After that came 9/11, and we jumped into Afghanistan, Iraq, and Pakistan, not to mention "the war on terror." Those were just the most obvious threats.

For economic purposes, real threats are best, but imaginary ones, and minor ones, which can be spectacularly overstated, serve almost as well in hard times. The United States has also had invasions of Panama, the Dominican Republic, and Granada to fill in some threat gaps and produce minor military dramas, as well as Bosnia and Kosovo, which were "peacekeeping missions." More recently there's been Libya, with North Korea and Iran still waiting their turn. If all else fails, there is always the "Venezuela threat" in the wings to arm up against, and some see Bolivia and Honduras as other emerging threats sufficient to justify a few hundred million dollars or so. Not to mention China.

That last one has everyone shaking in their boots, as we aggressively expand our military bases all over the Pacific. All instruments are pointed at China, which, on the other hand, still has a total military budget barely one-sixth of ours, and a *per capita* military spending level that is one-twenty-eighth of ours. Nonetheless, when China announced in late 2010 that it might limit exports of its rare earth minerals—crucial ingredients for the world's new high-tech industries, of which China has more than 90 % of the world's very scarce reserves— the American military establishment reacted almost as if it were Pearl Harbor all over again.

Both secretary of state Hillary Clinton and then–U.S. defense secretary Robert Gates quickly made not-so-veiled threats about the unacceptability of this move by China, and about the grave consequences that might follow. Gates said that the United States might soon need to expand its defensive postures in the Pacific, increasing speculation that we would hurry to create a kind of "NATO of the Pacific" to contain China. Clinton flew to Honolulu and reminded the world that the United States "is both a transatlantic power and a transpacific power," and that "security concerns underlie our mission." Was she actually implying that we might go to war to protect our supply of rare earth minerals to build computer batteries? I think she was. I wish she had stated that it was "economic concerns" that were primary, of which "security concerns" are only a subset.

Clinton did make reference to resources and economic matters in Papua New Guinea, where our own ExxonMobil is trying to nail down a $15 billion natural-gas contract in competition with Chinese companies. In any case, by her lights, economic competition from China is a good enough justification for advanced military "readiness." China backed off on the rare earth export issue, for the moment, at least. But I kept wondering, shouldn't the secretary of *commerce* have been the proper person to react, rather than the secretaries of war?

In response to China, the United States and other countries filed a complaint in the WTO that it was in violation of WTO rules of free trade for China to *not* export its minerals. The WTO finally ruled, in January 2012, that China could not continue to follow this policy and faced sanctions if it did, thus confirming the WTO's takeover of national sovereignty on trade issues. In any case, the current global supply of rare earth minerals is expected to run out within the next ten years, no matter who uses them up—another global warning on fantasies of unlimited economic growth.

Meanwhile, Clinton is keeping the rhetoric high. In March 2011, in testimony to the U.S. Senate Foreign Relations Committee, she argued against budget cuts for U.S. activity in the Pacific. "The U.S. is at risk of falling behind in a global battle for influence with China," Clinton warned. She highlighted the "unbelievable" competition with China for influence over islands in the Pacific, and for development of Papua New Guinea's "huge energy reserves." She argued against any cuts to the state department budget. "We are in a competition for influence with China," she said. "Let's put aside the moral, humanitarian, do-good side of what we believe in, and let's just talk straight realpolitik. Beijing has wined and dined these small Pacific nations . . . for more than a decade. If anybody thinks that our retreating on these issues is somehow going to be irrelevant to the maintenance of our leadership in a world where we are competing with China, that is a mistaken notion." Since then, new secretary of defense Leon Panetta has come out even more strongly against cuts in military spending.

So, the questions remain in focus: How much of the motive for our level of hyper-preparedness is due to actual military threats to the United States? And to what degree are the dominant motives economic? Which tail wags that dog? Are we *still* trying to avoid sinking back into a depression?

The Stealth Economy

Why the gargantuan military dimensions of the U.S. national budget are not more a part of the general economic discourse remains puzzling. The financial pages of major newspapers, including the *Wall Street Journal* and *Financial Times*, do report on government-military contracts and war budgets, but not nearly to the extent to which they do the normal manufacturing, services, and financial economies. Even at a time when elections are won by deriding profligate government spending, rarely is the fact noted that the single-largest government discretionary-spending program is for military activities. This spending is even promoted by the same conservative elements that generally deride all other spending.

Military spending continues to be supported by right-wing ideologues in the United States, as if it were some kind of a sacred expression of free-market libertarian capitalism. In reality, it is clearly the opposite of what its proponents state are their fundamental free-market principles.

Many military contracts are made without even a semblance of competitive bidding. And when contracts are awarded, government's rules and standards are routine. There is not much free-market about it. For military contractors there is generally only one market. If this is capitalism at all, it's because it continues to express the nonstop corporate need for market expansion, which, in this case, is done mainly by influencing government officials and persuading them of expanding military imperatives.

Perhaps defense spending activity achieves such special handling because military activity is generally thought of as being outside usual economic domains. The public is led to view it more as being in the realm of "necessity"— something a nation *must* do, though it doesn't really want to.

The perception is that any urgency for military production is *reactive*, mainly responding to dangerous (or fake) outside threats. Unavoidable geopolitical circumstances determine what activities and contracts are necessary in military spending, as compared with normal market activity's supply and demand, market seeking, or profit considerations. At least, that is how the story is told.

But is this true? With U.S. military spending approaching half of the entire annual taxpayer dollar, is it possible to believe that corporate interests, profits, and growth are *not* among the main determining factors?

What makes the absence of discussion about military expenditures so important is that the scale of the expenditures is astronomical. Making matters worse is that a high percentage of these military expenditures is completely useless, apparently assigned only to subsidize corporations, provide economic stimulus, add jobs, serve local congressmen whose districts gain from the jobs, and, possibly more than anything else, to service campaign donors.

Doing the Numbers

The scale of military spending by the United States is breathtaking. The following are a few highlights.

- Between 2006 and 2011, U.S. military expenditures have accounted for over 45% of all discretionary spending of U.S. tax dollars—a total military expenditure that even the Pentagon publicly acknowledges as now being well over $720 billion per year. (That figure does not include "national security" spending hidden in the budgets of other U.S. departments—i.e., Energy, State, Treasury, Veterans Affairs, CIA, NSA, et al., for a variety of military projects. Adding these would likely make the total more than *$1 trillion* per year.)

- Even if the oft-quoted $720 billion official figure is accurate, that's roughly *half of all the military expenditures of all countries in the world, combined.*
- As mentioned above, the United States now spends about six times as much on the military as our next largest competitor, China, which, despite having a population roughly four times larger than ours, spends only about $114 billion annually. According to the Stockholm International Peace Research Institute (SIPRI), using 2009 numbers, the top fifteen countries for military expenditures were these:
  - United States: $698 billion (43% of world total, since increased)
  - China: $114 billion (7.3% of world total)
  - United Kingdom: $59.6 billion (3.7% of world total)
  - France: $59.3 billion (3.6% of world total)
  - Russia: $58.7 billion (3.6% of world total)
  - Japan: $54.5 billion (3.3% of world total
  - Germany: $45.2 billion (2.8% of world total)
  - Saudi Arabia: $45.2 billion (2.8% of world total)
  - India: $41.3 billion (2.5% of world total)
  - Italy: $37.0 billion (2.3% of world total)
  - Brazil: $33.5 billion (2.1% of world total)
  - South Korea: $27.6 billion (1.7% of world total)
  - Australia: $24.0 billion (1.5% of world total)
  - Canada: $22.8 billion (1.4% of world total)
  - Turkey: $17.5 billion (1.1% of world total)

As for our arch enemies, Iran and North Korea, according to the CIA Fact Book, in 2008 they spent only $7.04 billion and $7 billion, respectively, on their militaries, about 1/100th of what we did.

Since the Vietnam War, total U.S. military expenditures have exceeded $20 trillion. And according to the Congressional Budget Office, the U.S. Department of Defense spending between 2001 and 2010 increased an average of 9 percent per year. The usual explanations for this recent spectacular growth in military spending were, of course, 9/11, the al Qaeda threat, and "the war on terror." But terrorism is not conventional warfare requiring multibillion-dollar aircraft carriers and $80 million jet fighters. Yet most of the U.S. budget has gone to this traditional weaponry—far more helpful for corporate capitalist needs than for fighting suicide bombers.

U.S. defense expenditures are distributed among many hundreds of corporations, but over the last decade, a high percentage of total spending was concentrated on a small number of repeat contractors. During 2009, for example, the top fifteen corporations receiving U.S. defense contracts accounted for more than a quarter of all U.S. military/defense spending. And although the ranking among them shifted somewhat from year to year, the majority of these corporations have been the same over the last decade, suggesting a close working relationship between these companies and the U.S. military procurement process. In 2009, the top fifteen were:

- Lockheed Martin: $38 billion (represents about 70% of total company sales)
- Northrop Grumman: $24 billion (77% of company sales)
- Boeing: $23 billion (48% of company sales)
- General Dynamics: $16.4 billion (78% of company sales)
- Raytheon: $16.1 billion (90% of company sales)
- United Technologies: $7.5 billion (17% of company sales)
- L-3 Communications: $7.5 billion (82% of company sales)

Also among the top fifteen were BAE Systems ($7.5 billion), SAIC ($7.4 billion), Oshkosh Trucks ($7 billion), McKesson ($6.5 billion), KBR/Halliburton ($6 billion), Bechtel ($5.2 billion), Computer Services Corp. ($4.3 billion), and General Electric ($4.3 billion), according to the the U.S. General Services Administration's Federal Procurement Data System.

A further expression of government support for aerospace/defense industry contractors is that the effective tax rate for the average defense industry corporation is 1.8%. For all other corporations in the United States, the average tax rate is 18.4%. That differential amounts to yet another hidden subsidy for militarization that doesn't get included in the overall military budget.

Christopher Hellman, of the National Priorities Project, formerly with the Center for Defense Information and the Center for Arms Control, disputes the Pentagon's publicly reported $720 billion figure. He argues that the actual amount is closer to $1.2 trillion. Writing for TomDispatch ("The Real U.S. National Security Budget," March 1, 2011), Hellman reports a long list of war and national-security expenditures that never show up in the totals reported by the Defense Department.

For example, in the FY 2012 federal budget projections, the Department of Energy receives $19.3 billion for keeping nuclear weapons properly maintained and for cleaning up waste from the weapons; spying and intelligence-gathering functions of the National Intelligence Program, including assignments from the CIA and NSA, total $53 billion; expenses by NASA for spy satellites add $18.7 billion. Another $53.5 billion goes to pay carryover expenses for past wars, and for "general support for current and future national security strategy" via various other federal accounts, including the Department of Homeland Security ($37 billion), the Department of Health and Human Services ($4.6 billion), and the Department of Justice ($4.6 billion). It is important to remember that most of these military expenditures actually wind up in the hands of private corporations performing services in each of these categories.

According to Hellman, the $117.8 billion war-funding request for the Department of Defense (which was authorized by Congress and is supposed to cover Iraq and Afghanistan war expenditures) doesn't include certain other actual "war-related fighting" costs, including the counterterrorism activities of the State Department and the U.S. Agency for International Development.

Commercial Arms Trade

Another very important dimension of this story is that U.S. corporate arms manufacturers also do very big business selling to *other* countries. Total arms sales to global markets (in 2008) represented about 68.4 percent of all global arms sales in the world, and that percentage is increasing. In October 2010, the Obama administration authorized the sale of some $60 billion in armaments to the government of Saudi Arabia, where 9/11 was born. These include Apache attack helicopters, tactical Black Hawk helicopters, and F-15 fighter jets. It is the biggest commercial armament sale in U.S. history. Not announced, but expected by most observers, is that the U.S. will likely make an offsetting sale to Israel so its own military readiness will remain superior to Saudi Arabia's. All of this can only be viewed realistically as yet more economic stimulus.

Other countries may not match our level of arms sales, but they are also significantly involved. Alex Sanchez, of the Council on Hemispheric Affairs, reported in February 2011 that Russia and China, and several European countries, have been finding good sales opportunities in South America. Venezuela is a particularly big buyer of Russia's Sukhoi fighter jets, helicopters, Kalashnikov and Dragunov rifles, and shoulder-fired antiaircraft missiles. Venezuela calls them "defensive," and Moscow calls them part of its "military diplomacy" program. Whatever you call it, it's highly profitable business.

Other South American countries buying military hardware include Brazil, Bolivia, Peru, Ecuador, Colombia, and Chile. Some of these countries say it's to deal with "narco-traffickers." The sellers include France, Israel, Germany, and Spain, as well as China, Russia, and, of course, the United States. Items in demand include helicopters, tanks, fighter planes, rifles, and radar equipment. One notable item is that Brazil is buying two nuclear-powered submarines from France.

A cynic might say that the good news about such deals is that they make it far more likely that countries will eventually start using this increased supply of modern equipment on each other, or on some of their suppliers. That would mean that more places will be destroyed, and more equipment will have to be built and bought, and wherever destruction has taken place will have to be rebuilt. All of this is very good for the business cycle.

While the United States makes sales to South America, many here have complained about the other countries that are intervening in South America, particularly those that support Venezuela. In a June 2010 report issued by the right-wing Heritage Foundation, Peter Brookes argued that "Chávez is spending billions on arms from Russia in the absence of any valid threat coming from Washington." But most worrisome, according to Brookes, is the Venezuelan leader's interest in nuclear power, where he is seeking assistance from both Russia and Iran. This conjures up the deeply disturbing image, says Brookes, of "a nuclear threat not far from our shores."

Meanwhile, the United States claims to remain the most peaceful of all nations involved in that region. But that's not how South Americans view it. South America experienced two centuries of U.S. intervention, assassination, and overthrow during the 1800s and 1900s. As recently as 1973, Henry Kissinger engineered the overthrow and effective assassination of Salvador Allende in Chile, and the ascendency of the brutal dictator Augusto Pinochet, who lasted until 1990. South Americans have not forgotten. When the United States requested in 2007 to open negotiations with Ecuador to build a new U.S. base there—theoretically as a buffer to Venezuela—Ecuador's president, Rafael Correa, answered, "Yes, of course you can, if we can build a base of our own in southern Florida." Negotiation plans quickly broke off.

Military Keynesianism

Former U.S. intelligence officer and author of *Blowback* Chalmers Johnson loves to point out that a gigantic percentage of military hardware (and software) is utterly out-of-date for modern "fourth-generation warfare," the kind we see in Afghanistan and Iraq. Much of it exists only for the purpose of subsidizing arms manufacturers. They are essentially bailouts and job stimulus programs for an economy that doesn't seem to be able to sustain jobs other ways.

Sometimes the motives are very direct and clear, as with the production and purchase of the Lockheed Martin F-22 stealth fighter plane. Lockheed Martin began construction of the F-22 in 1986, at a cost of $200 million each, which later went up to $339 million and a total cost of $620 billion.

Like so many other examples in the Cold War arms race, the F-22s were designed specifically to directly counter an expected new, ultra-fast, highly maneuverable Soviet fighter, ostensibly so we could sustain air superiority. But by the time the U.S. F-22 planes were actually rolling off the line, in 1997, the Cold War was long over, the Soviet Union no longer existed, and production on that super-hot Soviet aircraft had never even begun. The F-22s were built anyway, fulfilling what was probably the main goal—subsidizing Lockheed Martin—but they are now mostly unusable. Now we are trying to cut our losses by unloading them onto other countries.

Another case concerns production of the B-2 bomber, which was originally meant to replace the Fairchild A-10 "Warthog," which had performed well in the first Persian Gulf War. Northrop Grumman and the Pentagon argued that what we really needed now, rather than A-10s, were new, superfast (less maneuverable), high-altitude bombers that flew in straight lines. Three of these new Northrop Grumman B-2s cost the equivalent of 715 of the A-10s, and, according to Chalmers Johnson, "the Air force regularly inflicted heavy casualties [in Afghanistan] on innocent civilians, at least in part because it tried to attack ground targets from the air with inappropriately high performance equipment." Johnson continued, "The B-2 stealth bomber has proven to be almost totally worthless. They are too delicate to deploy to harsh climates without special hangars first being built to protect them, at ridiculous expense; and they cannot fulfill any combat missions that older designs were not fully adequate to perform; and, at a total cost of $44.75 billion for only twenty-one bombers."

In a *New York Times* article entitled "The Pentagon's Biggest Boondoggles" (March 13, 2011), John Arquilla cites eight more of the most excessive and utterly useless Defense Department projects. Here are my four favorites:

F-35 Lightning II Fighter: $325 billion (Lockheed Martin Corporation)

Noted for its "off-boresight" targeting, this plane does not have to be aimed for the missile to shoot accurately. The original estimate was that 2,443 of these planes, begun in 2000, would cost merely $178 billion. By 2006, the cost was up to $200 billion. By the end of 2010, the cost was $80 million for each plane, a total of about $325 billion. One Pentagon report concluded that "affordability is no longer embraced as a core pillar." Lockheed Martin is supposed to start delivering the planes in 2016. The Arquilla report concludes, however, that "the F-35 is simply not needed. Only one American fighter plane has been shot down in nearly 40 years. Our fighter aircraft are already a full generation ahead of anyone else's."

Even without these new planes, by the end of this decade our fleet is fifteen times the size of China's and twenty times Russia's. Also, according to the *Times*, the targeting technology, if we want it, can easily be adapted to existing planes.

Gerald Ford–Class Supercarrier:
$120 billion (Northrop Grumman Corporation)

The estimated cost for this giant, one-hundred-thousand-ton aircraft carrier was initially budgeted at $5 billion per ship when work began in 2007 but has increased to $12 billion each. Ten of them are supposed to be ready by 2015. The distinguishing features of the Ford include "an electromagnetic catapult for aircraft launchings, a better nuclear reactor, and a reduced radar profile." Big carriers are increasingly vulnerable to enemy attack—"China's 'carrier-killer' ballistic missile is just one of many threats—meaning too much striking power is concentrated in a handful of big ships." In other words, kill one or two of them, and the war is over. We lose.

Future Combat System: $340 billion (Boeing and SAIC)

This program combines a large variety of "interconnected vehicles, robots, and communications and sensing devices . . . including drones and various manned and unmanned vehicles." The original budget for this program was $92 billion, but it grew to $340 billion by 2009, when the program was canceled. The project was summarized as a "laudable concept of networking the Army and making it faster and leaner, derailed by runaway costs." Then it was pointed out that for achieving connectivity, "an inexpensive alternative has been demonstrated by the success of the Tactical Web Page—a simple, secure web-based tool initiated by special-op soldiers in Afghanistan in 2001."

Littoral Combat Ship: $38 billion (Austal USA and Lockheed Martin)

By 2015, each company is supposed to deliver ten high-speed, shallow-draft, catamaran-hulled vessels intended to fight running battles in shallow coastal waters of the Pacific, presumably against China. The initial budget was $220 million per ship, which has risen to $650 million. The full complement is expected to eventually be fifty-five of these vessels. A prototype version of this boat was introduced by Austal as a high-speed ferry in Hawaii in 2007, the Hawaii Superferry, which at that time had reportedly been built for a mere $80 million. (Prices go up when it's for the military.) The Hawaii Superferry had been loudly rejected by a huge Hawaii protest movement, led by environmentalists and surfers, worried about the boat's many appalling environmental consequences, notably the extreme threat of high-speed vessels to whales, dolphins, sea turtles, and other wildlife in the waters surrounding most Hawaiian islands.

The Superferry was eventually banned by the Hawaii Supreme Court when its (private) owners, led by former defense secretary John F. Lehman, refused to do an environmental impact statement, which would likely have failed. No less a military expert than Sen. John McCain "excoriated the Littoral project for building ships that 'are not operationally effective or reliable.' For example, the aluminum superstructure 'will burn to the waterline if hit'—highly problematic in an age of increasingly potent anti-ship weaponry."

We have barely mentioned the best example of all, the Big Daddy of insane spending within military Keynesianism programs: "Between the 1940s and 1996," according to Chalmers Johnson, "the U.S. spent at least $5.8 trillion on the development, testing, and construction of nuclear bombs. By 1967, the peak year of its nuclear stockpile, the U.S. possessed some 32,500 deliverable atomic and hydrogen bombs, none of which, thankfully, was ever used. This perfectly illustrates the Keynesian principle that the government can produce profits for giant corporations, and provide make-work jobs to keep people employed. Nuclear weapons were not just America's special weapon, but its special *economic* weapon. There is today, of course, no sane use for them, while the trillions spent on them could have been used to solve the problems of Social Security, health care, (and) quality education."

In *Dismantling the Empire*, Johnson summarizes the situation this way: "In our devotion to militarism, despite our limited resources, we are failing to invest in our social infrastructure and other requirements for the long-term health of our country. . . . Most important, we have lost our competitiveness as a manufacturer for civilian needs . . . an infinitely more efficient use of scarce resources than arms manufacturing."

Domestic investment would certainly have increased our chances of keeping up with China, India, Japan, and parts of eastern Europe, and other countries that are quickly filling vacuums in many industrial areas in which we were once in the forefront.

Johnson quotes historian Thomas E. Woods, who said that "during the 1950s and 1960s, between one-third and two-thirds of all American research talent was siphoned off into the military sector." Woods added that "it is impossible to know what innovations never appeared as a result of this diversion of resources and brainpower into the service of the military. But by the 1960s we began to notice Japan was outpacing us in the design and quality of a range of consumer goods, including household electronics and automobiles." This situation has not improved, as China and India and lately South Korea have also advanced to take the lead in all manner of technological innovations, especially in the area of high-tech research and production.

Chalmers Johnson goes into great detail about how U.S. military spending—

often of no practical use, sometimes poorly produced, and with inflated production costs—is introduced and sustained. It's a process characterized by shameless lobbying, self-interest, political-campaign debt payments, handouts, and bailouts. The very shoddiness of the procedures and programs becomes a kind of excuse for redundancy of production: If you make enough of it, some of it has got to work.

Johnson reports on the work of Franklin "Chuck" Spinney, a former high-level analyst with the Pentagon's Office of Systems Analysis, who explained the irrationality of the military purchasing process, featuring "inadequate amounts of wildly overpriced equipment." He described a contracting process featuring two corrupt and distorting tendencies: (1) "front loading," in which powerful corporate-military lobbies join forces to achieve huge up-front government payments for unproven technology that often ultimately fails, and (2) "political engineering," the practice of seeking contracts in as many congressional districts as possible simultaneously to solidify congressional support for over-budgeted and frequently useless equipment.

Johnson offers an example of the effectiveness of this "all-voting-districts" strategy, as it came to be called, when Congress attempted to cancel the completely useless B-2 bomber in 1990. After the disintegration of the Soviet Union, the B-2, which had been designed specifically against Russian defense systems, lost its raison d'être. However, the Pentagon and the Northrop Grumman Corporation created a gigantic lobbying campaign that emphasized that tens of thousands of jobs and hundreds of millions in profits were at risk in forty-six states and 383 congressional districts. As a result, the B-2 is still with us today.

U.S. Military Bases

During 2008, according to the Pentagon, the United States maintained 5,429 military bases in the world, including in all fifty states, seven U.S. territories, and thirty-eight foreign countries. The number of bases outside the U.S. was officially acknowledged as 761, including 124 bases in Japan (forty-seven troops on Okinawa) and 87 bases in South Korea, reports David Vine in "Foreign Policy in Focus" (February 25, 2009). These numbers do not count U.S. bases in Iraq, Afghanistan, Kosovo, Israel, Jordan, and England whose existence is not officially disclosed by the Pentagon. Most estimates are that the total number of U.S. bases on foreign soil should be listed as more than one thousand.

The total annual cost of maintaining all of these foreign bases is about $250 billion a year, approximately 25 percent of the military budget.

Sales by food-service industries on U.S. *foreign* bases alone equaled $5.6

billion in 2009. Ten million customers. Eighteen thousand employees. Leading contractors are Burger King, Subway, Baskin Robbins, Charley's, Taco Bell, Popeyes, and Pizza Hut. Bases are good for business.

Citing such figures as above, Chalmers Johnson loved to ask, provocatively, "What harm would actually befall the United States if we decided to close those hundreds of bases, large and small, that garrison around the world?" Would we suddenly face massive invasions? he asked. Or grave interventions into our economic domains? Does this worry justify a U.S. military budget larger than all the rest of the world's countries combined? Or is it just simply in the grand cause of economic bailouts, subsidies, and job stimulus for a country suffering the inevitable limits of a growth economy? He argued it was the latter, and that our bases were just the kind of provocation that could actually lead to war.

In her book *The Bases of Empire*, Brown University professor Catherine Lutz points out that "as late as 1938 the U.S. basing system was far smaller than that of its political and economic peers, including many European nations as well as Japan. U.S. soldiers were stationed in just 14 bases," mostly in the Caribbean. Everything changed after World War II with the creation, in 1947, of the National Security Agency, the National Security Council, the CIA, and the official merger between economic and military policy, mentioned earlier.

From that point forward, it was go-go-go for military-industrial collaboration and the expansion of our overseas bases, beginning with the decision to try and keep all the existing World War II bases in Europe, Asia, and elsewhere, *permanently*. For a short time, Russia maintained its own (far smaller) empire of bases, which provided U.S. military planners with further excuses for our deployments during the Cold War. Except for a small number within former Soviet territories, the Russian base program has since been abandoned.

For perspective, Lutz organized her findings by region, based on a 2007 map showing the 761 officially acknowledged U.S. military bases on foreign soil, according to the Department of Defense's "Base Structure Report: Fiscal Year 2007." A more recent report, by the *Nation*'s Katrina vanden Heuvel (June 15, 2011), put the number of officially acknowledged bases at 865, without counting Afghanistan or Iraq.

Here is a rundown of U.S. base deployments around the world:

Asia Pacific

The U.S. already maintains 84 bases in Hawaii and 166 in Alaska. We also continue to operate 87 bases in South Korea, 124 bases in Japan (including 47,000 troops on Okinawa), and several each in the Philippines, Singapore, and New Zealand. Most importantly, another 40–50 bases are on U.S. territories like

Guam, Saipan, Tinian, Kwajalein, and a supremely controversial one on Diego Garcia, nominally an English colony in the Indian Ocean. (Most of the bases in these regions are the subject of fierce protests from local populations.) Meanwhile, China, like almost all other countries, maintains *zero* foreign bases in the Pacific or, for that matter, anywhere else (except Tibet, if you count that as "foreign" soil). Russia has one military base in Syria, and about twenty-five within former Soviet states in eastern Europe and western Asia.

More recently, military activity in the Asia-Pacific region has increased very rapidly, because of the accelerated pace of economic competition and the alleged growing military threats from China. In a series of statements in late 2011, President Obama famously announced a "Pacific Pivot" in U.S. policy. Supposedly in reaction to China, new U.S. bases were announced in January 2012 to be built in Darwin, Australia, and the Philippines. Meanwhile, a giant protest against the United States has been ongoing since 2010, on Jeju Island in South Korea, a UNESCO World Heritage site. Local farmers and oyster divers are attempting to block construction of a new gigantic military seaport and airport being built by South Korea but designed specifically to serve as a port for U.S. missile-carrying warships, five hundred miles from China.

Western Europe

The U.S. still maintains about 500 U.S. bases in western Europe, left over from World War II and the Cold War: 227 in Germany, 89 in Italy, 57 in Britain (an estimate—the exact figures are not published), 21 in Portugal, etc. Within some of these countries there is active opposition to the bases. For example, in Italy there have been very large ongoing street protests against the U.S. expansion of its base in Caserma Ederle, in Vicenza. In the latter case, local people in Caserma protest loudly, asking why they need to cater to the U.S. military, sixty years after the war ended and NATO has taken over. No other western European country maintains bases in other countries, with the exception of Great Britain in the Falklands, where it recently fought a short war.

Middle East

About 66 U.S. bases are in the Middle East, including 19 in Turkey, 16 in Kuwait, and 8 in Bahrain, which is home to the U.S. Navy's Seventh Fleet, as well as bases in Saudi Arabia, Oman, Yemen, Qatar, the United Arab Emirates, Uzbekistan, Pakistan, Tajikistan, Kyrgyzstan, and others. Such U.S. military presences are presumably to protect Middle East oil supplies, and they're conveniently located between Russia and China. However, in quite a few of these countries there is fierce opposition to these bases, notably in Turkey, not to mention Saudi Arabia, where somebody named Osama bin Laden took the matter into his own hands.

In Bahrain and Yemen, popular democratic uprisings are being violently crushed, and there remain questions about why the U.S. base personnel do not assist the protestors to prevent them from being slaughtered. The official base numbers in this region do *not* include an estimated half dozen more in Israel, and those several hundred "secret" bases in Afghanistan and Iraq, none of which are officially disclosed by the Defense Department.

Africa

U.S. bases throughout Africa include Gabon, Niger, Côte d'Ivoire, Liberia, Sierra Leone, Mali, Senegal, Mauritania, Morocco, Equatorial Guinea, São Tomé, Ascension, Djibouti, Ethiopia, Tanzania, Uganda, Egypt, Tunisia, Algeria, and Chad.

Why should we have bases in those places? Are we helping solve local conflicts? We did fire some missiles from aircraft carriers in the Mediterranean into Libya. What about Nigeria? What about Somalia? Rwanda? Are we defending our friends against intimidation and insurgencies? Apparently not. Do we imagine these bases as effective military launch pads for actions elsewhere? Doubtful. Most likely, we are there to show our muscle and protect our interests in local resources, especially oil, lithium, and other minerals, especially against forays by China, as Mrs. Clinton warned. But China has *no* military bases in Africa. One wonders how they are able to keep thriving without them.

South America

We have three bases in Peru and six in Columbia—where we helped the right-wing government fight the left-wing guerrillas—with others in Paraguay, Bolivia, Ecuador, and Curaçao. Not to mention nearly one hundred bases in the Caribbean, mostly on U.S. territories, such as Puerto Rico, as well as eight in Haiti, where our troops assisted in the removal of at least one democratically elected president, Jean-Bertrand Aristide, in 2004. And, of course, we have one base in Cuba, at Guantánamo Bay.

The U.S. military and government like to say that all these bases are established at the invitation of the host countries. But this is rarely true. Catherine Lutz enumerates various incentives offered "host" countries, including high rent payments (except in Japan, where *they* pay *us*), lots of jobs for local people working on the base, benefits to local businesses (notably, restaurants, bars, and brothels), as well as the sale of armaments, military aid, and trade incentives, not to mention the prospect of direct military assistance if needed. Sometimes host countries will give up these incentives and insist that the United States abandon one or more of its bases. According to Lutz, this has happened over recent decades in France, Yugoslavia, Iran, Ethiopia, Libya, Sudan, Saudi Arabia, Tunisia, Algeria, Vietnam, the Philippines, Indonesia, Peru, Mexico, and Venezuela.

Occasionally countries will ask us to leave as a bargaining chip for increased rent payment, or for political support in certain international conflicts. But even when local populations express great outrage at the presence of U.S. bases, these bases are rarely shut down. The Asia-Pacific region is a particularly good case in point.

Focus on the Pacific

When the Obama administration announced, in 2011, the Pacific Pivot in U.S. economic and defense policies, it sounded like something new. While it is true that the United States has been focused in other parts of the world over the last half century, the Pacific has never left the agenda. As the title of their book on the subject, *American Lake*, by Peter Hayes, Lyuba Zarsky, and Walden Bello, suggests, the United States has actually considered much of the Pacific virtually its private property since at least the late 1800s. The Pacific program really got going when we "annexed" the independent nation of Hawaii (1893), surely one of the more outrageous and illegal acts of corporate oligarchic colonialism in history.

To satisfy the desires of three or four super-wealthy sugar planters in Hawaii, actively supported by powerful Christian missionaries, the U.S. military overthrew a very popular Hawaiian monarchy. They managed this despite the fact that throughout the mid-1800s, Hawaii was considered by most countries of Asia and Europe as a friendly, well-functioning, independent nation—embassies were exchanged, and there were many treaties and trade agreements.

Hawaii's population strongly opposed the takeover, the overthrow of the queen, and, later, annexation. But not even U.S. president Grover Cleveland, who understood it was a violation of international law, could stop what the dominant sugar oligarchs and missionaries were determined to do. Cleveland sent an envoy to Hawaii—ten days by boat—who tried to get the queen put back onto the throne. But by then the U.S. Congress had approved annexation and made the oligarchs happy, just as they do today. Given the remoteness of the islands, and the financial power of the plantation owners, the seditious act was soon a fait accompli and has remained so. However, a very active Hawaiian sovereignty movement still retains considerable energy and support. Other powerful movements opposing U.S. military presence exist on dozens of islands throughout the Pacific.

Kyle Kajihiro, of the American Friends Service Committee and DMZ Hawaii in Honolulu, hosts a Demilitarization Tour for visitors to Hawaii, surveying dozens of military sites on Oahu and reporting their history and implications. Kajihiro points out that the U.S. military had its eyes on Hawaii as early as 1875, specifically citing the strategic location of Pearl Harbor. Kajihiro's tour includes going up into the hills above Pearl Harbor, to the gates of the offices of the U.S. Pacific Command. USPC has articulated its mandate as ensuring "security" for the entire Asia-Pacific region, all the way to the westernmost reaches of the Indian Ocean. That covers about half the earth's surface, 50 percent of the global population, about thirty-six nations, and thousands of small islands.

In September 2011, at the World Affairs Council in San Francisco, I heard a lecture by Admiral Robert F. Willard, who heads the U.S. Pacific Command in Honolulu. Admiral Willard put it quaintly, I thought, by saying that the U.S. views the entire region, all the way to the Indian Ocean and beyond, as a "commons" that we are obliged to protect and control. "Commons" normally implies that lands (or waters) are the equal property of all the peoples who live in the region, to make joint use of and benefit from as they see fit. I don't think Admiral Willard sees it that way. He didn't actually say it was *our* commons, meaning our region, under our control for solely our benefit, but I would say that is the reality.

U.S. early aspirations in the Pacific extended far beyond Hawaii. In a notorious act in 1898, the United States pressured Spain, which had colonized the Philippines, to cede the islands to the United States, rather than return them to the Philippine people, as Spain had earlier promised. This led to war between America and the Philippines, resulting in a half century of U.S. occupation and rule until the end of World War II. It was interrupted only by a brief takeover by Japan, in tandem with the bombing of Pearl Harbor—causing the U.S. commander in the Philippines, General Douglas McArthur, to flee. But not before he made his famous pronouncement: "I will be back. . . ."

Further south in the Pacific, during World War II the U.S. defeated Japan for control of all of Micronesia. This encompasses more than 2,000 atolls and islands (many uninhabited), spread out over an area the size of the United States, among three major island groups: the Western Marianas; the Caroline Islands, including the independent indigenous islands of Chuuk, Yap, and Pohnpei; and the Marshall Islands. We established military bases throughout these island groups. In the Marshalls, we famously evicted the native populations of Bikini and Enewetak Atolls at the end of the war in order to use the islands as testing grounds for nuclear and hydrogen weapons, which continued for a decade. A half century later, radiation levels remain so high that families are still not able to return home.

By 1947, the Micronesia occupation by the U.S. was put under United Nations mandate: the UN Trust Territory of the Pacific Islands, which continued to be managed by the U.S. Department of the Interior. The UN's stated goal was always for the U.S. to quickly grant Micronesia full independence. But it wasn't until 1981 that we finally agreed to political freedom for the region, under a Compact of Free Association.

However, we conditioned the freedom on a few humiliating concessions. Most important was that the United States retained the right to military bases in the islands, including ports for nuclear aircraft carriers and a gigantic military base occupying most of the once beautiful island of Babelthuap, in Palau. The deal was not easily achieved. Micronesia held a series of plebiscites about granting permission for the nuclear ports, and the vote was always overwhelmingly "no." The United States wouldn't budge: No U.S. bases, no freedom. Finally, the U.S. offered to pay what is today about $92 million a year, about a third of the yearly operating budget for the Federation of Micronesia, and the people swallowed their pride (and a good deal of their sovereignty).

The U.S. wasn't so magnanimous in other cases. Guam, for example, which was designated one of only sixteen UN "non-self-governing territories" (or colonies), came fully under U.S. control. Previously occupied by Spain (twice) and Japan (once), Guam became the U.S. mid-Pacific military headquarters, with bases covering a third of the land, and with military ports constructed where several spectacular coral reefs and great forests and beaches had remained in pristine condition.

In an article in the *Nation* (April 15, 2010), Koohan Paik quotes the U.S. Defense Department calling Guam "the tip of the spear" aimed at China. Military noise—planes, live-fire practice, vehicles roaring around—have replaced the former lush sounds of the tropics. Traditional fishing grounds have been put officially "off-limits," leaving a formerly self-sufficient Chamorro people, officially U.S. citizens with a record of great support for and service in the U.S. military, engaged in huge protests against the extensive U.S. "occupation" of their land. The story here is not nearly resolved.

Similar resistance movements opposing an unwanted U.S. military presence have also been ongoing for nearly a decade on the spectacular South Korean island of Jeju, in a region known for its historic oyster-gathering economy. Traditionally, the oyster farmers are women, deep divers (without the aid of diving equipment), and they are the ones leading the local protests. Several hundred are massing every day to block construction of a new military base, and they are met regularly with police clubs. The huge facility would host U.S. nuclear warships, as part of an expanding display of military might aimed at China. Technically, the base is being constructed and will be operated by the South Korean military, but it is clearly under pressure from the United States, which remains hungry for ports near the China Sea. Continuous protests are also taking place over the island of Diego Garcia in the Indian Ocean—technically an English colony, which was "loaned" to the United States starting in 1964 to build a military presence near India, a short plane-hop to China. It was part of America's "Strategic Island Concept." The U.S. ejected about two thousand local residents to make way for this, its most luxurious base, which looks far more like a San Diego country club than like a former part of India, featuring beautiful swimming pools, bowling alleys, fancy restaurants, and, of course, Burger Kings. The residents, who were exiled to other islands or to England, are furious. For three decades they have been taking legal actions and mounting demonstrations in England—thus far to no avail.

Protests are also under way throughout the Marianas and the Marshall Islands. In the latter case, the people of Bikini and Enewetak are demanding to go home. And the people of Kwajalein—who supported themselves for centuries by reef fishing—have been forcibly moved to the miserable, reefless island of Ebey, where they can no longer fish and are reduced to seeking jobs at McDonald's on the base. Or else they go on welfare. They also want to go home. But so far, the United States is unresponsive to any of these appeals on any of these islands. And American media scarcely report it.

Given all this upheaval and upset, let's return to the question Chalmers Johnson raised about whether, if we withdrew from the region and left its peoples in peace, China would come sailing in. Johnson said he didn't think so—but the point is essentially moot. The United States is *not* withdrawing. The Pacific Ocean and many of its islands, and its hundreds of bases, are essentially considered the property of the United States, and withdrawal from the region would dramatically diminish our ability to control goings-on in the Pacific and Pacific Rim countries. This would include access to their and the ocean's resources, as well as shipping routes and trade opportunities. But most important, perhaps, are the positive economic-stimulus effects of our military contracts at a time of recession. What would happen to such "free market" icons as Lockheed, Northrup, Raytheon, and Boeing? We have contracts with them. Where would we house our thousands of nuclear and other warships, airplanes, and missiles?

As for the local populations and islanders—it's as if we had captured and held hostage thousands of innocent peoples, as if they were war criminals, trespassing on our property, when the opposite is more likely the case. So much for the Pacific commons.

"Comparative Advantage" of War

So. How does this all add up? We have thousands of fancy airplanes and ships that cost hundreds of billions of dollars but that we don't really need. We have thousands of bombs that can destroy the planet but that we can never use. We are occupying many hundreds of far-flung bases all over the world, and small islands from which we have expelled populations against their will, or else made them into colonized restaurant workers and janitors. We've redesigned the islands into militarized versions of Las Vegas. We continue to occupy these islands because of, we now say, growing threats from China. But China occupies *no* islands and is still gaining on us economically. So are other countries. Why do we still do this?

Actually, the best answer may lie in classical Ricardian economic theories, especially theories of "comparative advantage," as follows:

Not every country produces everything that it might produce. For example, the United States could certainly produce more stained-glass windows and high-quality wines, instead of military hardware. We could try to compete with Italy on those. But we don't have much of a history of that activity, and we don't have the artists or the production mechanisms; we don't even know how to think about it.

Neither do we have much experience making small, light, inexpensive cars, as Japan and China are doing, or 200-mph, highly efficient trains to substitute for auto and plane travel. Neither are we good at making inexpensive high-quality textiles, like China, India, and Indonesia are. We don't have the industrial history for any of that—though apparently, given the price of gas, we have begun to try, so far without too much headway. We used to be good at high-tech innovation, but most of our focus of late, and most of our talented technologists, have been seized by the military work. That has helped us lose our lead in most green-tech areas as well, leaving it to China, India, Japan, and eastern Europe to seize those flags. China in particular is rapidly becoming the world leader in wind, solar, all manner of computer technologies, and, according to recent reports, desalination of water, perhaps the most important economic opportunity of all, despite its environmental dangers. To do that, China is making use of state funds that it is *saving* by not having to build forward military bases throughout the Pacific and everywhere else. China lets us use up our money for that. In fact, it loans us money so we can do that.

But there is one thing the United States still *does* know how to do well: make armaments. We are a big country and are still pretty rich. (Any country involved in the armaments industry has to be very big and rich to indulge in it.) We *can* afford it, while few other countries can. We already have a highly developed military-industrial infrastructure well in place, and have a constant market in all those bases around the world, requiring nonstop material replenishment.

In terms of capitalism, therefore, *military* production and marketing may actually be our *best* economic opportunity—we already dominate it, we can depend on it, and it seems like we can keep it growing at 9–10 percent per year. Republicans and Democrats are all good with this. What's more, this steady market doesn't need real customers. *We are our own customers.* We do sell a small percent of this military production to other countries—more than the rest of the world combined—but mostly, we ourselves consume the products our companies produce, deploy them, and use them up ourselves, or leave them in storage somewhere forever. Anyway, there are always new wars to eventually use up our stockpiles, or new threats of wars to provide profitable new markets and good jobs.

So, speaking economically, we are better off concentrating on what we know and what we do best, letting other countries deploy their more advanced skills in light cars, solar panels, wind arrays, fast trains, green technology, good food, good wine, stained-glass windows, and fine inexpensive fabrics. We have a "comparative advantage" in military production, and an "absolute advantage" as well. Very few countries are in a position to compete with us for this important economic opportunity. And we have a good excuse, considering all our so-called "enemies" in the region that we need to arm up against, including North Korea, Russia, and China. They may someday threaten our "Pacific commons" resource base, or push for new shipping lanes.

Military production is one economic area where we can easily dominate global supply, production, distribution, and deployment and achieve constant renewal of the process. It is American capitalist genius at its best.

IX.

Privatization of Democracy

Forbes's annual issue on the world's billionaires has become like the Oscars for the arts of wealth creation. On public display are the winners and runners-up for capitalism's greatest acts, with the results widely reported in all media with a fervor nearly equal to the world soccer championships. The winners are treated as heroes and role models.

In 2011, *Forbes* reported that the planet now has 1,211 billionaires, up from only 982 the year before, more than a 20 percent growth in billionairism. Does that strike you as too many? How come there were 20 percent more billionaires during a time of deep recession while jobs are being lost in the millions and employee salaries are plunging?

The standings had shifted markedly in only one year. Bill Gates dropped to #2, at $56 billion. Mexico's Carlos Slim, a telecommunications czar who has dozens of other enterprises, became #1, at $74 billion. The infamous Koch Brothers (U.S. right-wing oil and Tea Party heroes) were #18 and #19, respectively, but if combined together, as they really ought to be, would be #3 (a combined $42 billion).

Also sprinkled among the billionaires' list are four members of the Walton (Walmart) family. If we combine them, they would be #1, at $89 billion. There are famous entertainers, like Oprah Winfrey (#400), as well as quite a few high-tech entrepreneurs, various sports heroes, and some super-oligarchs from Russia (though lately some have been put in jail by Mr. Putin for trying to steal his show). The U.S. share of the oligarchy is highest, but there are also impressive numbers from other countries, especially the "BRIC" countries—Brazil (29), Russia (102), India (55), and China (115)—up by 56 percent in only one year, bypassing Europe. Only three are from Africa.

How did these people get so rich? Some became wealthy by inheriting huge amounts of money; now they usually spend their days managing and investing it to become even more rich. Quite a few of them have invented and/or launched fantastic levels of technological innovation that have swept the world. Bill Gates is the most spectacular example of that. And there's Mark Zuckerberg (#52) of Facebook, Larry Ellison (#5) of Oracle, and the Google boys, among others. Telecommunications entrepreneurs have also thrived, including one African billionaire, Mohammed Ibrahim (#692), and retail innovators, such as the Waltons, who discovered that dominance leads to more dominance.

Others have managed by military means or geopolitical deals to control a crucial scarce-resource supply, such as oil, like the Saudi princes, the Koch brothers, or the new Russian oligarchs. Or they dominate the supply of key minerals or steel production. Still others made their wealth mainly by making *bets* on the values of others' wealth, or of currencies, or stock trends in the market. George Soros (#46) is one of those. So are most of the hedge fund, banking and finance industry billionaires and mega-millionaires. And Shelley Adelson (#16) made his in Las Vegas, owning casinos.

But now, something new has been added to the process of capitalist wealth creation, enabling a rate of wealth expansion like nothing that came before it. That is the role increasingly being played by so-called democratic governments in catering to and facilitating the interests of the ultra-rich. It's nearly as if government itself has become a subordinate division of a far larger capitalist enterprise. The outcome from this new trend is a startling decline in the practice of democracy, and its near replacement by an alternative form of governance in which 1% of the population, the wealthiest, controls the economy entirely: *plutonomy*.

Rule by the Rich

Binghamton University professor emeritus James Petras sums up the new growing problem this way in "Canadian Dimension" (April 7, 2011): "The current concentration of wealth exceeds any previous period in history; from King Midas, the Maharajahs, and the Robber Barons to the Silicon Valley–Wall Street moguls." Petras argues that in most countries, including the United States, the sudden emergence of a large, super-rich class of billionaires has been significantly promoted by nation-states and lower-level governments, conspiring with the wealthiest classes to serve their interests over all others:

"What is striking about the recovery, growth, and expansion of the world's billionaires is how dependent their accumulation of wealth is based on pillage of state resources; how much of their fortunes are based on neo-liberal policies which led to the takeover at bargain prices of privatized public enterprises . . . that the state—not the market—plays the essential role in facilitating the greatest concentration and centralization of wealth in world history. . . . The sources of billionaire wealth are, at best, only partially due to 'entrepreneurial innovations.'"

A similar view was expressed by Bill Moyers in 2010 in a daring speech to the Environmental Grantmakers Association (an organization comprising more than seven hundred wealthy philanthropists and foundation executives), in which he cited a 2005 publication by Citigroup entitled "Revisiting Plutonomy: The Rich Getting Richer."

> *Plutocracy* is rule by the rich. *Plutonomy* is an economy where the government helps them do it. . . . The world is dividing into two blocs: plutonomy and the rest. . . . Asset booms, a rising profit share, and favorable treatment by market-friendly governments have allowed the rich to prosper . . . and to take an increasing share of income and wealth over the last twenty years. . . . The top 10 percent, particularly the top 1 percent of the United States, have benefited disproportionately, especially from globalization and the productivity boom, at the relative expense of labor.

Since 2005, the figures have gotten even more distorted. And, predicts Moyers, the ultra-wealthy "are likely to get even wealthier in the coming years, because the dynamics of plutonomy are now intact. Plutocracy and democracy don't mix. Plutocracy too long tolerated leaves democracy on the auction block." Democracide.

Moyers adds, "After the Reagan years and the Bush tax cuts, by 2007 the wealthiest 10% of Americans were taking in 50% of the national income. A fraction of people at the top now earn more than the bottom 120 million Americans." Public Citizen, the Ralph Nader–founded political action group, puts the exact number at "1% of Americans, who earn more than the bottom 120 million Americans."

Chrystia Freeland, in her *Atlantic* article "The Rise of the New Global Elite" (January/February 2011), points out that "before the recession, it was relatively easy to ignore this concentration of wealth among an elite few. . . . But the financial crisis and its long dismal aftermath have changed all that. A multibillion-dollar bailout and Wall Street's swift reinstatement of gargantuan bonuses have inspired a narrative of parasitic bankers and other elites rigging the game for their own benefit. And this in turn has led to wider—and not unreasonable—fears that we are living in not merely a plutonomy, but a plutocracy, in which the rich display outsized political influence, narrowly self-interested motives, and a casual indifference to anyone outside their own rarified economic bubble." She quotes one woman at a dinner party complaining that though she made $20 million in the prior year, she was disgusted that after taxes it would be only $10 million. It seemed like theft to her.

Freeland believes that two factors have recently accelerated the trend. The first is the set of recent technological breakthroughs that have converted previously small players into gigantic economic superstars and have allowed bankers to operate instantaneously across oceans. A second ingredient, by now most important, has been the actions of governments which have served their wealthiest plutocrats—let's call them clients—with favors, subsidies, and good deals. Freeland describes it as very worrisome that "individual nations have offered contributions to income inequality—financial deregulation and upper-bracket tax cuts in the United states; insider privatization in Russia; rent-seeking in regulated industries in India and Mexico."

Freeland quotes economists Emmanuel Saez, of UC Berkeley, and Thomas Piketty, of the Paris School of Economics, who say that "between 2002 and 2007, 65 percent of all income growth in the United States went to the top 1 percent of the population. The financial crisis interrupted this trend temporarily, as incomes for the top 1 percent fell more than those of the rest of the population in 2008." They quickly recovered. After that down year of 2008, "the top 25 hedge fund managers were paid, on average, more than $1 billion each in 2009."

A later report, from the Congressional Budget Office, confirmed that "from 1979 to 2007, average inflation-adjusted after tax income grew by 275 percent for the 1 percent of the population with the highest income." For the top 20 percent of the population, the growth rate was 65 percent. Meanwhile, according to the *New York Times* (October 26, 2011), "people in the lowest fifth of the population received about 5 percent of total after-tax household income in 2007, down 7 percent from 1979. People in the middle three-fifths of the population saw their shares decline by 2–3 percentage points." The gap between rich and poor is rapidly accelerating. This has become a rallying point for the Occupy movement.

Doing the Numbers

There is a mountain of data on the amazing growth of extreme inequities in both the United States and the rest of the world, during the last few decades. One is seriously tempted to do a whole book of just these astounding numbers, because they so exquisitely reveal the state of things these days. Author and filmmaker Koohan Paik is seriously thinking of doing exactly that. She says she may call it *The Plutonomy Fun Book*.

But the mind boggles when poring through too much of this stuff. So we decided to reduce the citations to just a *dozen* of our top favorites, and we will take it from there, as follows:

- According to Credit Suisse Research Institute (2010), "The bottom half of the global population together possess less than 2% of global wealth. . . .

In sharp contrast, the richest 10% own 83% of the world's wealth, with the top 1% alone accounting for 43% of global assets."

- Also from Credit Suisse: "To be among the wealthiest half of the world, an adult needs only $4,000 in net assets. . . . To belong to the top 10% of global wealth holders, each adult requires $72,000 in net assets." Let's repeat that one: If you have $4,000 in personal wealth—a bank account, property, machinery—that amount is sufficient to put you in the upper half of wealthiest people in the world. If you have $72,000, you are in the upper 10%.
- Credit Suisse says that being a member of the top 1% of global wealth holders "requires net assets of only $588,000." In other words, if you own a paid-for house, or an almost-paid-for house, in the United States, you are probably among the top 1% of wealthiest people in the world. I am sure you are as surprised to learn that as I was.
- "Members of the top decile [10% of the world's wealth] are almost 400 times richer, on average, than the bottom 50%, and members of the top percentile are almost 2,000 times richer" (James B. Davis, Susanna Sandström, Anthony Sharrocks, and Edward N. Wolff, "The World Distribution of Household Wealth," a report by the United Nations University World Institute for Development Economics Research).
- "The average income in the richest 20 countries is 37 times the average in the poorest 20—a gap that has doubled in the past 40 years" (World Development Report 2000/2001 Overview).
- "The world's richest 500 people earn more than the 416 million poorest" ("Poverty to Power: Shocking Facts," Oxfam, U.K.).
- "The world's four richest citizens—Carlos Slim (Mexico), Bill Gates (U.S.), Warren Buffett (U.S.), and Mukash Ambani (India) . . . control more wealth than the world's poorest 57 countries" (Carl Pope, *Foreign Policy*, January, 2011).
- "The income of the richest 25 million Americans is the equivalent of nearly 2 billion of the world's poorest persons" ("Poverty and Inequality in the Global Economy," Michael Yates, *Monthly Review*, February, 2004).
- In 2008, "the richest 1% of Americans [held] wealth worth $16.8 trillion, nearly $2 trillion more than the bottom 90%" of Americans" ("The Rich and the Rest of Us," by John Cavanagh and Chuck Collins, *The Nation*, June 30, 2008.).
- Also from Cavanagh and Collins: "A worker making $10 an hour would have to labor for more than 10,000 years to earn what one of the 400 richest Americans pocketed in 2005."
- "In 1962, the wealth of the richest one percent of U.S. households was

roughly 125 times greater than that of the typical household. By 2004, it was 190 times" ("By the Numbers," Inequality.org).

A few more figures help demonstrate the degree of inequality among countries: The richest countries in the world, including, for example, Norway, Sweden, the United States, and Luxembourg, enjoy a per capita GDP ranging from $45,000 to $122,000 per person. The poorest countries, including most of Africa, have per capita GDPs below $500. The average is at the level of Mexico, which is the sixtieth-wealthiest country (among 187), at $10,800 GDP per person, according to the World Economic Outlook Database, International Monetary Fund, September 2011.

All GDP per capita figures in poor countries are actually misleadingly *high*. A small handful of the richest people have skimmed most of their wealth off the top by controlling wealth-producing mineral resources or land or the government itself. So the poorest half of society really has nearly nothing.

Summing things up in *Foreign Policy* (March 2012), Charles Kenny, of the New America Foundation, adds this comment on prevailing inequities: "To make it into the richest 1 percent globally, all you need is an [annual] income of around $34,000. . . . The *average* family in the U.S. has more than three times the income of those living in poverty in America, and nearly 50 times that of the world's poorest. Most of America's 99 percenters, and the West's, are really 1 percenters on a global level."

What *Is* a Billion Dollars?

In a *Truthout* article, "Nine Pictures of the Extreme Income/Wealth Gap" (February 14, 2011), Dave Johnson points out that quite a few people now make over $1 billion per year, every year, and then asks: "How much is a billion dollars? Can you visualize such an amount of money?" It's not easy.

If you earn the median income in the United States, which Johnson estimates at about $50,000 (we have quoted others who put it lower), "and don't spend a single penny of it, it will take you 20,000 years to save a billion dollars."

Johnson goes on to ask what people *do* with all that money. Well, there are luxury cars, like the Maybach, that cost up to $1 million each. "Rush Limbaugh, who has 5 homes in Palm Beach," owns six Maybachs. "Your billion [could] buy you a thousand Maybach Landaulets."

There are hotels where a one-night stay costs $20,000–$30,000. Some people pay it. "A billion dollars will buy you a $20,000 room every night for 137 years," Johnson points out. But in each of those years, you earn another billion, so cost doesn't really matter. You can also buy a private jet for $40–60 million; you could actually buy quite a few of them. Private islands seem to go for another $25 million or so, give or take a few million. You could buy forty of them with this year's billion alone. And voilà—you'd be a major landholder.

And there are yachts. There was even a famous "yacht war" that got started in 1997 among the super-wealthy, competing with each other for the biggest. First, Leslie Wexner of Limited Brands bought a 316-foot vessel, some 110 feet longer than anything in its category. That cost about $300 million. But Russia's Roman Abramovich outdid him, buying three super-yachts of the same kind. Then Paul Allen, cofounder of Microsoft, outdid them both, with a 413-foot yacht that boasts a basketball court, a heliport, a movie theater, and a submarine in the hold.

The "Problem" of Surplus Capital

Jack Santa Barbara is a retired businessman. He is wealthy, though not in a class with the kind of oligarchs we have been discussing. He has lately been writing on the consequences of plutocracy. In a 2011 special report published by the International Forum on Globalization, "Outing the Oligarchy," Santa Barbara contributed an article about the pressures that the very wealthy feel as they search continuously for ways to profitably spend their mounting surplus capital:

> Extreme inequality means that a small number of people have much more financial wealth than they can use for their own pleasure, or even for a comfortable life. They need to find places to park their excess capital. If they let their money just sit in a normal low interest bank account, they would consider that a business loss. They feel they must maximize the growth potential of every dollar; that's endemic to their training and way of life. This often leads them to speculation in high-risk investments and bubbles, which sometimes collapse. The speculative mortgage housing bubble, which burst in 2008, is an example.
>
> That excess money also becomes available to influence the political process. The very rich are easily able to intervene on a broad scale. They not only fund various political campaigns (often backing opposing candidates to ensure influence), but they contribute to drafting party platforms, supporting special interest groups, and setting up think tanks to push their narrow self-interested agendas.

In internal correspondence from IFG, Santa Barbara reports, "The oligarchs are smart. They have realized that the global economy is starting to die. It's short on resources, and the costs for what remains are skyrocketing. The prospects for rapid economic growth in the real economy, and for sustained high-level "surplus value," are sharply diminished. So, many of the wealthy are coming to the view that they will no longer seek business growth, per se. More and more of them are seeking political control as a way of gaining economic expansion. They can squeeze out more by controlling the political process—toppling unions, gaining subsidies, cutting their taxes, gaining offshore havens—and, perhaps most of all, by privatizating services like education, transportation, the military, security, Medicare and Social Security, health services, and many aspects of the natural commons, like fresh water. That's their big new market: commodification of the commons."

Republicans and especially Tea Partiers are now also advocating for privatizing whole government agencies, even those providing welfare services, for example. It represents a very profound shift in corporate/state/oligarch strategy, and is potentially much more pervasive and dangerous. All of it has been made *necessary* by the reality of declining resources and the stunted growth potential of the usual means of wealth expansion.

Through campaign contributions, this class of super-rich already "owns" many of the U.S. state houses and legislatures, the House of Representatives, and, as we said, an alarming number of U.S. senators. The election of 2012 has a fair chance to also bring them control of the Senate, and quite conceivably the presidency. If so, we should probably start calling it *neofeudalism*. A *privatized* country.

Investments in Government

In the context of resource depletion, diminishing corporate growth, and the need to find new investment opportunities for surplus wealth, the two best investment bargains now available in any market for the ultra-rich are: (1) to buy lobbying services that create or protect their tax breaks, and (2) to buy individual politicians outright.

A special *TIME* magazine report by Steven Brill (July 11, 2010), "On Sale: Your Government. Why Lobbying Is Washington's Best Bargain," notes that the Private Equity Council—an organization dedicated to keeping taxes low for some of the richest finance capital managers in the world—spent about $5 million, in about a year and a half, on lobbying Congress to sustain the present low tax rates on "carried interest." Presently they are taxed as if carried interest were a form of "capital gains," rather than as percentage fee income—a kind of management fee—for providing investment services among a small, rich community of investment bankers in the United States. Groups similar to the Private Equity Council paid out about $10 million more, with the same goal of keeping carried interest income at a low tax rate, bringing the total spent on this lobbying effort to $15 million. If that sounds like a large expenditure, consider the benefits. "What did the money managers get for their $15 million investment?" asks Brill. About $10 *billion* in lower taxes.

While lawmakers did manage [in 2010] to boost the taxes of some hedge fund managers and other folks who collect "carried interest" as part of their work, they also agreed to a compromise that will tax part of those earnings at the regular rate, and another part at a lower capital gains rate. The result was a tax bite about $10 billion smaller than what tax reformers wanted. That is $10 billion in taxes that will have to be made up with taxes on other people. That payoff is all the more remarkable when you realize that this tax break is going to some of the wealthiest Americans, and that all the reformers originally wanted was for those folks to pay the same graduated income tax rate that normal wage earners do.

This battle over "carried interest" shifted directly over into the great Republican-Democratic conflict over the United States debt limit in mid-2011. Obama and the Democrats were eager to require that hedge fund managers and others who still use the carried interest 15% tax rate, as if it were investment income rather than fees, should be required to pay taxes on the tens of billions they earn at the same rate that you and I would have to pay on ordinary earned income. According to Pat Garafolo of ThinkProgress (July 6, 2011), the top hedge fund managers in the United States earned a combined $22 billion in 2010. It would take the combined income of 441,000 middle-class families to equal the income made by just the twenty-five richest hedge fund managers. "If this small group," says Garafolo, "operated under the same rules that apply to other people—police officers, for example, or teachers—the country could cut its national deficit by as much as $44 billion in the next ten years."

Former labor secretary Robert Reich writes, in the *Christian Science Monitor* (May 26, 2010), that closing the hedge fund loophole could contribute as much as $20 billion a year toward deficit reduction. Nonetheless, Republicans refused to go along with any change on this. With the control of the House of Representatives firmly in the hands of Tea Party activists, who would not budge in their ideological belief in the lowest possible taxes for the rich, President Obama backed off. The whole opportunity flopped.

Exactly what rationale could a congressperson use to justify voting for such benefits for some of the richest people on Earth? Do these financial managers at hedge funds create jobs? Or aid national security? Or provide terrific new green-energy plans? They do none of it. Their work is almost entirely within the "virtual economy" and has no public service benefit. The products that they work with—derivatives, hedge funds, and the like—are gambling instruments, provided and sold to other super-rich investors who need to do *something* with their excess capital, now that economic expansion in the "real" economy has become more difficult. Nothing useful comes from this activity. In fact, quite the opposite, it was a principle cause of the 2008 financial collapse, the greatest recession since the 1920s. Millions of people lost their jobs and their homes. Despite that, $10 million spent on lobbyists to buy congressional votes succeeded in producing a $15 billion wealth gain for a relative handful of individuals. That's a 1,500-to-1 "profit" ratio, benefit to expense.

Another good example reported by Brill in *TIME* concerned the battle over the Volcker Rules, a package of financial regulations on investments bankers proposed by Paul Volcker, former head of the Federal Reserve, intended to prevent a repeat of the worst excesses and irresponsibilities that led to the financial crash of 2008. More than two thousand lobbyists—that's about four times the number of lobbyists than there are members of Congress—worked tirelessly sending a daily barrage of word changes for the proposed rules, slowly eating away at the vitality of the plan. "By the time the bill was finished," according to *TIME*, "lobbyists seeking Volcker rule 'carve-outs' had won complete exemptions for most mutual fund companies, and a provision allowing banks to manage other peoples' funds and still make [risky] investments of up to 3% of their capital, and to take up to seven years to sell off investments they already had."

According to the Center for Responsive Politics, the total now spent on lobbying Congress in the United States is about $3.5 billion annually—and increasing. The spending emerges from many industries and affects just about every person in Congress. It's become a great game to hear a congressional speech and then look up the speaker's campaign donors. My favorite example is when congressman Joe Barton (R-TX) apologized to BP for how it had been treated by the White House after the Gulf of Mexico oil spill. Look him up, and you'll find that Barton's primary financial support for his campaigning comes from the oil industry.

TIME reviewed the lobbying and campaign donations of a wide cross-section of industries, including these:

- *Derivatives Trading*. A senate bill would have required U.S. banks to spin off their derivative-trading desks, which might have cost the banks $5–7 billion. So, they hired more than six hundred lobbyists for fees totaling $28 million. The lobbyists were able to deplete the rules sufficiently to delay implementation for two years, allowing them to keep derivatives trading in-house. This saved the banks many billions. Then, in two years' time, they will do the battle over again.
- *Auto Dealers*. The White House wanted to add regulatory oversight, controlling auto dealers' propensity to add interest and fee kickbacks on loans, a practice that gains auto dealers a hidden $20 billion annually. The industry spent about $6.3 million in 2009 and 2010 lobbying against any change. It also donated $3.4 million congressional campaign contributions. The result was that Congress exempted the auto dealers from these consumer-protection regulations. So, for about a $10 million total

expenditure, they realized a $20 billion benefit, a 2,000-to-1 ratio, benefit to expense. Very efficient.

- *Big Banks.* This concerns the Volcker rule, which tried to bar banks from high-risk trading for their own gain, confining them to trading only on behalf of clients. "Three mega-banks—JPMorgan Chase, Morgan Stanley, and Goldman Sachs—stood to lose $4.5 billion yearly in potential profits." Those three banks together invested $15.4 million in lobbying against the rule, and also gave $2.6 million in 2010 campaign donations. Congressional negotiators finally gave in, allowing the banks to continue to invest up to 3 percent of their capital in private-equity and hedge funds, thus saving themselves about $2.9 billion annually.

Another big subject that reformers tried to put on the table during budget negotiations in 2011 was the issue of "offshore tax havens." Certain banks that the super-rich use, in such places as the Caribbean, Monaco, Lichtenstein, the Cayman Islands, or Luxembourg, are sworn to secrecy. Remarkably, in those places banks are not required to report how much of a balance their depositors maintain, or how much interest they pay, thus permitting the wealthiest individuals to hide otherwise taxable income from their home countries. Investors also take advantage of differential tax rates between countries; they would far rather show their earnings in Ireland, for example, than in the United States. Democrats and the Obama administration have been working to alter some of these arrangements, but have been overpowered by lobbyists.

According to Allison Kilkenny, writing for the *Nation* (June 14, 2011), "The IRS estimates that individuals and corporations currently hold $5 trillion in tax haven countries. Nearly two-thirds of corporations pay no taxes at all . . . and the great vampire squid, Goldman Sachs, negotiated [with the government] to lower its tax rate down to one percent." Kilkenny reports that the entire tax haven scam costs taxpayers as much as $100 billion per year.

By now we know that General Electric, one of the biggest companies in the world, made $14.2 billion in profits in 2010, of which $5.1 billion came from the United States, reported the *New York Times* (March 25, 2011), but paid no taxes at all. Neither did Bank of America, though both companies paid plenty of bonuses. The CEO of GE during this period was Jeffrey Immelt, who has now become Obama's chief of staff. We will see if he eventually shows signs of a change of heart.

Kilkenny reports that 115 companies among the S&P 500 paid less than 20 percent in taxes. Thirty-seven companies in the S&P, including Citigroup and AIG, paid less in taxes than they gained in government tax credits, another form of subsidy, effectively transferring wealth from the middle class to the rich.

Paul Buchheit, writing for *Buzzflash* at *Truthout* (May 6, 2011), points out that oil company behavior is particularly egregious. "Over the last five years, Exxon paid federal taxes at 3.6%.... Chevron was a little better at 5.6%, Marathon paid 12%, Conoco Phillips 17%." Nonetheless, says Buchheit, "They use American research infrastructure and national security to make record profits. ExxonMobil, BP, Shell, Chevron, and ConocoPhillips realized a combined 42% increase in profits in the first quarter of 2011 [in the midst of the recession]. Together, the five biggest oil companies made almost $1 trillion in profits over the past decade." They are also the leading campaign donors among corporations.

Activity of this kind is certainly not confined to U.S. taxpayers. The BBC reported that Sir Philip Green, one of British prime minister David Cameron's advisors, already the ninth-richest man in the UK (#132 on the *Forbes* list, at $7.2 billion), avoids British taxes by claiming his income is really earned by his wife, who technically lives in the tax haven of Monaco. In 2005, according to Kilkenny, the BBC calculated that Green earned £1.2 billion (nearly $2 billion) and paid nothing in taxes—dodging more than $300 million that he should have paid. A new movement has formed in England, called UNCUT, which is devoted to figuring out and exposing the way the super-rich hide their money. The movement has recently advanced to the United States and begun activities in twenty states.

In the United States, millions of dollars in campaign donations come from the wealthy beneficiaries of these special favors. The candidates then steer all kinds of government special deals in the direction of their supporters: subsidies, no-bid contracts, loopholes in environmental or health regulations, and military contracts that may not actually be necessary. And deregulation of their activities—a crucially important factor for Wall Street's financial performance, for example, in the economic crisis and since. Often, wealthy people act second-handed, through surrogate organizations that they finance, such as the very aggressive Tea Party lobbying campaigns.

In the end, all of this amounts to simple massive transfers of wealth from the middle class and the poor to the rich, and has brought us to a situation of the greatest schism between rich and poor in history—the utter breakdown of democratic government in favor of the "new feudalism."

Politicians for Sale

While writing this chapter, I recalled some conversations I had on similar issues about twenty years ago, with Doug Tompkins. The former co-owner of the clothing company Esprit, Tompkins sold his interest in the company, during the 1990s, for an estimated $500 million–plus. By today's wealth standards, it was a pittance, not even enough to get him onto the *Forbes* richest list. But still he found it somehow more than enough to live on, and soon began giving lots of it away to environmental and progressive activist causes, especially for wilderness preservation and land restoration. In our conversation, I was suggesting that he change his spending to include buying some politicians. He was appalled.

I had been friends with Doug and Suzie Tompkins since long before they became wealthy. We lived in the same San Francisco neighborhood, and our children played together. At that time Doug owned a small ski shop in North Beach and was in training for the Olympics as a downhill racer. He became injured and couldn't continue that activity. Meanwhile, Suzie started a small fashion company together with Jane Tise, called Plain Jane, which later morphed into Esprit, which Suzie and Doug operated together, with spectacular success. In 1990, Doug formed the Foundation for Deep Ecology to facilitate his giving to environmental and progressive activist causes (especially for wilderness preservation and land restoration), and he invited me to be his first executive director and, later, program director.

About midway through my ten-year tenure I suggested to him a far more efficient way to serve the environmental cause in the United States, rather than only giving to membership activist groups. Such groups typically have to struggle for years to just get a good public hearing on some key issues—like stopping the development of big dams, or nuclear power plants, or CO_2 emissions. Why not shift some of our spending to simply giving campaign money directly to politicians? Of course that expenditure would not be tax-deductible for him, as it could not come from a 501(c)(3), nonprofit foundation, but from him personally. So the relative cost would go up.

But it was so much more effective to give a senator, say, $25,000 (the going price has gone up since then, to about $100,000) to get him/her to sponsor legislation and fight for it, and win it. And you would thenceforth have complete personal access to him/her at all times. Giving to activist groups, while certainly useful in building movements, cost much more, and then they might anyway fail to get their issue effectively exposed. I recommended to Doug that he devote a substantial part of his donation portfolio, outside of the foundation, to simply buying senators and congresspeople, who would thenceforth be likely to do what we asked on key issues. I gave him lots of examples. (House members back then cost only about $10,000 for similar services; now the price has gone way up there as well, as the Koch brothers and many others have been bidding up the costs. Even so, it was far less than a typical grant to a national environmental group.)

Anyway, as I told Doug, that's how our democratic system really works. Even so-called "progressive" senators are bought off by special interests. You didn't hear a single word of support in 2010 from the usually liberal Charles Schumer when it came to voting on a bill that would have restricted Wall Street practices and possibly prevented the kind of outrageous practices that brought on the recent financial meltdown. Schumer was quiet because he has been well bought by Wall Street. Democratic senator Joe Manchin, of West Virginia, is owned by the coal industry. According to the Center for Responsive Politics, says the *Huffington Post* (April 30, 2009), a lot more of Congress is owned by real estate and banking industries. Senator Mary Landrieu received $2 million from the real estate and banking sectors over twelve years, about $200,000 per year. Sen. Birch Bayh took in about $3.5 million, and Sen. Ben Nelson got $1.4 million from them and another $1.2 million from insurance. After that, you could think of these people as employees of those industries.

Senator Joe Lieberman, of Connecticut, is employed by the health insurance industry. In fact, the health insurance industry has bought a lot of Congress, including Sen. John McCain ($546,000), Sen. Mitch McConnell ($425,000), Sen. Max Baucus ($413,000), Rep. John Boehner ($257,000), Rep. Eric Cantor ($245,000), Rep. John Dingell ($180,000), Rep. Earl Pomeroy ($104,000), et al.—Republicans and Democrats.

I think we could fairly say that just about *all* senators are owned, or nearly so, by some special interest, except possibly ex-senator Russ Feingold, of Wisconsin, who lost his seat in 2010 to a senatorial candidate owned by the Koch brothers. Congress is bought and paid for. So are state legislators and lots of governors.

Doug Tompkins thought over my strategic suggestion for a few days, but found the whole idea too immoral and repulsive to pursue. I argued further, but he was adamant. He has never changed this policy.

In our current system, *all* special interests—left to right, environmental to social—are now utterly dependent upon the degree to which they can gain leverage or can influence the White House or Congress or local governments. The whole process is impressively bipartisan. For example, I was especially fascinated by the surprising role of a handful of very wealthy Republican donors in the New York state legislative battle to legalize gay marriage in the state.

At a key moment in the debates, these wealthy Republicans persuaded a small number of fence-sitting Republican state senators and assemblymen to vote in favor of gay marriage; this was sufficient to put the bill over the top and establish the new law. These wealthy Republican donors had been brought into the discussion by liberal democratic governor Andrew Cuomo. Included among them, according to a *New York Times* report (June 26, 2011), were billionaire Republican donor Paul Singer, "whose son is gay, joined by the hedge fund managers Cliff Asnes and Dan Loeb."

They "had the influence and the money," said the *Times*, "to insulate nervous senators from conservative backlash if they supported the measure. And they were inclined to see the issue as one of personal freedom, consistent with their more libertarian view." According to the *Times* report, "Each of them [the Republican donors] cut six-figure checks to the lobbying campaign that eventually totaled more than $1 million . . . behind the scenes it was really about a Republican Party reckoning with a profoundly changing power dynamic, where Wall Street donors and gay-rights advocates demonstrated more might and muscle than a Roman Catholic hierarchy, and an ineffective opposition."

But what it was *really* all about was this: Whether it's protecting tax cuts for the rich, or it's super-wealthy people just looking for more wealth, or it's gay-rights advocates left and right, or, for that matter, if it's proposals for carbon trading, it's increasingly just a matter of money being generated for congressional campaigns and individual congress-people. Political control, from which myriad benefits emerge, is really not very expensive for the people now doing the buying. It's a buyers' market, and an affordable one at that. Our collected democratic leaders, and our democracy itself, are increasingly subordinated to the wishes and gifts of a small number of super-rich people who can make things happen. Or not.

Koch Brothers: Role Models for Neofeudal Expression

There is considerable variation of interests among the new class of super-rich. Many of them find far more imaginative ways to move their excess wealth around, beyond just buying yachts or more vacation houses or congressmen.

Let's take the case of the famous Koch brothers, #18 and #19 on the *Forbes* billionaire's list, with a combined worth of about $42 billion. They are known for the breadth of their giving, including many millions to museums. They surely deserve credit for that. It's traditional among feudal lords, actually, to support the arts, but not all do it.

David Koch donated $100,000,000 to Lincoln Center's New York State Theater, several million more to the American Ballet Theatre, and $20 million to the Museum of Natural History, "whose dinosaur wing is named after him," according to Jane Mayer writing in the *New Yorker* (August 30, 2010). He gave another $10 million to the Museum of Modern Art. He also, according to Mayer, "serves on the board of Memorial Sloan-Kettering Cancer Center. After he donated more than forty million dollars to the Center, an endowed chair and a research center were named for him."

On a more politically philosophical front, according to a report by the Center for American Progress Action Fund, David and his brother Charles Koch have demonstrated a great interest in promoting a philosophy: libertarianism. They have directed funds to a very long list of nonprofit groups "promoting an anti-tax, anti-regulatory ideology." Some of the groups they give to are also devoted to challenging "the science behind climate change," thus incidentally benefiting the Koch brothers' oil industry profits by delaying environmental regulations on oil production and on climate change.

The Koch brothers are among the leading funders for Tea Party groups, currently the dominant libertarian activists in the United States. Many observers give the brothers credit for effectively having created the Tea Party. They have funded Citizens for a Sound Economy (now called Freedomworks, headed by former conservative congressman Dick Armey) and the Americans for Prosperity Foundation, giving about $12.5 million and $5.6 million, respectively. Other libertarian and right-wing groups on the list of at least fifty organizations receiving Koch brothers largesse are the Heritage Foundation, the Federalist Society, the Competitive Enterprise Institute, the Bill of Rights Institute, the Tax Foundation, and, my personal favorite, the Ayn Rand Institute, among dozens more.

Meanwhile, on the liberal side, we see George Soros, Warren Buffett, and Bill Gates also giving away staggering amounts, but mostly on various anti-AIDS, antipoverty, and "pro-development" strategies for places like Africa. This is one reason why Glenn Beck characterized Soros as a communist, which may be the most ignorant charge in all of human history. It is also why the conservative donors are more influential politically than the liberals; they give to political action and think tanks that are plotting long-term economic strategy. Liberals give to people and humanitarian causes. Do-gooder stuff. Not nearly as effective in political terms.

But, the most exciting new thing this new class of super-rich likes to buy is direct political control. According to Jane Mayer, the Koch brothers have personally given "over $2 million in political contributions" to candidates over the last 12 years, while their political action committee, KochPAC, "has donated $8 million to political campaigns, 80% of it to Republicans." In 2010, "David Koch was the biggest individual contributor to the Republican Governors' Association, with a million dollar donation," toward the campaign that produced a large majority of Republican governors for the first time in decades.

The Koch brothers also financed most of the organizations leading the Tea Party revolt of 2010, and most of its right-wing, antigovernment, ferociously antideficit political candidates. Most of the Tea Party candidates backed by the Kochs ran on platforms specifically focused against the government deficit, or, more precisely, against the government itself. They had tremendous success in 2010 and immediately joined the forces advocating giving the top 2 percent of the wealthiest individuals a gigantic tax break, *increasing* the federal deficit. By late 2011, several potential 2012 presidential candidates had emerged from this pool, including Michele Bachmann, Rick Santorum, and Rick Perry, supporting nearly identical policies. The Koch brothers' support helped make such people "legitimate."

Meanwhile, according to Frank Rich of the *New York Times* (February 27,

2011), "since 1998, Koch Industries has spent more than fifty million dollars on lobbying," expressed through a combination of campaign donations and direct pressure on Congress.

Koch Industries and its employees form the largest bloc of oil- and gas-industry donors to members of the new House of Representatives' Energy and Commerce Committee, topping even ExxonMobil. And what do they get for that generosity? As a down payment, the House budget bill not only reduced financing for the Environmental Protection Agency (which had levied several fines against Koch Industries in the past for causing heavy pollution in its oil operations) but also prohibited the agency's regulation of greenhouse gases. And they lower taxes in various ways. Here again, the dollars that will be saved are minute in terms of the federal deficit, but the payoff to Koch interests from a weakened EPA is priceless.

According to the International Forum on Globalization, the Koch brothers' lobbying efforts are very broad-gauged, including pushing for continued ethanol subsidies—the Koch brothers have a huge financial stake in biofuels. They also seek limits on many regulations of toxic substances, including dioxin, asbestos, and formaldehyde, all of which have been linked to cancer, and all of which are by-products of the operations of Georgia-Pacific, a subsidiary of Koch Industries. That is surely another example where libertarian activists, who speak of governments staying out of business, are nonetheless lobbying hard for government to help *their* business.

Koch Industries also lobbied against carbon reduction proposals—on behalf of its subsidiaries INVISTA, Flint Hills Resources, Koch Carbon, Koch Nitrogen, and Georgia-Pacific—and lately in Canada, in support of oil sands production in Alberta. Koch Industries imports 25 percent of the Canadian tar sands oil that is brought into the United States, and is fighting hard for the new pipeline that would carry tar sands oil from Alberta to Texas. Koch lobbyists also actively supported the Bush tax cuts for the wealthy and are against any effort to regulate financial industry initiatives.

On another front, buying governors also seems to be remarkably inexpensive and cost-efficient. When the Koch brothers, through their political action committee, supported the election of Scott Walker as governor of Wisconsin, they granted him only $43,000, but he won with ease. Frank Rich called this "merely a petty cash item on the Koch ledger."

Just after being elected, Gov. Walker immediately turned to busting the public service unions of the state, particularly their collective bargaining rights, a very important issue for the Koch business enterprises, and for the libertarian values the Koch brothers stand for. Other states quickly got the idea and followed suit. What a good buy. One small donation, and the whole country was turned around.

The billionaire brothers also chipped in $320,000 for advertising to support

Walker's anti-union legislation. The whole effort was very brilliantly conceived, and so cheap. Highly efficient. These people should go into business.

We could offer dozens of other examples from the Koch brothers, and from other oligarchs in the United States and around the world. But here's the main point: For the emerging class of super-rich oligarchs, buying politicians is cheap and easy. All of the Koch brothers' political efforts together probably cost less than a couple more yachts, or a few months in a fancy hotel in the Seychelles, or a new Picasso, or another jet airplane. Politicians and governments are this decade's bargain-basement opportunities.

Democracy?

Ultimately, the question comes down to whether or not we accept that wealth should be allowed to be the determining factor as to who gets to direct "democratic" processes and who does not. Up till now, most Americans have been limited to expressing their democratic choices by voting for a governor, congressman, senator, or president over two or four years. Then we sit back and watch while the representative or president whom we voted for is far more responsive to those who paid for his advertising campaign than he is to the people who put him in office.

Ideally, in democracies, all adult citizens should have an approximately equal say on issues and outcomes that affect their lives. Means tests should not apply. And some people and/or institutions should not be able to dominate the public commons as they do now. I like to think of the ideal democracy as no larger than what will allow any individual to personally interact with every other individual, where every citizen is within easy distance of every other. In that ideal world, we would all have the opportunity for more or less equitable impact as to the way things are done, and who benefits from them. But obviously this would only be possible on the smallest scale.

Short of that, in large societies, a system must offer all adult individuals, if not an equal say, at least a *meaningful* say in the most important decisions by any government that affects them. But what, exactly, is a "meaningful say"? Right now in the United States and most Western democracies, our voices are reduced to those periodic votes on candidates and issues—every two years, or four. And these votes are so highly influenced by oligarchy-backed campaign spending that we really don't know what or who we are voting for. In large societies, where you are unlikely to know a candidate personally, there is little opportunity to have any personal impact—save through expressing oneself in media, if that is available to you, or through lobbying activity, or in public protest demonstrations of some kind. This is what we have called "representative democracy": a highly reduced, compromised version of democratic process.

The problem is obviously not only domestic, but global. The schism between the rich and poor is both *within* countries and *among* countries, as our statistics make clear. And it is getting steadily worse.

It is important to be aware that if these global equity issues are not resolved and the world continues to be driven as it is now, with most wealth (and with most remaining resources) moving upward toward a small number of people, while huge numbers of people are deprived of a fair share of resources, no ultimate sustainable solution will be possible. Without a solution, the world will sink into irretrievable conflict, chaos, and war.

If applicable solutions do ultimately emerge, they will surely involve agreements on how wealthy countries and individuals can dramatically diminish their over-accumulation and over-consumption, while poor countries and individuals are aided to increase their circumstances at least to a bare level of economic "sufficiency." As the climate negotiations have made clear, this will certainly require direct transfers of wealth, as partial payment of our climate debt and resource-depletion debt, as well as of know-how and technology (which poor countries have been seeking).

Will capitalism allow such changes? Will political leaders dare to propose such action, defying the needs of their own industrial base and their benefactors? Within the prevailing system that celebrates self-interest over all else, it is difficult to imagine that they would. But if not, what comes next?

There is some good news. Circumstances *are* definitely beginning to change. With the democracy revolts across the world over the last two years, and since November 2011 and the sudden impact of the Occupy movement in the United States, questions of extreme inequity have moved onto the front pages of newspapers for the first time in decades. And the movement has succeeded in articulating a "headline" that everyone understands: the 99% vs. the 1%. New possibilities have become visible. We begin to imagine changes of structure and power. And the world is bursting with new energy, ideas, and programs for democratic change. We will review and discuss some of these in chapter XII—Which Way Out?

X.

Privatization of Consciousness

Is advertising legal? Most people agree that it is an uninvited intrusion into our lives and our minds, an invasion of privacy. But the fact that we can be aware of this without being furious, and that we do little to change the situation, is a good measure of our level of submission. There is a power relationship in advertising that is rarely, if ever, looked at, and yet it is a profoundly corrupt one. Some speak; others listen.

A. J. Liebling famously said, "Freedom of the press is guaranteed, but only if you own one." Freedom of *speech* is also guaranteed. But only if you have a few million dollars for an effective media strategy. Soapbox oratory doesn't sway the public anymore. But the powers of advertising go well beyond the amount of money spent. The true power is in the nature of moving-image media, projected for hours every day into human brains. It's a form of intrusion we have never before in history had to face. Even now in the Internet age, the powers of television and advertising are undiminished and insufficiently examined or discussed.

Very early in my advertising career, it became clear to me that I was being paid to stop you from doing or thinking whatever else you might want to do or think, and instead get you to focus on the piece of information that was of interest to my client. All advertising is an attempt by one party to dominate the other. More than $150 billion is now spent annually in advertising in this country—$450 billion in the world. Every dollar of that has the same purpose: to get people to do what the advertiser wants. Very few people have a similar opportunity to *speak back* through media, to make demands on the advertisers. Or to suggest some other way to find happiness besides buying things. This makes it a very one-sided deal. Advertisers say that you have the choice of *not* buying their products, as though that's satisfactory. You get to say yes or no, like voting a one-party ballot. And you get to say it thousands of times per day.

Advertising is now literally everywhere, interrupting our lives at every turn, requiring that we deal with it. We walk through life as a kind of moving target; hawked at by media, hawked at by signs on the street—blinking, flowing, five stories high. Even clothes have ads on them, and we wear them proudly. Corporations have become like "community" for us. Steve Jobs was our guru. We mourn him as we once mourned Martin Luther King. What a transition.

The situation has advanced to a capitalist utopia: a giant, nonstop global marketplace that carries itself into all our experiences. Life has become a process of constantly avoiding things that people are trying to sell us. Yet most people don't complain.

Why do we tolerate this? What right do advertisers have to treat us this way? When did we sell the rights to run pictures in our brains? If the airwaves are *public*, then why are they filled with people selling things all day without our permission? In fact, the "public airwaves" are supposed to be a "public commons." We own them. In the early radio days, you and a few friends could throw up an antenna behind the house and *speak* to the world. It was like the early Internet days—YouTube, radio-style.

That stopped when the broadcast frequencies got crowded and capitalists realized what a crucial instrument this could become. The FCC fell quickly in line with the corporations during the 1920s and started selling off our public rights to the airwaves, granting licenses to commercial interests who could pay. Over the years it made little rules about "fairness and balance" and "equal time," but those rules and rights were soon overpowered and, under Ronald Reagan and then Bill Clinton (who helped launch the infamous Telecommunications Act of 1996), effectively eliminated. The "public airwaves" are now nearly totally privatized. Even the remnants of public airwaves, like PBS and NPR, now have commercials. When the *PBS NewsHour* reports some horror story about Chevron's behavior in the Amazon, it feels obliged to say, "Chevron, a 'sponsor' of the *NewsHour*, was today accused of . . . " I turn off the program the minute I hear that.

The fact that advertising can be occasionally entertaining does not mitigate matters. You could also enjoy a visit from Jehovah's Witnesses, or from an entertaining vacuum cleaner salesman who came ringing the doorbell five times daily. But you would do that only if you had nothing else to do. Your public airwave commons have been invaded, as has your mental space. If that is not a constitutional invasion of privacy, than what is?

In 1975, I convened a small meeting in my living room in San Francisco, which included some of the leading public interest attorneys in the Bay Area, to ask them if they thought advertising was legal. The way I read the First Amendment, I said, was that its intention was clearly to promote democracy by assuring that all people have equal rights to free speech—at least a fair amount of equality in opportunities for expression—and a similar ability to access all other points of view. As I mentioned briefly in chapter IV, when the Bill of Rights was written, in the late 1700s, there were no national broadcast networks that could project one political point of view to millions of people. There was no advertising, either, except for the occasional handbill, to project a particular vision to those same millions of people.

If the goal of the First Amendment was to sustain a democratic flow of information, those days are long gone. The commercial broadcast media speaks to everyone all day and night, and we don't get to speak back. And those media outlets are owned by a tiny group of megacorporations.

As for advertising, that's a medium that, by definition, is confined *only* to the people who can afford to pay for it. The First Amendment wasn't conceived to give powerful advertising conglomerates power over the people. The advertisers speak their imagery, and we absorb it. Shouldn't that qualify as a violation of the Constitution? Isn't that illegal? The group in my living room thought maybe it was, or ought to be, but, given the way the Supreme Court was ruling in those days, they decided there was not yet much opportunity there. Since then, things have only gotten much worse, especially since the Supreme Court's passage of Citizens United.

Who Needs Advertising?

Capitalism can exist without advertising, of course, and did so for its early years. The spice traders of East India and the railroads laid across the American continent during the 1800s did not need much in the way of advertising to promote their offerings. The benefits were obvious and clearly understood—and word got around. The offerings themselves were relatively scarce at the time, so their availability was itself news.

When capitalist enterprises provide products and services that everyone needs and wants, advertising is not necessary. You don't need to advertise food: basic grains, vegetables, fruits, meats. Everyone wants and needs a certain supply of those and will search them out and buy them wherever they might be available.

However, no one has an intrinsic need for packaged frozen lasagna, Coca-Cola, Cheetos, or Burger King. Those have to be advertised, promoted, and packaged in appealing ways. No one needs to advertise fresh water, but you do need to advertise Perrier. You don't need to advertise clothing—people know they need clothing—but Macy's needs to advertise; so do the Gap, Walmart, and Christian Dior. Nor is there any need to advertise transport services; anyone needing to get from here to there will make the effort to find out how. But you certainly do need to advertise a new Ford Fiesta in some artful way, or a Cadillac, to justify the expenditure. And once you have successfully sold that one, you may need to persuade a buyer to upgrade to the latest model. Meanwhile, the wider system needs to persuade the broad public that it is selling a way of life that equates with happiness and fulfillment.

The dominant delivery system for mass advertising in our society even in the age of the Internet, is television. As with all other commercial media in capitalist societies, the specific assignment of television is to attract as large an audience as possible and to fixate that audience for as long as possible every day. Television has exceeded all expectations on that score. The average American watches more than four and a half hours per day, all year, every year. Most important for the corporate world is that television and its programming have proven to be the best possible packaging for their *real* product: the advertising. If certain programs do not attract advertisers, they will soon be off the air.

Television commercials have characteristics that are especially useful for instilling desire and commitment in a mass population to buy things that it could mostly get along without. American culture and the entire global economy have been built around these unnecessary exchanges. More important, it is built around the constant *expansion* of these exchanges for as long as possible, or at least until they combine to reach a level of near saturation—a global *bubble* of commodity production and consumption that, if it falls off by a percentage point or two, which it recently did, is catastrophic.

Advertising first asserted its prominence in the early twentieth century through radio, then exploded into its heyday in the 1950s and '60s, when television took hold. It was in that post–World War II period when America and the world were desperate for some means to avoid crashing back into the Depression. It was a matter of economic survival that our economy should expand at a rate sufficient to make use of its surplus industrial capacity, as well as a huge labor surplus that existed after the war.

Factories that had formerly made armaments were now empty. They needed to be converted to producing consumer goods, to be hyped and sold. Speaking in the language of moving images, television offered capitalism its greatest opportunity ever to accelerate consumer consciousness.

Over the last half century, the combination of television and astronomical advertising spending has effectively reshaped the consciousness of the United States and the entire planet: our self-image, the way we aspire to live, our habits, our thoughts, our references, desires, memories. Total U.S. advertising spending, which was only $2 billion in 1940, grew to $12 billion by 1960, then $54 billion in 1980. By 2010, even while recovering from the recession, the U.S. advertising industry was still spending well above $150 billion, with by far the largest percentage of that going to television, says *Adweek*. This represented more than one-third of total global advertising spending, which by 2010 reached $450 billion. Despite competition from the Internet, as well as from magazines, radio, and newspapers, television today remains by far the largest and fastest-growing ad medium in the world, increasing by more than 9 percent in 2010, says eMarketer (March 29, 2011), more than double the total of online advertising.

Meanwhile, the U.S. Bureau of Economic Analysis indicates that the U.S. (GDP) showed corresponding growth, from $100 billion in 1940 to $525 billion in 1960, to nearly $3 trillion in 1980, to $14 trillion in 2007.

Living Inside Media

According to the Nielsen Company, the primary assessor of most of these matters, 99 percent of American homes have television sets and 95 percent of the population watches at least some television every day. Two-thirds of U.S. homes have three or more sets, arranged for separate, private viewing. The average home has a TV playing for about seven hours per day, even when no one is watching. While the average adult watches about five hours per day, the average child aged two to eleven watches nearly four hours per day. The average adult over age sixty-five watches about seven hours per day.

Sixty-six percent of Americans typically watch television while eating dinner. Thirty-five percent of local TV news broadcast time is devoted to advertising. (The percentage devoted to crime and disaster is 53.8.) These figures have varied over the last couple of decades, but not by much. The average television viewer watching television for four-plus hours per day is hit with about twenty-five thousand commercials per year, and by age sixty-five, that number exceeds two million. That would be twenty-five thousand annual repetitions of basically the same message: *You will be happier if you buy something.*

If the average adult is watching nearly five hours per day, this means that roughly half the U.S. population is watching *more* than five hours, day after day, for years. How is that even possible? (By heavy viewing every night, and then all weekend.)

Ours is the first generation in history to have essentially moved its consciousness *inside* media, to have increasingly replaced direct contact with other people, other communities, other sources of knowledge, and the natural world—which is anyway getting harder and harder to find—with simulated, re-created, or edited versions of events and experiences.

Some people argue that the situation has improved now that we have cell phones, computers, iPads, Twitter, and other social media. A Pew Research Center study found that most American teenagers send fifty or more text messages per day, and one-third send more than one hundred per day. All of this *non-*TV technology is good, they say, because information gathering and exchange have become far less passive than TV, and more intellectually engaging. Our minds are more "alive." But the advent of computers and the Internet, for all their interactive features, has not diminished the total amount of time that people watch television. What the Internet has achieved is only to *add* to the time that people with access to computers spend physically and mentally attached to information machines as their sources of imagery and ideas. The science fiction image of the disembodied brain seems ever more appropriate.

In the United States, aside from time spent sleeping and working, television viewing is still the main thing people do with their days. It's replaced community life, family life, culture. In many ways, television has *become* the culture, and by this, I do not mean so-called "popular culture," which sounds somehow democratic. Television is *not* democratic. Viewers at home do not make television; they *receive* it. Television does not express culture; it expresses *corporate* culture.

Advertising to Children

A lot of advertising is aimed at children aged eight to thirteen. One relatively new category of ad expenditures is directed toward children younger than eight years old.

Psychologists Tim Kasser and Allen Kanner, co-authors of *Psychology and Consumer Culture*, have reported that advertising targeted at small children now represents $12 billion–plus per year in the United States, with $95 million of that coming from just Burger King and Quaker Oats' Cap'n Crunch cereal. Tens of millions more dollars go into psychological research on what gets kids to push their parents into certain buying decisions.

Even from ages two to four, children watch television for about three hours daily, not counting the television they see in preschool. Meanwhile, the "number of minutes per week that parents spend in meaningful conversation with their children is about 3.5."

A report by Paul Nyhan in the *Seattle Post-Intelligencer* (May 7, 2007) described a University of Washington study called "Babies and TV," finding that even "babies are glued to television sets these days, with 40% of 3 month olds and 90% of 2 year olds regularly watching TV." The Kaiser Family Foundation in 2003 reported that 65 perent of children over eight years old have a TV in their bedroom, and confirmed that not even infants are free of television. About 20 percent of U.S. parents leave a TV on next to their baby's crib all night. It certainly has some kind of hypnotic effect, keeping the infants quieter.

Of course, many researchers have established this hypnotic effect as functioning to some degree in all age groups among heavy viewers. Studies also show that small children, far from being quieted by TV, seem quieter only when watching; turn off the TV, and they revert to hyperactive behavior caused by the heavy viewing. According to a famous study from the 1960s by the Australian National University, it works like this: Kids watch the screen and see some lively or dangerous activities; they have the instinct to respond, but it's television, so they repress the response. After a while there is a build-up of go-no-go energy, then the set goes off, and *splat*—they're all over the place (and we have a problem).

According to Nielsen, "by the time an average child finishes elementary school, they see 8,000 murders on TV. The number of violent acts seen on TV by age 18 is 200,000." A 2010 study by the American Academy of Pediatrics discovered that "children's shows had the most violence of all television programming . . . twenty acts of violence in one hour, and that by the age of eighteen, children will have seen 16,000 simulated murders." The Kaiser Foundation confirmed that "violence was more prevalent in children's programming (69%) than other programming (57%)."

In the late 1970s, during the presidency of Jimmy Carter, the Federal Trade Commission, under Michael Pertschuk, was so shocked at the mounting revelations about industry practices in relation to small children, it decided to hold public hearings to establish any negative effects of ads directed at kids under six years old. There was particular alarm about techniques that urged children to bug their parents to buy them unhealthy sugary cereals, for example.

But before the first FTC hearing could even take place, a unified uproar arose in the media—from the Right *and* the Left, even including the *New York Times*, to its shame and disgrace—denouncing and editorializing against the whole effort. The *Times* said it would inhibit the free-speech rights of advertisers. President Jimmy Carter, a liberal, gave in to the concentrated media pressure, canceled the FTC hearings, and fired Mike Pertschuk and his assistant, Tracy Westen, who was the man in charge of the children's advertising project for the FTC. Westen went on to a distinguished teaching career at UCLA. No one has since attempted to revive such hearings aimed at protecting children.

Global Reach

As we suggested earlier, it's a primary drive of corporate globalization that every place on Earth should become like every other place on Earth. This creates new investment opportunity for global capital and promotes efficiency in resource management, production planning, marketing, and distribution for millions of commodities and their producers. But the *external* homogenization process also requires an internal homogenization process—a remake of human beings themselves—our minds, our ideas, our values. The ultimate goal is a global monoculture of human beings that fits nicely with the redesigned external landscape, like so many compatible computers. In the end, corporations seek a mental landscape that nicely matches the physical landscape of freeways, suburbs, franchises, high-rises, clear-cuts, and the sped-up physical life of the commodified world.

Internationally, the situation is little different from the United States. About 80 percent of the global population has access to television, with most industrialized countries reporting viewing habits very similar to those in the United States. In Canada, England, France, Germany, Italy, Russia, Greece, Poland, and many other countries in Europe and South America, the average household watches 3 to 4.5 hours per day. According to the OECD Communications Outlook (2011), the comparable "household TV viewing time" in the United States is 8.35 hours, more than double that of most OECD countries.

In any case, in many parts of the world, the TV that people watch often comes from the United States and from other countries in the West; local programs are few. Even in places on Earth where there are no roads—tiny tropical islands, icy tundras of the North, log cabins—millions of people are sitting night after night, watching urbanites in Los Angeles or Miami or New York driving sleek cars, standing around swimming pools, or drinking martinis while plotting ways to do each other in. Life in the States is made to seem the ultimate achievement, while local culture in other places, no matter how vibrant and alive, is made to seem somehow backward, less fun, not good.

Merging with TV values is quickly replacing other ways of life. People everywhere carry identical images and crave the same commodities, from cars to hairsprays to Barbie dolls to iPhones. TV is turning everyone into everyone else. It is effectively cloning cultures to be alike. In *Brave New World*, Aldous Huxley envisioned a global cloning process taking place via drugs and genetic engineering. We have those too, but TV does just as well, because of the medium's reach and power, and because of the intentions of its owners.

The Powers of Received Images

It's not only the volume of television viewing that matters, but also the nature of the experience and the powers of the imagery that we ingest daily.

It was a half century ago, in 1963, that I first entered the world of commercial advertising. Only then did I personally grasp the nature and power of moving-image media. I realized it's possible to create and project purposeful images into millions of brains at the same time, and to get people to view and believe things in the way you wanted them to. I *loved* that—at least, at first. It was lively and fun and brought a sense of omnipotence.

Advertising people don't talk about it much, but as a group they generally accept that if they had sufficient funds, they would have the ability to enter and redesign human consciousness according to commercial intention, and that the whole process of injecting imagery has transformative capabilities. And since it can also change worldviews, the process should ultimately be understood as potentially deeply political, with great powers of persuasion and influence, concerning not only products but also political philosophies and choices. Neil Postman was right in *Amusing Ourselves to Death*: "Advertising is the most important subject we don't discuss and that we do nothing about." This is especially so now that advertising has taken on such a huge role in political campaigning and the information movement.

Are You Immune?

Most people, especially if they are well educated, still believe that advertising (or television, for that matter) has no effect on them or on their beliefs. Their intelligence protects them against invasive imposed imagery, even when an image is repeated a hundred times in their heads. People believe in their immunity even though the imagery does not actually communicate through the language of logic or contemplation. Images ride a freeway into your brain and remain there permanently. No thought is involved. Every advertiser knows this. As a viewer, you may sometimes say, "I don't believe this," but the image remains anyway.

My late partner in the advertising business, Howard Gossage, spoke frequently to audiences about "the dirty little secret" among advertisers: that their silly superficial meaningless trivial imagery nonetheless goes into your brain and doesn't come back out. "It doesn't matter how observant or intelligent you are," he said. If you are watching television, you will absorb the images. Once the image is embedded, it is permanently embedded. You cannot get rid of it.

"If you don't think so," said Gossage, "how come if I say 'Jolly Green Giant' most people will instantly get a picture in their heads of this huge green character wearing green leotards, selling peas?" Of course you do. Well, actually, maybe *you* don't. Gossage was speaking in the 1960s.

But contemporary examples abound: How about images of a giant gecko? Did you think of Geico insurance? How about the Taco Bell chihuahua? Or Ronald McDonald? Or the Energizer Bunny? Or that M&M candy that doesn't want to be wrapped around a pretzel? Did you know you were carrying all these images around in your head?

The effects of this stream of invading images apply as much to noncommercial images as they do to commercial—Donald Trump? Glenn Beck? Dominique Strauss-Kahn? Sarah Palin? *Oh God, get those people out of my head.*

Is Television Real?

Television imagery rides into your brain as a vast potpourri of mixed image forms that is otherwise not experienced anywhere in life. Dozens of categories of information are strung together as though they were all in the same domain of reality. Because of that, the viewer is disadvantaged, trying to sort out or discern what is "real" and what is not. It's one reason why the instrument produces such a high degree of passivity among viewers. After a while, the best choice is to give up, sit back, and just let it come.

In a normal couple of hours of television viewing, you are likely to see a combination of fictional images from drama or comedy shows, as well as scripted reenactments of historical events; reality shows that show real people doing things they would be unlikely to do without cameras pointed at them; news programs, which are supposed to be real but cover events that happened an hour or days or weeks ago, and that are edited and cut down from many hours to fifteen to twenty seconds, with a *commentary* to tell you how to understand them.

This river of mixed-up imagery is further interrupted every few minutes by advertisements that sometimes have well-known real people in them—actors or celebrities—who are paid to tell you things they otherwise would not and probably don't believe. Or else it's cartoons, or dancing words, and loud music flashing in and out, and fast cuts to mountains or beaches or deserts, then nightclubs, then battlefields. And then it's all suddenly interrupted by the next commercial and the next; then back to the "real" news or reality show or fictional police show. Next, you might see an image of a couple walking on a hillside, a quarter of a mile away, though you can hear their words as if they were next to you—and then, the music rises.

All of this variety of imagery and sound comes through the same image stream, largely undistinguished, and becomes the weird DNA of moving-image media. How are you supposed to keep up with all that, making distinctions on each point, thinking it over? You cannot keep asking yourself, "Is this real?" "Do I believe this?" Anyway, the images *are* real, at least in the sense that they are physically composed of the pixels on the TV screens, but the content of the images breaks down into dozens of categories. If you did ask yourself questions intended to sort things out, you couldn't keep up with what's happening on the screen. You wouldn't keep watching at all. So instead, most of it enters as one flowing ephemeral stream of "reality." It's captivating. Literally. Once you see it, you can't un-see it. The only way to avoid it is to stop watching.

Of course, repetition also has an important role. Each time you see a replay of a commercial—that you may wind up seeing hundreds of times—it has the cumulative effect of adding vitality to the stored image, especially if it's well executed. While that may not make you go out and buy the product or vote for the candidate, advertisers are just playing a numbers game across a wide audience. The more people who see it, and the more times they see it, the more likely they are to react. Repetition adds "heat" to the image. The viewer becomes more familiar with it. It gradually becomes part of him or her. In the long run, across a wide public, it makes the advertiser's desired outcome more likely. If this weren't true, why would they continue spending hundreds of millions of dollars doing it?

Here's the point: Your intellect cannot save you. You don't really want that imagery, but you've got it anyway. The imagery enters your brain, whether it's advertising imagery or general programming. Once in, it's impossible to erase. It becomes a kind of internal billboard, ready to flash at appropriate moments. You may not believe everything Glenn Beck had to say, but he continues to say it inside your head. You are not in control.

There's a second point: Information transmitted in this way, in the absence of counterpoint imagery and argument, especially when repeated over and over, takes on an undeserved element of authority—"seeing is believing." And whoever controls that technology has powers that no one before ever did. Hitler controlled a nation largely through the power of his amplified voice broadcast on the radio night after night. It would have been even easier with television.

"Truth" in Advertising

Most commercial advertisements are pure imagery. That is, they don't try to make factual arguments. This is especially true during the most expensive prime-time hours, which the biggest national advertisers use. Soft-drink ads tend to display a lot of very attractive people laughing and smiling or playing volleyball while drinking Coke. Insurance commercials may show darling children or families that need protection. Even auto ads, which we would expect to have something concrete to say, are far more focused on glamorous curves, or speed, or good-looking people. Very little is said about anything you might consciously agree with or disagree with, using a logical perspective. It is pure form, image, and mood. This is an important point.

In the 1960s, there was a burgeoning "reform" movement focused on advertising that demanded *counter-advertising* when commercial messages were false. The problem with that effort, however, was that most advertising does not dwell in the realm of truth or fiction; most ads don't say anything that you can agree or disagree with. Not even ads for hard technological products—cars, washing machines, computers—promote their wares on the basis of their superior technology, life span, or reliability. Mostly it is for their timeliness or style. The exception to the rule is usually found only on late-night low-budget television where, say, a car dealer will announce the unbelievably low price of a new car, which by noon the next day turns out not to be anywhere on the lot. *That*, you could identify as false advertising and attempt to legislate. But it's a very minor part of the advertising industry.

Most advertising, especially in expensive prime time, doesn't make claims about product performance. It's all innuendos, associations, and images. The cute couple is happily drinking Pepsi on their first date. The pug dog is breaking down the door to get his Doritos.

The problem with *commercial advertising* is not whether the ads are truthful or not; the problem is the image itself. Once it is ingested, it becomes our frame of reference. Over time, we begin to imitate the image. We see the mannerisms from the TV show *Friends* turning up among our own friends. We slowly begin to merge with the imagery. Like the Novice who contemplates the Buddha for decades, hoping to absorb his nature, we absorb the advertising. We become what we see. And we share its values.

On the other hand, the problem with *political ads*, especially campaign ads, whether Republican or Democrat, is that they are almost always lies. We are left to base our votes on false information. If there is any domain of public speech that ought to demand laws requiring absolute truth, it is political expression. But the opposite seems to be the case.

Some people predict that the 2012 presidential campaign will see over $1 billion being spent on advertising, by *each* side. Political ads are typically wildly overstated and frequently make things up. At the very least, all points are magnified or distorted. Always, they leave out relevant facts that might weaken their arguments. The total imagery we receive from those distorted ad expenditures totally overpowers most impressions we get from "live" debates, for example, or press conferences, where we see the candidate through less of a filter.

You may remember the patently false "swift boat" TV spots against Senator John Kerry when he ran for president against George W. Bush in 2004. The ads sought to destroy Kerry's record of military valor, claiming that he never deserved the major medals for combat bravery that he won in Vietnam, and that he was soft on defense. In one powerful ad, the images showed military equipment suddenly vanishing from a battle landscape, leaving our soldiers undefended. This was to show what would happen to our unprotected troops under a Kerry presidency. Meanwhile, other ads showed George Bush as a tough, clear-minded, military leader.

The swift-boat ads seemed so silly that the Kerry camp did not at first respond. By the time Kerry did respond—weeks later—it was too late. His public ratings had collapsed. Kerry had forgotten the cardinal rule of political advertising: In the absence of a counter-ad, people will always believe whatever images they see. How could it be otherwise? In the absence of an alternative set of images, the public will *always* accept the apparent "evidence" of imagery.

All advertisers know this. They know that even the dumbest products and ideas can gain acceptance because advertising imagery does not appeal to intellect but exploits a human, genetic, sensory predisposition to believe what we see. That's the way premodern humans protected themselves. In that sense, we are all still premodern.

A follow-up story in *USA Today* interviewed voters in seventeen swing states who had seen the false ads. The story revealed that the public accepted the patently false ads as true. Interviewees mimicked exactly the language from the advertising. Here's another advertising homily that Kerry didn't know: *Logic will never overcome imagery*. Press conferences were useless. The images were in, and they had not been answered soon enough.

In a *New Yorker* article, "State for Sale," (October 10, 2011) Jane Mayer described the way ultra-wealthy North Carolina oligarch Art Pope used his enormous wealth to finance advertising campaigns against democratic candidates for North Carolina state office. It is a model for ultra-conservatives in many states, who have begun to use a particular kind of advertising to throw out democratic candidates.

In many cases, Pope's funding for North Carolina Republican candidates totally overwhelmed opposition candidates, who had never faced that kind of financial infusion. But it was not only the amounts of the financing, but also the messages, that were so unique. They were very often based on totally misleading innuendos that were hard to counter.

Mayer gives the example of Margaret Dickson, "a sixty-one-year-old retired radio broadcaster and executive who'd been married for thirty-one years and had three grown children, and was seeking election to the state senate." She had served in the state general assembly, had the backing of the state business community, and was politically centrist. "Then came what she calls 'The Hooker Ad.' Her Republican opponent released an ad suggesting that Dickson was using her seat to promote personal investments. As Dickson describes it, 'They used an actress with dark hair who was fair, like me. She was putting on mascara and red lipstick. She had on a big ring and a bracelet.' A narrator intoned 'Busted!' and the actress's hand grabbed what appeared to be a wad of hundred-dollar bills. 'The thrust of it was that I am somehow prostituting myself.'"

More ads of a similar kind followed. By the time Dickson fought back, it was useless. She had been dramatically outspent and victimized by negative imagery. She lost the election, as did other democratic candidates who were similarly attacked. There are no laws about misleading innuendos or false statements in political campaigns, and no legal avenues available to respond.

Is this a good way for democracy to run its electoral processes? Some countries—most of Scandinavia, for example—ban all paid advertising in election campaigns and provide candidates an equal amount of free television exposure. It would be nearly impossible to implement such a system in the United States, where the television industry depends on the income and has the lobbying power to demand it.

Virtual Reality

Most of our lives are contained within physically reconstructed, human-created environments—cities, buildings, streets—where nature is no longer visible. It's as if we have moved inside the minds of the people who imagined these constructs and realities. In this way, generation to generation, we go more deeply into human thought and creation: *mediated reality*.

Now that our direct contact with the sources of reality are highly diminished, our sources of usable information are parents, friends, schools, offices, and media—print, electronic, radio, television, and the Internet. The final result is that we cannot any longer have personal certainty that the information we get is entirely reliable. All mediated information is processed, edited, and altered in various ways as described above. TV commentators tell us what to make of it all. We make guesses about who is best to believe. Rachel Maddow? Sean Hannity? Limbaugh? Colbert? There is also "science," of course, which makes wider observations about natural forms and interactions and tells us what to think of it all. But we can't know the reliability of that, either, since scientific certainty varies from year to year. It tends to be wrong at least as much as it's right. Mammograms are necessary every year to stop cancer. Annual mammograms cause cancer. Prostate screening stops cancer. Prostrate screening is unnecessary and causes other awful conditions. Coffee is bad for you; coffee is good for you. Now we find that a lot of Einstein's theories about the universe are wrong. If Einstein is wrong, who isn't?

Finally, we make our own judgments. We guess. It sounds either right or wrong. We believe one side of the science debate or the other.

With most of our information mediated—that is, processed and edited and changed by human beings who have specific purposes for the image—and without any direct contact with the true circumstances of an issue, how can anyone possibly know what is right and what is wrong? And yet we are asked to make our country's major decisions based on the knowledge we receive from the machine. So, it's Murdoch or Eisner, or Shell Oil and GM, or democratic media consultants, or Republican media consultants, who enter our brains, leave their viewpoints, and firmly implant their images. Then they each spend millions of dollars' worth of political ads, most of which are wildly distorted. We can only guess what to finally believe.

I once tried to prove the point that we cannot separate truth from fiction when the information is brought to us solely through media. In my book *In the Absence of the Sacred*, I tried a little experiment on the reader. Early in the book, I described an event of some significance, which was designed to help make my case in a certain discussion. But then later in the book, I reported to the reader that what I had indicated earlier was made up. I was simply demonstrating that readers have no way of knowing whether information in media, even books, is true or false. They pretty much take it all on faith. This came as a real shock to some readers, who hadn't thought about this possibility before. In fact, right now, I might be lying to you again. I just told you I did an experiment in a book of mine, but maybe I didn't do that. How could you possibly know if it happened or didn't, without direct knowledge? Certainly, you could read that book and find out the truth, but in most media you cannot double-check.

All mediated information is wrapped in doubt, especially moving-image media. We tend to always believe the image, because images seem real. But they're not. The images we see in moving-image media are redesigned, rearranged, edited, sped up, slowed down, reorganized, sometimes reenacted; dialogues are changed, music applied.

If we base our democracy on such processes that are intrinsically unreliable and infinitely alterable, always approximations, can we expect effective public participation and engagement? Making matters worse, these processes are controlled by a very small number of people, whose total intention is to get us to behave and think in ways that will expand their wealth. These people are capitalists.

Global Control

The single-most-alarming fact about global communications today—given the immensity of its reach, power, and effect—is how few global corporations control it. The concentration of global media ownership rivals that of the global oil industry. But the difference between oil and media is that the former deals with tangible things, while the latter deals with consciousness. As such, it may be even a more central factor shaping how societies evolve and whether democracy functions right now.

One amazing expression of this power and control, though little noticed at the time, was the way the telecommunications industry gathered its forces in the 1990s and forced the eventual passage by Congress of the landmark Telecommunications Act of 1996. It was a tour de force that merged three dominant trends of our society: the grand promise of great new technology, the powerful capitalist drive for nonstop profit, and the already-advancing capitalist takeover of government and media.

The law was passed after tens of millions of dollars were paid by industry lobbyists to compliant congressmen, and with practically no public debate. It mandated that by the end of 2006 (later stalled to 2009), the entire country would junk our "ancient" analog TV sets. Less than a decade later, we would all be required to buy new, digital TV sets or substitute auxiliary equipment, enabling the complete instant national conversion to a new technology that, really, nobody needed. The financial benefits to the corporate-tech community were stratospheric: instant obsolescence for a technology in every American home; new (forced) equipment purchases by an entire population; a tremendous economic stimulus for the economy (particularly technology companies); an instant congressional payback to campaign donors; and an effective subsidy to corporate executives and stockholders. (It also greatly benefited the shipping industry, which got to collect and lug those obsolete analog TV sets to ever-more-expansive waste-disposal fields in Africa and India.) What a vast, thoughtful undertaking, involving direct costs to every household in the country, with no public debate (or lawsuits) about the government mandate to buy, and doubtful benefit to consumers!

But the Telecommunications Act was not even primarily about selling more hardware. President Bill Clinton had promised that the act would also advance the democratizing of media ownership. But, after staggering levels of industry lobbying, it proved to have exactly the opposite effect. In radio, for example, it *lifted* ownership limits beyond the previous standard and made possible a new level of concentration. One company, Clear Channel, now owns more than forty radio stations, notes Common Cause's "Facts on Media in America."

In cable TV, five companies—News Corporation, General Electric, Disney, CBS/Viacom, and AOL Time Warner—would soon own twenty-four of the top twenty-five cable channels in the United States. Together, they account for 85 percent of prime-time viewing, and 74 percent of programming expenditures, according to "Against Media Consolidation: Evidence on Concentration, Localism and Diversity," edited by Mark N. Cooper, of the Donald McGannon Communication Research Center at Fordham University, 2007.

Meanwhile, only twelve companies gained control of 61 percent of U.S. movie theaters, according to the National Association of Theatre Owners (2009).

University of Illinois professor Robert McChesney points out that every medium is now dominated by a very small number of corporations and people. Often, the names are the same in several media. "But concentrating upon specific media sectors fails to convey the extent of concentrated corporate control," says McChesney. "The dominant trend since the 1970s or 1980s, which accelerated in the 1990s, is the conglomeration of media ownership."

Giant media companies began to own two or more distinct sectors, such as film production, recorded music, radio, newspapers, book publishing, cable TV, and broadcasting, globally. According to Ben Bagdikian in *Media Monopoly*, by the end of the twentieth century, ownership within the whole media sphere was heavily dominated by eight companies: Time Warner, Disney, Viacom, Seagram, News Corporation, Sony, Bertelsmann, General Electric (which owns NBC, AT&T, and TCI, among dozens of others). Also rising very quickly is Vivendi Universal.

In his book *Rich Media, Poor Democracy*, McChesney names the biggest three of those media giants as AOL–Time Warner, the News Corporation, and Disney, with Seagram's very close. To give you an idea of the extent and breadth of their domination, here is a small part of McChesney's already abbreviated list of these companies' major holdings:

AOL–Time Warner

Warner Brothers films and TV, CNN, TNT, TBS, Court TV, HBO, Comedy Central, Hanna-Barbera, Cartoon Network, Cinemax, New Line Films. Control of 22% of the one hundred largest cable TV markets. Magazines include: *TIME*, *Fortune*, *People*, and *Sports Illustrated*. Warner Music Group (one of five companies that dominate global music market), 90% ownership of Time Warner Telecom, 37% of Road Runner Internet service, 40 percent of Towani (Japanese movie/TV producer), 23% of Atari, 31% of U.S. satellite TV company Primestar. It also owns the Atlanta Hawks and Atlanta Braves, as well as major shares in movie theater companies, distributorships, and satellite and cable companies, not only in the United States but also in the U.K., Asia, the EU, Africa, and elsewhere.

Disney

Disneyland, Disney World, Euro Disney, Disney Channel, ABC TV, ABC Radio, ESPN, ESPN NEWS, ESPN International, A&E, Entertainment and History channels. They own Miramax, Touchstone, and Walt Disney Pictures, as well as 660 Disney stores, Club Disney, Disney Cruise Line, the Anaheim Angels, and the Anaheim Mighty Ducks. Disney also owns 20–33% of such Euromedia companies in other countries as Eurosport TV network, the Spanish Tesauro SA, the German terrestial channel RTL2, the German cable TV channel TM3, the Brazilian TVA (pay TV), and Patagonia Film (Argentina).

The News Corporation

Fox TV Network, Fox News Channel, 20th Century Fox Film Studios, Golf TV channel, 22 U.S. TV stations, 130 daily newspapers, including the *New York Post* and the *London Times*, 23 magazines, HarperCollins publisher, and the L.A. Dodgers. It has large interests in satellite companies like United Video Satellite Group and Echostar, and large interests in British Sky Broadcasting, British Interactive, Sky TV, and Latin American TV channels including El Canal Fox, Fox Sport, and Latin Sky Broadcasting. Fox owns majority shares in Munich TV station TM-3, Vox TV Network, Italian pay-TV venture Stream, Fox TV Channel, Netherlands, New Zealand Natural History Unit, Asian Star TV satellite, dozens of broadcast channels in India, China, Japan, New Zealand, Australia, Taiwan, and Indonesia, and 52% of New Zealand's newspaper circulation, among many dozens of others.

Nobody in any democratic society voted to put a few advertisers in charge of all these media. Nonetheless, this handful of giant corporations, all representing roughly identical worldviews, get to speak and project their information and imagery into our brains night after night, all year, using the public airwaves.

For decades, large media conglomerates have also been pressuring the FCC in the United States to permit a much higher degree of cross-ownership among forms of media. They argue that companies should be free to own newspapers, radio, and TV in the same markets. Finally, under George W. Bush in 2007, the Federal Communications Commission loosened the restrictions on a thirty-five-year-old ban on newspaper-broadcast cross-ownership in single markets. If this ruling remains operative, it allows for any company that can afford it to buy and operate both a major newspaper and a radio and/or TV station(s) in the same market. The FCC move was immediately challenged by public interest advocates, including the Prometheus Radio Project and Media Alliance, and is now plodding through the courts. It will doubtless eventually reach the same great U.S. Supreme Court justices who gave us the Citizens United decision.

My prediction is that before long, the world's largest media companies, which may already own TV stations in a given market, will, for the first time, also be allowed to own the local newspaper and at least one or two radio stations, thus capturing an entire information environment. In effect, Rupert Murdoch already nearly does this in the New York City area, with his ownership of the

New York Post and the Fox News network. Fortunately, in that market there is also strong liberal opposition in all media. But in most places there is not.

Current negotiations within the WTO's General Agreement on Trade in Services (GATS) may soon advance the trend toward concentration even further. New rules are currently proposed that may require that all countries allow unlimited entry by global media conglomerates, enabling them to buy up local media outlets and local corporations and to control local standards of reporting, content, and ownership. New rules may also challenge any country's support for public broadcasting networks, such as PBS in the United States and those that still survive in England, Germany, Scandinavia, France, Canada, New Zealand, and elsewhere. Global corporations would prefer that all media be privatized, or, more accurately, that all *minds* be privatized, under their control. If this new GATS rule passes, government-supported nonprofit media could be classified as an "unfair trade practice."

Crisis Point

"How do we fight back against the incessant flow of logos, brands, slogans and jingles that submerge our streets, invade our homes, and flick on our screens?" This is the question being asked by the editors of *Adbusters*, Kalle Lasn and Micah White in their series of articles in 2010 and 2011, "A Unified Theory of Mental Pollution."

"We could wage a counteroffensive at the level of content. . . . But this approach is like using napkins to clean up an oil spill. It fails to confront the true danger of advertising—which is not in its individual messages but in the damage done to our mental ecology by the sheer volume of its flood. . . .

"To say that advertising is metaphorically mental pollution is one thing. To say that advertising is literally a kind of pollution and that TV commercials and highway billboards are more closely related to toxic sludge than to speech, is another matter entirely. The commercial media are to the mental environment what factories are to the physical environment. One cannot be an environmentalist without also being a mental environmentalist. Seen in this light, the fight against advertising is the defining struggle of our era. Info-diversity is as critical to our long-term survival as biodiversity. Both are bedrocks of human existence."

Over the years, there have been a variety of consumer movements and government efforts to counter the control of advertisers over media and its content. There was the old Fairness Doctrine, which established, for a time, that if erroneous information regarding public health were presented in advertising, then consumer groups could apply to run free counteradvertising, but only up to one-seventh of the insertion rate of the original. There was also the "equal time rule," which tried to be responsive to false statements in political advertising. And I have already mentioned above the "truth in advertising" movement, which was a pathetic effort, dating back to the 1920s, for the industry to regulate itself. All of these have been temporary palliatives, soon killed by the capitalist political process. The Citizens United case was the coup de grâce, allowing unlimited political spending by nonhuman entities of unimaginable degrees of wealth.

In that historical context, it was highly optimistic, I thought, of Zoe Gannon and Neal Lawson to add some new suggestions on how we might reform matters in relation to control of advertising. In the *The Advertising Effect*, (Compass, 2010) they make seven proposals, as follows:

(1) Ban advertising in public spaces. The idea here is to eliminate all billboards, bus-cards, taxi-ads, and the like. Such a plan was introduced in Brazil with great popular success, and versions of it also exist in Hawaii, Alaska, Vermont, and Maine, not to mention many parts of Europe, and Beijing, China, where the mayor put it this way: "Many of the ads use exaggerated terms that encourage luxury and self-indulgence which are beyond the reach of low-income groups, and are not conducive to harmony."

(2) Control advertising on the Internet. "The area of greatest concern," say the authors, is the way that Google collects information on all its users' viewing habits—perhaps the greatest data collection on all of us anywhere on Earth—and then sells that information to advertisers, to help them target and profile their potential customers. The possibility also exists, of course, that this data could be summoned by governments or hackers. Google defends this practice," say the authors, "on the basis that it makes for better targeted adverts—you get a better service because you are more likely to get the adverts you want to see. . . . The second line of argument is that 'free content' has to be paid for, so why not put up with a few adverts? However, both of these arguments only tell us the content is *not* free." We pay for it with our personal privacy.

(3) End the commercialization of childhood. We briefly discussed this problem above, describing what happened to an earnest effort to regulate ads promoting harmful sugary cereals and high-fat-content foods aimed at the minds of our most vulnerable population. Though this very modest U.S. effort was killed, far more blanket regulatory restrictions against ads directed at young children remain popular in Scandinavian countries, especially Sweden.

(4) Tax advertising. The social and environmental costs of advertising must now be seen as another corporate "externality." Businesses cause real harm through various pollutions to the community or to the environment but don't get stuck with the cleanup costs. The taxpayers get stuck. Advertising should be recognized as causing "mental pollution" and taxed on its volume.

(5) *Introduce a time and resource levy.* Authors Gannon and Lawson argue that it is not sufficient to merely tax the industry for the harms it creates; the industry should also be made to express its penance by devoting a significant percent of its productive hours and efforts to persuading the public to believe the opposite of what the advertising intends. It's a kind of counter-advertising produced by the same people who did the harm in the first place. (This is the one proposal among these seven by Gannon and Lawson that feels to me hopelessly undo-able. You can't train vultures to be vegetarians. A fund for counter-advertising done by community groups would be far more practical.)

(6) *Require ad agencies to put their name on their ads.* Perhaps this would help "out" the people who are sending inappropriate messages. Perhaps their photos should also run in the corner at the bottom.

(7) *Introduce statutory regulation of the ad industry.* The authors point out that, at the moment, in the United States, there is essentially no regulation on advertising, other than media outlets' discretion. Well, if an ad ran saying to go assassinate someone, probably very few media outlets would run it, and there could be a case brought for inciting murder or mayhem. But there is no longer any process to review lies in ordinary ads, or seriously misleading innuendos or statements, especially in political advertising, where it is rampant. This is clearly a very serious cause of misunderstanding of reality that has left the public in the dark about many important challenges. It is a direct challenge to the workability of democracy.

Among the above, numbers 2, 3, 4, and 7 are my favorites, though I might add a couple of my own suggestions: No advertising at all should be permitted in political campaigns—only a fixed amount of *free* television time for each candidate. No advertising of any kind on television. No selling of consumer information by Internet companies. And the establishment of a public board to judge lying and deliberately misleading statements in advertising—with fines and bans to follow.

Actually, I would also be okay with dropping advertising entirely, save for small classified-type ads in print media or on the Internet, listing commodities and services that may be available in specific categories. Some from businesses, others from individuals—a Craigslist kind of thing.

But are such reforms achievable? Certainly not judging by the history and fate of far less profound efforts at reform over the last half century, at least in the United States. The entire corporate community would oppose them, as would the mainstream political community and, of course, the media itself, left to right. They would see any of these as a direct threat to capitalist "free" markets.

Advertising is a crucial component of the capitalist economy, to keep itself functional and growing. Without it, and other marketing efforts that keep society addicted to visions of consumer culture and its joys, the economy would be far worse than it already is. So I am not optimistic that the above reforms can be achieved, though it is certainly worth the effort. Perhaps it's time for something even more awakening. How about *Occupy Madison Avenue*? Or *Re-occupy Our Minds*?

XI.

Capitalism or Happiness

My son Kai once proposed to me that we do a book together in which we interview fifty or so of the wealthiest people who are willing to talk with us, and ask them only one question: "Why do very rich people want to be richer?"

Does getting richer make them happier? Apparently not, as we will discuss below. One definitely doesn't seem to go with the other. Is it security? Ego? Power? Hubris? Freedom? Respect? Sexual access? Maybe it's like a sport or competition? Maybe it's just really satisfying to do better than the next guy, even if it means cutting down a bigger forest. Some say it's about achieving immortality. *New York Times* film critic A. O. Scott, in his review of the movie *Wall Street: Money Never Sleeps* (September 23, 2010), suggests it might be the "sheer fun of predation." The question remains: What's the appeal of accumulating more wealth than can ever be used for personal or family purposes?

It didn't occur to us that it was simply that capital *itself* needs to grow. The demand is so strong, it controls our behaviors, like the puppet manipulating the puppeteer. We have little choice. You would never invest your wealth in a local bank account at 1 percent interest if some other bank in Des Moines pays 3 percent or a hedge fund pays 20 percent. We didn't do the book, but we still might.

Grace Kim is a physician in California, in partnership with several other doctors in a private medical practice. She once told me of a frustrating conversation she had with her partners. She asked why they stay late every night, rather than keeping to just daytime hours; why did they feel it necessary to do that? Why not confine themselves to regular daytime office hours, she said, except in emergencies?

Her colleagues argued that working nights saved money on extra doctors and clerical help. "Let's hire those people," Kim said. "Why add three hours to our own long day? Do we need to make every dollar humanly possible? I already make good money. I don't want to work every night. I have a life I want to live.

There's so much I want to do. I'm on the board of a great museum. I love that." Her partners found her protestation hard to understand, she said. Things got left in the air.

Laissez-Faire

As a dominant economic strategy, and as a model for how we live on the planet, the inherent drives of capitalism pretty well assure it cannot ultimately serve the general public welfare. Anyway, it was never designed for that. It has only one purpose—to accumulate ever-expanding wealth for its owners by whatever means it can.

In their New Economy Working Group report, "A Main Street Fix for Wall Street's Failure" (December 2011), coauthors John Cavanagh and David Korten do not use the "c"-word to name this flawed system. They prefer to use "free-market fundamentalism." But they do a great job describing the system's inherent drives to profit "from eliminating jobs and worker benefits, depressing wages, evading taxes, denying health insurance claims, and pillaging the retirement accounts of the elderly."

That hardly seems a formula for widespread happiness. In practice, free market fundamentalism, and laissez faire really mean that government limits its interventions, reduces regulations, minimizes accountability standards, lowers taxes, and provides as few social services as possible, demonstrating maximum faith that free markets will solve all problems. While the U.S. does not yet live up to the full dreams of its arch-conservatives, among the world's industrial nations, U.S. corporations are given far greater freedoms than elsewhere. For example, corporate tax rates are low, and there are a myriad of ways to escape them completely, as we have discussed. We also have far lower rates of employee protections than other western industrial nations, less meaningful maternity leaves, or guarantees of meaningful vacations, or health-care support. As for public programs, spending on social services is similarly limited, with much lower public spending on public education, mass transit, public media, child-care and elder care services and public housing. And we are among few countries without universal national health care guarantees. The "free market" is, in fact, left in charge of most of all those, and of military allocations as well, which are very profitable for corporate players—the main goal of the system—and so are treated with far greater enthusiasm and priority. If all this was a route to happiness, or to general well-being, then the United States would be the world's poster child for laissez faire capitalism—the capital of happiness, contentment, satisfaction. So. Are we happy yet?

Meanwhile, nearly all European countries, as well as quite a few other highly industrialized countries, like Japan, have much higher corporate and individual tax rates than the United States and have retained substantial government support of public services, including free lifetime healthcare; inexpensive public education all the way through college; free care for children and the elderly; inexpensive, highly efficient public transportation; excellent worker guarantees for annual *six-week* vacations; significant maternity leave; good protections for the unemployed; and government financing for election campaigns, so as to minimize the role of small groups of wealthy special interests. That is only a partial list.

Such public commitments are precisely why so many American political leaders, especially on the right wing, love to call European countries "socialist" or "communist" and make fun of them in political campaigns.

In fact, many of those countries practice what they call "social democracy," or "democratic socialism." And yet it turns out that these more socialized countries, like most other democracies, report much higher rates of overall well-being by most standards of measurement including *voter turnout* at all levels of democratic elections than our own democracy does. The United States has by far the lowest voter turnout among the forty leading industrial democracies, itself a grim demonstration of alienation from the larger society and its abilities to serve its people. There are others.

Doing the Numbers

In terms of human well-being and happiness, how does American-style capitalism fare compared with the somewhat less capitalist, more socialized versions—and with other systems? If the figures don't finally suggest the system is making us a whole lot happier than everyone else, then we might want to ask—why on earth are we continuing to do things this way? Here is a sampling of some important indicators of well-being:

- *Divorce*: The U.S. has the highest divorce rate in the world, 54.8 per 100 marriages (UN Demographic Yearbook, 2009). Runners-up are Russia and Sweden.
- *Suicide*: According to the World Health Organization (2009), the United States was 41st in *suicides* among 107 countries reported, putting us in the upper 38%.
- *Adult Obesity*: The United States has the world's highest rate of adult obesity (34%) followed by the United Arab Emirates, Egypt, New Zealand, Mexico, Canada, Slovakia, Greece, and Australia (CIA World Factbook, 2010). The overall U.S. figure for "overweight" people was 75%. The lowest rates of obesity were in Italy, Norway, Switzerland, and Japan. (Japan was less than 3%.) The U.S. states with the highest rates were Mississippi,

Alabama, and West Virginia, according to the Centers for Disease Control (2011). Perhaps we just have too much food available, or McDonald's and Kentucky Fried Chicken are the wrong kinds of food.

- *Maternal Mortality*: In 2008, says the CIA World Factbook, among the leading industrial nations, the United States was worst in the rate of *maternal mortality* (deaths during pregnancy and childbirth), with 24 deaths per 100,000 live births. The next-most-negative numbers were from Canada and the U.K., who reported half the U.S. death rate: 12 deaths per 100,000. The best records came from Italy, Japan, Spain, Denmark, Belgium, Sweden, Austria (all under 6 per 100,000), and Ireland (with only 3 per 100,000). Most observers attribute this poor performance to lack of adequate healthcare.

- *Infant Mortality*: Similarly, the United States was worst among industrial nations in *infant mortality* (deaths within one year of birth) at 6%, followed by Canada, Portugal, and the U.K. The best records were from Norway, Spain, Italy, France, and Japan (which was only 3%) (World Health Organization, 2009). Measured globally, among 193 nations, including less developed countries, the United States was worse than forty other countries, including Malaysia, Slovakia, Cuba, and Poland. Worst of all was India, at 27.8%, said ABC News, quoting PLOS Medicine's "Neonatal Mortality Levels for 193 Countries in 2009" (August 30, 2011).

- *Childhood Poverty*: According to UNICEF (2005), the United States has a childhood poverty rate of 22%, second only to Mexico, which leads the world with 28%. Third on the list was Italy, with 16%. In this category, among rich countries, Denmark was best (only 2%), then Finland, Norway, Sweden, Switzerland, the Czech Republic, France, Germany, Spain, et al. (all under 8%).

- *Prison Incarceration*: In 2009, the United States had the highest prison incarceration rate of any other country in the world: 743 per 100,000 people. Second-highest was Russia (577 per 100,000). China had 120 per 100,000, about one-seventh of the U.S. rate. (International Center for Prison Studies, 2010).

- *Murder Rate*: According to the UN Office on Drugs and Crime, in 2010, among highly industrialized nations, the United States is second in murders, with 4.8 per 100,000 people. Russia is first with 13. Canada is third, with 1.2; Scandinavian countries, Italy, and the Netherlands are all below 1.0; and the lowest are Finland and Japan.

- *Rape*: Based on 1991 figures, the United States is first among highly industrial nations, with 37 reported rapes per 100,000 people per year. Sweden is second, but with less than half of the U.S. rate. Below 9 are Germany, Norway, the U.K., and Finland. Japan is lowest, with 1.4 ("Where We Stand," a project of the World Rank Research Team, 1991).

- *Armed Robbery*: The United States is first, with 221 per 100,000 people. Canada is second, though with less than half the U.S. rate, at 94 per 100,000. Sweden, Germany, Denmark, Finland, and Norway are all below 50. Japan has only 1 per 100,000. (Ibid.)
- *Home ownership*: Though this is frequently mentioned as such an important part of the "American dream," among the 20 leading industrial nations, the United States ranked 12th, with 59%. The highest percentage of home ownership was in Ireland, with 82%, followed by Spain, Luxembourg, Norway, Belgium, Greece, Italy, the U.K., Canada, Japan, and Portugal. (Ibid.)
- *Wealth Inequality*: As indicated in earlier chapters, the United States has the greatest inequality of income and wealth in the industrialized world. According to the World Bank's GINI index (where 0 equals the highest degree of equality, and 100 equals the worst level of inequality) the United States's rank was 99. Canada (83), Netherlands (82), and Switzerland (79) came next. The United States also had the highest pay differentials of any other country among top corporate executives versus office and production staff, averaging about 350 to 1. Japan's was only 10 to 1. Among the top 200 U.S. companies, the differential is 650 to 1.
- *Life Expectancy*: According to the CIA World Factbook, as of 2011, the United States ranked 15th in the world in average life expectancy (78.37 years), behind Japan, which was first (82.25), Italy (81.77), France (81.19), Spain (81.17), and ten others.
- *Middle class*: The highest middle-class percentage is in Japan (90%), followed by Sweden (79%), Norway (73%), and Germany (70%). The U.S. middle class is about 53% of the total population.
- *Voter Turnout*: Among 40 leading democracies, the United States ranks last in voter turnout in most kinds of elections (from 1960 to 1995), averaging below 55% of the electorate even in presidential elections, below 45% in congressional elections, and much lower in state and local votes. (23 other democracies enjoyed over 80% turnout in legislative elections; these included Austria, Luxembourg, Italy, Denmark, Sweden, Czech Republic, Netherlands, Norway, Bulgaria, and Romania, as well as such non-European countries as Malta, New Zealand, Iceland, Venezuela, and Israel, and five countries where voting is mandatory: Australia, Belgium, Chile, Brazil, and Argentina), according to Mark N. Franklin, "Electoral Participation," in *Controversies in Voting Behavior, 4th edition* (2001).

In addition to the above, in *Orion* (March 2012), James G. Speth, former director of the EPA under Jimmy Carter, now a professor at the University of Vermont, reported some important comparisons with the OECD countries (including the United Kingdom, Scandinavia, Germany, France, Canada, and Japan). His study found that the U.S. was worst among all these countries in terms of poverty, social mobility, wealth distribution, "material well-being" of children, mental health, inclusion in healthcare programs, and ability to learn math, among other measures similar to those we already indicated above.

Admittedly, there are nuances of difference from country to country in how they keep track of these matters. In some cases, these differences might slightly mitigate a few findings. For example, there are variations in the measures for obesity. And the reliability of rape reporting in some countries is questionable.

But we can surely conclude generally that none of the numbers above display much evidence of general contentment, well-being, or happiness, or successful democratic engagement in the world's *most* capitalist country. Our own greatest achievements seem clearly in the area of wealth creation for a small minority of the population.

Consequences of Inequity

In *The Spirit Level: Why Greater Equality Makes Societies Stronger* (2010), Richard Wilkinson and Kate Pickett give particular attention to the uneven distributions of wealth that characterize modern society, especially among industrial nations, including the U.S. and the U.K. Using data from the World Health Organization, the United Nations, the World Bank, and the Organization for Economic Cooperation and Development, they compiled extensive lists and charts of health and social indices that show positive increases as the level of overall societal equity increases. Included are such measures as life expectancy, infant mortality and child well-being, obesity, use of illegal drugs, teen pregnancy, imprisonment rates, math and literacy levels, social mobility, status of women, inventiveness and innovation, et al. In all cases, greater equality in society led to more positive measures in all categories.

> The contrast between the material success and social failure of many rich countries is an important signpost. It suggests that if we are to gain further improvements in the real quality of life, we need to shift attention from material standards and economic growth to ways of improving the psychological and social well-being of whole societies. For the vast majority of people in affluent countries the difficulties of life are no longer about filling our stomachs, having clean water, and keeping warm. Not only have measures of well-being and happiness ceased to rise with economic growth, but, as affluent societies have grown richer, there have been long-term rises in rates of anxiety, depression, and numerous other social problems.

Pickett and Wilkinson demonstrate their point with an array of dozens of charts on the relationship between excessive wealth—that is, standards of living that are beyond a level of sufficiency. "In poorer countries, life expectancy increases rapidly during the early stages of economic development, but then, starting among the middle-income countries, the rate of improvement slows down. As living standards rise and countries get richer and richer, the relationship between economic growth and life expectancy weakens. Eventually it disappears entirely, the rising curve becomes horizontal—showing that for rich countries [and rich people] to get richer adds nothing further to their life expectancy. That has already happened in the richest thirty or so countries."

According to Pickett and Wilkinson, "the richer a country gets, the less each increment of wealth adds to a population's overall happiness and well-being." The same result of course applies in individual reports, i.e., beyond an economic level of "sufficiency" in basics like food, housing, clothing, medical care, education, and security, additional increments provide less incremental expression of happiness. In fact, as many researchers have confirmed, at high levels of increased wealth there is an actual measurable decline in levels of overall happiness and well-being.

Among all countries, the U.S. now ranks second, behind Singapore, in overall inequality among the developed industrial nations. On a state-by-state basis in the U.S., even if the average income is higher in one state than in another, it is the uneven distribution of the wealth that matters more than the actual level of income . . . high *average* income level in the U.S. as a whole does nothing to reduce its health and social problems relative to other countries."

Using the Child Well-Being Index in rich countries, figures compiled by UNICEF show a strong negative link between child well-being and inequality. Somewhat less wealthy countries with less inequality (including Finland, the Netherlands, Belgium, Spain, and Italy) rate much higher in the index than rich countries with the greatest inequality (like the U.S., the U.K., New Zealand, and Israel). "Where income differences are bigger, social distances are bigger and social stratification more important." And, as they clearly suggest, people are less happy. "The best way of responding to the harm done by high levels of inequality would be to reduce inequality itself."

American economist Herman Daly concurs. He frequently points out that great numbers of research projects have shown that material gain increases happiness only up to the point of sufficiency. "Studies of self-evaluated happiness show that beyond a threshold annual income of roughly $25,000–32,000/year, further growth in personal income does not increase happiness by a corresponding amount. Happiness beyond this threshold is overwhelmingly a function of the quality of our relationships in community, by which our very identity is constituted, rather than the quantity of goods consumed."

Wilkinson and Pickett quote the work of Jean Twenge, a psychologist at San Diego State University, who has been researching anxiety. Twenge found that we are generally far more anxious than we have ever been. She reported on 269 studies measuring anxiety levels in the United States between 1952 and 1993, covering fifty-two thousand individuals. Despite the fact that during the forty-one years of the study, the United States and many other industrialized countries showed enormous economic growth, levels of anxiety steadily increased. It's also worth noting that the expanding per capita income levels during this period were mostly enjoyed by the upper 20 percent of society. Twenge found that the "average college student at the end of the period was more anxious than 85 percent of the population at the beginning of it, and even more staggering, by the late 1980s the average American child was more anxious than a child of psychiatric patients in the 1950s."

The negative correlation also extends into related conditions such as depression. Citing comparative studies among ten thousand people in their twenties, Pickett and Wilkinson found that depression was twice as common among those born in 1970 as those born in 1958. And among adolescents, this corresponded with a rise in the frequency of behavioral problems, including crime, alcohol, and drugs.

Economics of Happiness

In the feature documentary film *The Economics of Happiness*—cowritten and coproduced by Helena Norberg-Hodge, John Page, and Steven Gorelick, of the International Institute for Ecology and Culture—Norberg-Hodge describes her own awakening to the many false promises of modern industrial economics and consumer-driven, growth-oriented societies. Her awareness evolved during several years of extensive visits to Ladakh (the northernmost mountain province of India), which radically altered her views about what creates a "happy" society.

"I learned [in Ladakh] about social, ecological, and personal well-being, about the roots of happiness," says Norberg-Hodge in the film. "I was forced to reconsider many basic assumptions that I had always taken for granted, and to look at my own Western culture in a different light. There was this sort of radiance and vitality that I had never experienced anywhere else. Even the material standard of living was high. They had large spacious houses, plenty of leisure time, there was no such thing as unemployment—it had never existed—and no one went hungry. Of course, they didn't have our comforts and luxuries, but what they did have was a way of life that was vastly more sustainable than ours, and that was also far more joyous and rich."

The film's narration describes changes in Ladakh during the 1970s as the out-side commercial world reached through to this remote place and "bombarded Ladakhis with advertising and media images that romanticized Western-style consumerism and made their own culture seem pitiful by comparison." Says Norberg-Hodge, "I saw how people started thinking of themselves as back-ward, primitive, and poor. . . . The changes were so clear-cut, and I saw with my own eyes cause and effect. One minute you've got vital people and really sustain-able culture. The next minute you've got pollution, both of air and water, you've got unemployment, a widening gap between rich and poor, and perhaps most shocking of all, in a people who have been so spiritually grounded, divisive-ness and depression. These changes weren't the result of innate human greed or some sort of evolutionary force; they happened far too suddenly for that. They were clearly the direct result of exposure to outside economic pressures. These pressures created intense competition, breaking down community and the connection to nature that had been the cornerstone of Ladakhi culture for centuries."

The film goes on to report on the increasing levels of depression and stress in the Western industrialized world, as we seek material success and consumptive lifestyles that are broadly trumpeted as the roots of happiness. In the film, U.S. activist and author Bill McKibben cites U.S. studies on the matter: "Every year since the end of World War II, one of the big polling firms has asked Americans, 'Are you happy with your life?' The number of Americans who say, 'Yes, I'm very happy with my life'—the percentage peaks in 1956, and goes slowly but steadily downhill ever since. That's interesting because in that same fifty years, we have gotten immeasurably richer. We have three times as much stuff. Somehow it hasn't worked, because that same affluence tends to undermine community."

In his book *Authentic Happiness* (2002), Martin E. P. Seligman reported that "while real income in America has risen 16 percent in the last 30 years, the per-centage of people who describe themselves as 'very happy' has fallen from 36% to 29%. Money really cannot buy happiness."

In *The Economics of Happiness*, India's celebrated agricultural activist Vandana Shiva partly blames the shift toward a corporate-controlled export-oriented globalized food economy as the source of additional grief and alienation:

"I think the only people who are happy, deeply happy, and deeply secure, are people who know they can rely on someone else in life: people who know they are not alone in this world. Lonely people have never been happy people. Globalization is creating a very lonely planet. . . . Removing people from their land is the root of all unemployment. It is at the root of the creation of slums and the rural-urban migration. . . . Making people disposable in terms of working with the land is creating probably the biggest human crisis. No human rights community is noticing it, no Amnesty has noticed it, but 100,000 Indian farmers have been driven to suicide."

Australian ecologist Clive Hamilton adds this: "Before the modern era of consumer capitalism, people's sense of self, their personal identities, were shaped largely through their communities, their neighborhoods. Nowadays, where all of those supports have fallen away, the gap that was left has been filled by the marketers, who came in and said, 'Don't worry if you don't know who you are. We will provide you with a packaged identity, which you can use—by buying our products—to create a sense of self, which you can then project into the world.'"

The film makes a strong argument for transitioning from globalization toward economic *relocalization*. Norberg-Hodge explains: "When people turn away from the global consumer culture and start reconnecting with each other in their own local communities, they're providing very different role models for their children. The distant images of perfection in the global media and in advertising create feelings of inferiority . . . when children identify with real, flesh-and-blood people, they get a much more realistic sense of who they are, of who they can be.

"I saw this so clearly in Ladakh. There were no 'celebrities' there. Everyone was seen, heard, and appreciated; in effect everybody was 'somebody.' That sense of belonging built confidence and a deep sense of self-respect. . . . We have no right to tell people how to live their lives. But we can tell them that they are not stupid and backward or primitive if they live on the land, and that there's no need to blindly emulate a consumer culture in order to feel that you're worthy . . . at the deepest level, localization is about connection, it's about reestablishing our sense of interdependence with others and with the natural world."

Sufficiency

Scouring all the research in journals for the last half century, in 2007 a team of four university psychologists confirmed that just the basics of "sufficiency," like adequate food, shelter, clothing, friendship, family, and community services, promoted the greatest sense of well-being and happiness. Beyond basic needs, the drive toward higher levels of acquisition promoted less happiness.

In their report, "Some Costs of American Corporate Capitalism: A Psychological Exploration of Value and Goal Conflicts," psychologists Tim Kasser, Steve Cohn, Allen D. Kanner, and Richard M. Ryan decided to focus their research on "American corporate capitalism" (ACC), because it is the form of capitalism that now has "the largest worldwide influence."

More than any other national expression of capitalism, ACC actively encouraged "values based in self-interest, financial success, high levels of consumption, and interpersonal styles based on competition." It also undermines more pro-social goals and values that encourage positive relationships and a sense of self-worth.

The authors remind us that "the level of income and wealth inequality declined from the late 1920s until the early 1970s, but since then, inequality has increased dramatically." They cite Noreena Hertz, author of *The Silent Takeover* (2002), reporting that in the period of U.S. economic expansion between 1980 and 2000, 97% of the increased wealth was garnered by those in the top 20% of incomes, leading America today to become the most unequal society in the industrialized West.

The authors continue, "The winner-take-all mentality engendered by capitalism ensures that in the minds of those who have internalized the ideology of the system," this inequity seems fair. (*Think:* David Koch, Mitt Romney, Donald Trump.) "It follows the rule which proclaims that self-interest and competition are of primary importance."

Studies consistently show that quality relationships matter more than money to people's perceived happiness and quality of life. If this is so, then it again raises the questions of why economies should continue to seek growth after material sufficiency has been achieved, and why people continue to pursue wealth after maximum satisfaction has been delivered.

In a special issue of *Resurgence* on the subject of well-being (November/December 2011), Canadian author Mark Anielski remarks that two thousand years ago, "Aristotle defined happiness as 'well-being of spirit' . . . and that 'people's' happiness was the highest good."

Anielski argues, "Economists have forgotten the meaning of words like *wealth*, which, back in 13th-century Old English, meant 'the conditions of well-being.' Examining the origins of the word in either the *Oxford* or *Webster's New World Dictionary*, you will find that it comes from combining the Old English words *weal* (well-being) and *th* (condition). Therefore, the word wealth literally means 'the conditions of well-being' or 'the condition of being happy and prosperous.'" It doesn't mean getting rich.

Anielski reports on the work of Princeton University economists Alan Krueger and Daniel Kahneman (Nobel Prize winner in economics, 2002), who concluded that the "belief that high income is associated with a good mood (happiness) is greatly exaggerated."

When we examine the relationships between GDP and life satisfaction across 178 countries, we see diminishing returns to life satisfaction with incremental increase in GDP per capita. There is a relationship between income and life satisfaction, but that after a surprisingly low level of GDP per capita is reached, the increment in life satisfaction is marginal. People in Luxembourg, the United States, and Norway, while enjoying the highest GDPs per year, are no more satisfied with life than the average person living in Costa Rica or Bhutan.

In that same issue of *Resurgence*, Herman Daly explains that the whole subject is becoming anomalous, because growth "no longer really makes us richer; it has started to make us poorer." He didn't mean it metaphorically. "What used to be economic growth could become uneconomic growth—growth that in reality makes us poorer, not richer. . . . If we cut down all the trees this year, catch all the fish and burn all the oil and coal, then GDP counts all that as this year's income [growth]. The same can be said for aggregate growth beyond sufficiency . . . to maintain the same rate of growth, ever more matter and energy has to be mined and processed through the economy, resulting in more depletion and waste." In other words, the richer we get, the poorer we are.

And also in that issue of *Resurgence*, Anglican priest Peter Owen Jones adds a spiritual dimension to conclude the discussion: "Our well-being is inextricably linked with the well-being of everything else on the planet," he said. He lists some conditions of happiness that you don't see mentioned often as they have little to do with standards of wealth and acquisition. These two are my favorites:

(1) *Do no harm*: "I love what the Jain tradition has to say about our relationship with the natural world. First, we are asked to experience the natural world as something sacred and therefore something that we do not harm. In the west, we have never lived in peace with the natural world—it has been neither our tradition nor our way of seeing ourselves. We have instead been predators, despoilers, eradicators. Technological progress has largely been sold to us claiming that it will make living more easy. One of the main illusions that we have all subscribed to is that easy living will give us happiness and well-being. It hasn't."

(2) *Abandon ownership*: "The belief that we own things is actually an illusion. The weight of carrying that belief is far heavier than we have realized, and so many of us carry so very much: houses, cars, clothes, computers, paintings—it's a long and endless list. . . . Ownership is not a reality but merely a belief system. Our society functions on the belief in ownership, and part of the environmental crisis we face is that we believe in ownership of fields, woods, rivers, trees, sheep, and cats. One of the tenets of ownership is that if we believe it is ours, we will take better care of it, but just one look at the state of planet Earth is in now should be enough to show how flawed that argument is. Don't we tend to take better care of things when they don't belong to us? When we have borrowed from a neighbor? This belief in ownership is one of the greatest obstacles to well-being and happiness. But the good news is that it is relatively easy to find a way out of it. Just don't believe in it any more. That's all there is to it. You just let go. The belief we own anything is an illusion; it cannot make us happy."

Summaries & Afterthoughts

Ultimately, questions of happiness and well-being are subjective matters. But you know it when you see it. You know it when you feel it.

Capitalists continue to argue the opposite case, that the system is highly beneficial for all of us—"greed is good" remains the central ethic. As top echelons get ever richer, the benefits will trickle down to us all. *They* get a lot, but *we* get some, too. It's a win-win for everyone. *Happiness?* What's that? Let's get serious.

That line of argument on the universal benefits of a competitive obsessive pursuit of wealth is meant to defend against criticism of the system's built-in venality, amorality, social arrangements, and ecological harms. But during the 2012 Republican primaries, we saw a leak in the argument—the truly weird spectacle of Mitt Romney's having to defend against charges (by other Republicans!) about his behavior as a "predatory capitalist," during his early career as a corporate raider. I don't think there was, ever before, a presidential candidate so widely criticized in U.S. mass media for being too capitalist. In Romney's business career he had been deeply engaged in buying up businesses and firing huge numbers of employees to lower operating costs and presumably increase efficiencies. Then he would quickly turn around and sell the businesses for a profit.

Romney defended this as routine "free enterprise." That's how the system works, he said, and indeed it is. Sometimes you fire workers if it opens the way toward better profit opportunities for the owners. But that whole idea, once finally exposed, wasn't very appealing to potential voters, who identified more easily with the fired workers than with the predatory capitalists.

Newt Gingrich led the charges against Romney, using a $10 million campaign donation from Shelley Adelman, the arch right-wing oil and gambling casino billionaire who paid for the attack ads against Romney. Really, God doesn't make more "predatory free-enterprise" capitalists than Gingrich and Adelman. It turned the whole intramural dust-up into a stunning capitalist farce of majestic proportions. Finally the GOP itself demanded an immediate stop to it lest it would give the voting public negative ideas about capitalism and Republicans.

In order to avoid damaging indictments like that, capitalism has to repeatedly make the case for its many positive virtues, its great promise, and its potential benefits to everyone—visions of so much *more* to be attained—despite the little ups and downs and bumps of the process. In the end, great material reward might possibly await some of us.

One of the most celebrated advocates on the virtues of self-interest was the great philosopher from the Scottish Enlightenment Adam Smith—at least, so we have been told. Actually, however, as we describe in chapter IV, he never really praised *unfettered* capitalism. His written words and intent have been edited and distorted to mean nearly the opposite of what he intended. His infamous "invisible hand" line, where self-interested business activity sometimes brings unexpected economic benefits to a wider community, was actually intended to focus on the subtle benefits of *local* businesses, putting funds into *local* circulation. We can all agree with that, and we will discuss the benefits of local business in considerable detail in the next chapter. But Smith actually spoke in admonition, saying, in effect: *Watch out for corporations! Keep them well regulated! Keep them small, local, and under control! And don't let capital or corporations leave the neighborhood, or cross borders or oceans.* Smith was praising *local* shopkeepers, butchers, and furniture markets, not Walmart or Lockheed Martin or Citibank or Credit Suisse.

But surely capitalism does have its benefits. They say it built the world we live in, which is true enough. Never mind that capitalism also built the conditions for its inevitable collapse, and the oncoming collapse of the natural world.

And, of course, capitalism is very well celebrated for bringing the wonders of innovation. No system has ever promoted technological invention the way capitalism has. This is undeniably true. Technologies such as private automobiles, pesticides, chemicals, genetic engineering, and television—all of that bursting onto the scene—have within only one century transformed our planet. And the transformations are not over yet. It's all part of the greater modern narrative of never-ending "progress." All things get constantly better, and all problems are solved by human technological ingenuity.

Look at the glories of our new cyber-world, which has changed everything in only the last decade and continues to: computers, smartphones, tablets, e-readers, and new apps every week or so, making obsolete whatever gizmos you bought the month before. Think of it—now you can walk down a busy street or drive your car while listening to Lady Gaga on your iPhone while sending sexy text messages and photos to your girlfriend. And think of all the geniuses in Silicon Valley hard at work right now inventing the next great social-networking tool to make obsolete whatever they invented a few months before. It's little different from the old annual automobile-style change, or the raising and lowering of women's hemlines from year to year.

Then there's the evolution from VHS to DVD to Blu-ray, and that great revolution will surely go forward to who knows what further glory. The wide variety of Internet communications and networking opportunities have become, in only one decade, the absolute center of our lives—it's our way of making contact with friends, our way of doing work, our way of shopping—all of us everywhere, deeply connected and engaged with moving electronic information, data, and thoughts, communicating virtually nonstop for hours daily. We are evolving rapidly into info-bots, wired together like an electronic mosaic, unified in our minds and actions, like one single global creature. Surely this has made us happier. As for the prior living global creature—the global interconnectedness of living nature—well, maybe we can get along without that.

And what about the greatness of the new face-recognition, voice-recognition, and talk-back technologies? They are praised as helping the handicapped and stopping terrorists—virtuous purposes indeed. Now they may also eliminate all the keys you are otherwise obliged to carry in your pocket. No worries anymore about leaving them in the restaurant. Just speak out to your car, and it starts; speak to your TV, and on it goes . . . speak to your front door! Isn't that something you have been hoping for?

Then there is the genius of satellite communications and pilotless drone bombers. Some young fellow in Colorado gets to sit at his computer, using satellite technologies to zero in on some suspected terrorists in Pakistan or Yemen or anywhere. Push the button, and *poof*—they're history. How neat is that? Really, it's much better than a video game. And then it's home for a bite of lunch. *How did he get such a great job?*

Look, I am nearly as far into the cyber-revolution as the average person, but I ask myself constantly what has been gained and what has been lost by spending all these hours slowly morphing into an anti-sensual techno-human. Frankly, I doubt that it has added much to my pleasure or happiness . . . or wealth, for that matter. I often think maybe we should drop the whole thing and go back to radio, streetcars, movie houses, and nature. What's the point of all this? I think it's making us crazy. But, admittedly, I am a confirmed neo-Luddite.

I am ready to stipulate that of course some innovations are useful. I think antibiotics have been on the whole a good thing, for example. And I like trains, and radio and normal telephones, even rotary phones, and YouTube and email (though I really miss ordinary hand-written letters). But, as Doug Tompkins loves to point out, if you talk about email or computers or cell phones, you have to talk about coltan and lithium mines in Africa or South America, and rare earth minerals in China. Without such minerals, your cell phone is toast. Getting those mines operating requires shoving entire indigenous communities off their traditional lands into cities and remaking their landscapes.

And you can't talk about computers or cell phones without considering a vast scientific and industrial infrastructure that make them possible—Tompkins calls it "the scaffolding of civilization, that great train of invention, production, waste"—and the history of prior technological underpinnings, without which new technologies could not exist. "It's those that are as much of the problem as the cell phone itself, which is the tip of the iceberg; it's all that which has brought us climate change, and biodiversity loss, and ugliness."

Innovations do not exist simply because some idealistic visionary thought it would be good for the world, despite corporations' tendency to advertise their creations on that basis. Really, it's only about the creation of wealth. Even our high-tech hero Steve Jobs made a lot of his money by shifting his production facilities to China, laying off American workers and paying Chinese sweatshop laborers $1 per day so we could have our cherished iPads and he could make billions. Now his technical creations are celebrated everywhere. But look, if they didn't have the potential to make him rich, he might have dropped the whole idea and switched to making video games.

The drive for personal wealth is celebrated as a great thing that drives creativity, achievement, and innovative business. I have already reported how many corporations indicate that they give multimillion-dollar bonuses and $50 million salaries to their CEOs because that is what motivates them. In January 2012, the *New York Times* reported that Steve Jobs's replacement as CEO of Apple, Tim Cook, signed on for $378 million. Did it make him happy? Probably, at least at first. But imagine the poor CEOs at other companies who were offered only $5–10 million. How insulting. Surely they were raging at the inequity. They are not happy.

And what about the other executives further down the hierarchy, and employees at lower levels? It's a well-known virtue of capitalism that it keeps everyone on their toes, because every aspect puts the emphasis on competition. If one guy wins the job, others lose it. If one company gets the deal, others don't. If one person gets the promotion, others don't, and then they have to go home and tell their families. And, of course, every worker on the production line knows that however much she or he is being paid, it reduces the $378 million guy's salary and bonus. Maybe he will make only $375 million next year. He knows that, too. That's why he shifts production to China. Every win is also a loss. Someone gets happy and someone doesn't.

On the other hand, I have spent most of my adult life around thousands of people working in nonprofit organizations, and I've worked closely with dozens of such organizations. The typical executive director or program director of an environmental or social-justice nonprofit works at least sixty hours per week. If they are paid $50,000–70,000 per year, they are usually quite happy. And these are highly talented people. They are arguably, in many ways, more talented, and surely ultimately wiser, than the CEO of Apple, whose worldview is bounded by an absolute imperative for corporate advancement. The pay inequity between Tim Cook and the director of, say, Amazon Watch or IFG, illustrates that outside the corporate world, money is *not* the only reason people drive toward achievement; sometimes altruism is the motivating factor. Or creative vision. Or trying to help the community, or save the planet. I think those are goals at least as valuable and personally satisfying as selling more oil or cars or iPads.

What about Adam Smith's small local entrepreneurs? What about small local farmers? Are they happy? What about electrical workers and bus drivers? Are they all competing like mad and craving wealth, or are they just trying to do their thing and have a nice life and friends in the community and some reliable education for their kids, some transport to work, and healthcare for everybody?

What about writers, dancers, artists? Do you know any sculptors or painters? They may work like dogs for weeks to make, well, *one* painting. There is no guarantee anyone will ever buy the painting, or buy them dinner either, for that matter. The rewards are in another domain that the system has lost track of. They have nothing to do with wealth accumulation, but still the artists get up every day and work at their paintings, and if in the end they like it, and others like it, they are happy.

PART THREE

Epilogue

Solving problems in the context of outdated and crumbling models will dig us deeper into the hole. We are in an era of profound change that urgently requires new ways of thinking instead of more business as usual; capitalism, in its current form, has no place in the world around us.

Klaus Schwab, founder, World Economic Forum, Davos, Switzerland, January 21, 2012 (fortieth annual elite gathering of 1,600 political and economic leaders, including forty heads of state)

QUESTION FROM THE AUDIENCE: *Okay, Jerry, capitalism is causing terrible problems. Things have changed since the old days. Maybe we've reached the limit of all that gung-ho growth. Isn't there a way to fix it? I hope you're not advocating socialism. Wouldn't that be worse? Can you name a better way forward?*

XII.
Which Way Out?

Let's start with some good news. There is no shortage of good alternative ideas, plans, and strategies being put forth by activist groups and "new economy" thinkers in the United States and all countries of the world. Some seek to radically reshape the current capitalist system. Others advocate abandoning it for something new (or old). There is also a third option, a merger of the best points of other existing or proposed options, toward a "hybrid" economic model that can cope with modern realities. This chapter will review and discuss some of these options and opportunities.

Meanwhile, U.S.-style laissez-faire capitalists, who now dominate the politics and economy in this country, continue to argue that all solutions must be determined by the "free market." But the free market does not focus on the needs of democracy, or the implications of rampant inequity, or the catastrophic problems of the natural world. The free market is interested in one thing: expanding wealth. That is its only agenda. Nothing else matters, at least until the system collapses. Klaus Schwab had it right. And the situation is not much better abroad.

Ecological economist Brian Davey reported from the Beyond Growth Congress in Berlin (2011) that there was "much talk of the need for democratization to facilitate the *post-growth* economy. However, there was great skepticism for how much could be achieved. . . . The grip of corporate lobby interests over politics at national [U.S.] and European levels is too great. The state is a weak instrument for the kind of change that has to happen." (*Adbusters*, December 2011)

In the same issue, Simon Critchley, professor of philosophy at the New School, New York, concurred: "Citizens still believe that governments represent the interests of those who elect them, and have the power to create effective change. But they don't, and they can't. We do not live in democracies. We inhabit plutocracies; government by the rich."

So, the change will be up to us. And yet the puzzle persists: *How do we get from here to there?* How do we bridge the chasm from corporate, oligarchic, global dominance of governments, economies, media, and, not least important, military, all driven by the ideologies of consumerism, growth, and "progress," toward some new set of values and structures?

What struck me most about the Occupy Wall Street movement was the way the Occupiers initially resisted formally articulating the kinds of changes they hoped to see. By their very lack of expression, they deliberately seemed to imply that the problem is more extreme. Systemic. *Total.* They seemed to say that there was little point in describing ways to modify governance, because all the currently available forms and instruments of power are themselves inaccessible, and no longer valid. One of the precursors of the U.S. Occupy movement, the *Indignados* (the "outraged") of Spain—who've been doing mass demonstrations in Madrid's public squares since May 2011—put it explicitly: *"You do not represent us!"* It's their complaint about lack of responsive government, but also their desire to break with representation altogether, and to act for themselves. It expresses a loss of faith in the leaders and systems of governance as they now exist.

Living in the United States and watching the near dissolution of our own governance system over recent decades makes it hard to disagree with the perception that government is moribund, bought and sold by a small oligarchic class. As we try to describe good new approaches begging for application toward transformative change, the governing institutions of this society—corporate power, military power, media—continue to control all the levers of change as few systems before have done. These governing institutions are emphatically *not* interested in our transformative projects. This seems to apply nearly as much to the Obama regime as it does to Republicans. At most, each party gives systemic reform some lip service. But really, they prefer to co-opt, repress, or kill it in order to protect their benefactors.

In June 2011, the *Nation* published a special issue on "Reimagining Capitalism," edited by William Greider. In his introduction, Greider asked respondents to "imagine you have the ability to reinvent American capitalism. Where would you start?" Greider acknowledged that the political parties "are locked in small-minded brawls, unable to think creatively even to tell the truth about our historic crisis." As a result, he said, it would be extremely unlikely for the proposed ideas "to have any traction in regular politics. . . . [But] at some point, it will become obvious that our economy will not truly recover until American capitalism is refashioned, stripped of its self-aggrandizing excesses, and made to serve the interests of society rather than the other way around . . . this will require deep structural change, not simply new politics."

One response to Greider's call came from Villanova University professor

Eugene McCarraher: "*Why should we want to reinvent capitalism?* The nature and logic of capitalism are incorrigibly avaricious. As a property system driven by the need to maximize profit and production, capitalism is a giant, ever-whirling vortex of accumulation. . . . Capitalism compels us to be greedy, callous, and petty. It takes what the Greeks called *pleonexia*—an endless hunger for more and more—and transforms it from a tawdry and dangerous vice into the central virtue of the system. The sanctity of growth stems from this moral alchemy, as does the elevation of market competition into a model of human affairs."

As I suggested at the beginning of this book, certain aspects of capitalism seem okay to me, at least if they're small and local. For example, I don't see a problem with privately owned small businesses, in which someone begins an enterprise and it supports him or her, plus their family and community. But by "small," I mean *small!* Serving a single community. Rooted locally. No outside controllers. Predefined maximum size. Focused on a single line of products or services. Like the furniture store in the first graphs of this book. Or local farmers. Or the publisher of this book. Or the most marvelous small neighborhood coffeehouse/café located in Japantown, San Francisco, YakiniQ, run by a young woman who is there every day, Christy Hwang, and an ardent and cheerful young staff of students and artists. They are making a little profit but have no wish to be Starbucks.

Scale is paramount. We don't want Starbucks dominating the coffeehouses of the world. We don't want bookstores buying other bookstores in other towns— and we don't want any Amazon.com shutting down our local bookstores or turning reading solely into an Internet experience. We don't want banks buying other banks, or banks buying corporations, or banks or corporations buying governments. We don't want military contractors like General Electric buying up mass media. We don't want Rupert Murdoch owning hundreds of newspapers and broadcast outlets. We don't want some rich guy coming into our neighborhood and buying up all the property and local businesses for himself. We don't want a few companies like Google or Apple or Facebook dominating global communications in every form, as seems to be rapidly developing.

Some aspects of capitalism could be *easily* reformed, if only the laissez-faire, anti-government capitalist fundamentalists weren't depositing gifts into the pockets of legislators. Regulations could be advanced to control pollution and resource use, to prevent banking excess, to stop the buying of all politicians and government, and to promote equity.

Theoretically, we could quickly start mitigating inequity problems. We could require that the wealthy pay taxes at the same rate as the middle class, or at "surplus wealth" rates (graduated rates that went as high as 90 percent) that rose from the presidencies of Franklin Roosevelt and Harry Truman through

Dwight Eisenhower. We could/should have "excess profits" taxes on corporations to cover their *externalized* costs, or their *depletion* of the public-resources commons. We could ban tax havens and the many subsidized tax rates on financial transactions and inheritance. We could establish maximum and minimum guaranteed income levels. We could place controls on salary ratios within corporations. That's all good.

We could have better guarantees for workers' rights and better public services for everyone—health, education, transportation, childcare, elder care. We could prevent corporations from abandoning local communities and moving to China. And we could establish a new, more realistic relationship with the natural world, one based on equality, mutual dependence, and the full acknowledgment of limits.

Most people would appreciate these interventions. They're *all* good. I'm sure they would make us a happier society. Maybe Americans would start voting again and eating less junk food while permitting the natural world a deserved breather and long-term protections. Only oligarchs and "free-market fundamentalists" would oppose them. Unfortunately, however, they are in charge.

Those and a hundred others ideas are all doable by relatively simple acts of Congress and the President. Many other modern countries—like Norway, Sweden, Denmark, France, Germany, Italy, Spain, Iceland, and Japan—already enjoy many of those practices within their own versions of a kind of "hybrid" economics, an active collaboration of capitalist and socialist visions that most of these countries call "social democracy." Of course, they have problems, too—some of them caused, actually, by U.S. deregulation of finance under Clinton and Bush II—but, according to friends in Europe and members of my own family who live in Scandinavia, as well as the statistics we cited in the last chapter, these countries are in far better shape than we are in terms of public satisfaction, economic balance, environmental awareness, levels of equality, quality of public discourse, freedom from ideological domination, willingness to adapt, and happiness.

Could Americans living in the world headquarters of laissez-faire capitalism do anything like that? Obviously, such changes could happen in the United States only if the powers that be were willing to allow them. They won't. In the United States, ruled by the most ideologically rigid form of capitalism in the world, any level of government engagement, intervention, or partnership in anything but military adventures quickly gets labeled "socialist" or "communist." It makes transformation very difficult.

Unless there is an astonishing shift in political realities, or a massive uprising many times larger than the Occupy movement, viable changes would be incremental and politically unlikely. With government and media owned and operated by the super-wealthy, we can't expect much help from them. *They don't represent us.*

So then. What we can do right now is start discussing and creating alternative pathways, so we know what we agree on and what direction to start walking in. Hopefully each new path will fill with walkers and lead to others. Critical mass is the goal.

What follows, therefore, are a few of my favorites among ideas that are now being discussed among new-economy activists and thinkers.

Four Megashifts Toward a New Economics

1. Nature Comes First

Let's start with the most difficult point. *All* economic design must begin with and be forever bounded by a firm, articulated, and codified recognition that human beings and our economic patterns are embedded within nature. In fact, to our chagrin, human beings *are* nature, made of the same genetic and chemical materials as trees, bears, coral, fish, rats, cockatoos, centipedes, and neurons. We are one interlocked being. No more, no less. That, I believe, is the number-one-toughest reality for most of our society to accept.

It is the rankest absurdity to advance human-created economic systems that do not acknowledge the *carrying capacities* of the planet. Growth beyond carrying capacity is suicide. And ecocide.

"Human societies that presently dominate the world govern on the basis of a false understanding of the universe," says South African environmental lawyer Cormac Cullinen, author of *Wild Law*, who is the primary organizer in the drafting of The Universal Declaration of the Rights of Mother Earth.

"The core falsehood is that we humans are separate from our environment, and that we can flourish even as the health of the earth deteriorates. The governance structures, legal philosophies, and laws established by many societies reflect and entrench the illusion of separation and independence."

Ecological philosopher John Michael Greer, author of *The Long Descent*, says this: "To reverse course will require abandoning the core narrative of this society . . . the narrative of progress—the story that defines human existence as a single great upward trajectory from the caves to the stars, and insists that the present is better than the past and that the future will inevitably be better still, and that capitalism is [the] instrument for its achievement."

STEADY-STATE ECONOMICS

University of Maryland ecological economist Herman Daly has been the world's leading proponent of "steady state" principles. These are now incorporated into the programs of dozens of environmental groups, and actively promoted by the Center for the Advancement of the Steady State Economy (CASSE), as well as the rapidly advancing Transition Towns Movement, and most "new economy" think tanks. A steady state means that all economic activity that occurs within a finite context, such as the planet, must be contained well below the environmental carrying capacities of the earth, as expressed by limits to resource supply, maintenance of all biological and ecological balances, and waste capacities. No economy should attempt to expand beyond that point.

Some *individual* enterprises or types of production that are especially attuned to the economic realities and needs of a locale may continue to grow, at least for a time—e.g., local food systems, local clean-energy efforts, small retail and local services, and others—if they reflect specific community needs that are not otherwise fulfilled. That growth, however, is ultimately confined to the local. Larger enterprises that operate regionally or nationally—energy industries, transportation, public health, communications, resource gathering, etc.—will operate by rules that are consistent with a larger planning process. All environmental costs would be reflected in corporate accounting.

National measures of economic performance, now confined to measurements, such as GDP and GNP, and which indicate the totality of financial transactions for a nation, would have to be abandoned and replaced by new measures, reflecting levels of "sufficiency," equity, and general well-being. These must include accounting for beneficial unpaid services, such as family management, elder care, childcare, and the like, as well as negative externalities, and recognition of resource depletions from production. The genuine progress indicator (GPI) is one effective new measure among many others.

GPI goes well beyond GDP by measuring human and environmental costs of "uneconomic growth." The idea was developed by Herman Daly together with other ecological economists, including John Cobb and Richard Cobb (of Redefining Progress), and furthered by John Talberth, Noah Slattery, and Brian Czech and Rob Dietz of CASSE. The goal is to include potential negative indicators from excessive growth, including resource depletions, ozone depletion, various forms of pollution, and loss of farmlands or wetlands or forests, as well as social dangers, such as crime, health effects, family breakdown, the effects of overcrowding, among dozens of other impacts from overdevelopment.

GPI is now commonly used among environmentalists as a far better tool than GDP for defining and setting *limits to growth* compatible with natural carrying capacities, locally, regionally, nationally, and globally.

All of this activity is accompanied by a variety of campaigns consistent with the overall goal of *conservation*, rather than consumption: "Powering down" (the use of far less energy and the transition to "greener" systems), elimination of waste, recycling, shared community resources, and, most important, *crushing the ideology of consumerism*. Old-fashioned values like sufficiency and increased frugality will be the future social standards.

One more dimension, consistent with these necessities, is that *human population* has obviously grown far beyond any conceivable standard of viability on an Earth of disappearing resources. One effective way to relieve pressure on the planet would be to achieve a voluntary reduction in population, via far greater distribution and use of contraception, the easy availability of abortion, and/or abstinence where appropriate. If these are insufficient, more aggressive measures could be considered, e.g., much higher taxes on large families, to reflect their increased pressures on the public commons. In most countries today, including the United States, the opposite is now the case—we have *lower* taxes for larger families. This is almost certainly in hopes of generating more consumption.

CONTRACTION AND CONVERGENCE

A further consideration in any steady-state system is the matter of *distribution* of whatever resources that remain available. As the currently over-consuming nations of the world "power down" their energy and resources use, overall global consumption will need to be reduced to a level safely below what is sustainable for the planet.

Some nations and peoples already live at very low consumption levels, sometimes well below levels that can sustain well-being. Disparities like that are typically the result of centuries of prior exploitation or present neocolonial activity, making self-sufficiency impossible. The deplorable resource and land grabbing that we described in chapter VI is a good current example. Nations that have been historically deprived argue that they cannot reduce consumption as yet. In fact, they continue to need help in *increasing* consumption to a level of sufficiency—hence the emergence of an important new concept, making its way through environmental and social-justice communities: *contraction and convergence*.

The model goes like this: Work to achieve overall global economic *contraction* to a level safely below planetary carrying capacities. At the same time, within this lower level of overall consumption, work to establish an equitable plan for redistribution of sufficient available resources, until all remaining human societies are able to move toward *convergence* at an acceptable use level for everyone. That's a good one for the UN to try to work out. I hope it does better than it's doing with climate negotiations, which ideally should be operating on principles similar to the ones the G-77 (least developed countries) has long advocated.

I have heard this contraction-and-conversion discussion quickly dismissed by some ecology activists, who have said, in effect, "There will be no social justice on a dead planet." That's a good point; however, it's also true that there will be no living planet, and surely no viable societies, unless a greater degree of equity is achieved. People in desperate states are unlikely to sit still and see their families starved; the world might quickly fall into Armageddon. And with good reason. If we are to achieve a "steady state," then the operating formulas for it must obviously include a significant reallocation of the remaining resources and wealth to a level of "sufficiency" for everyone.

BIOLOGICAL RESTORATION AND THE PUBLIC COMMONS

Other important steps might include formal local and national initiatives toward *restoration* and conservation of nature. Many such initiatives are already under way, begun by environmental groups and private philanthropists. The most impressive that I have seen are those in South America on 2.2 million acres of the private lands operated by the nonprofit Conservacion Patagonia, created by Doug and Kris Tompkins in Chile and Argentina. They have succeeded over the past three decades in achieving full restoration of native wildlife populations, and native biodiversity, on a huge portion of these lands, and have then donated the restored lands to the appropriate governments. The lands have since been established as national parks with full protections.

Preserving large tracts of land by purchasing them has proved to be a good strategy. Ultimately, however, we will want to initiate public discussions on the very question of human "ownership" of any land or natural resources at all. If you believe in the idea of rights for all species, does it really make sense that one species of animal should have rights to "ownership" of the contributions of nature? This must also eventually apply to private ownership of land. These are "God-given" bounties for all creatures, and at best we might view ourselves stewards to protect nature, but *not* owners. As eco-socialist Joel Kovel argues in *The Enemy of Nature*, "No longer can the earth be privately owned." In socialist societies, of course, most ownership of land tends to be by the state, which hopefully acts in the interest of preservation and restoration, though this has not always been the case.

None of this discussion is new to most indigenous peoples of the world. Even today, it is generally not permissible for any individuals within traditional indigenous communities to "own" land, or any other part of nature, save for the small housing structures they construct and occupy, and a few personal tools and artifacts. This has been one important explanation for the fact, as mentioned in chapter VI, that indigenous peoples have succeeded to a far greater extent than any other societies or governments in retaining a high level of wilderness and biodiversity on their lands. It is estimated now that about half of the world's remaining resources, biodiversity, and genetic diversity are on lands that have been continuously occupied by indigenous peoples. This is also why the recent passage of the United Nations Declaration on the Rights of Indigenous Peoples (UNDRIP) was such a landmark achievement. It confirms that indigenous peoples have the rights of "free prior and informed consent," so as to be able to control any further outside intrusions onto their lands. The declaration also guarantees the right of indigenous peoples to practice and sustain their traditional governance forms and subsistence-based economic systems, which emphasize living well within the capacities of their immediate environments.

THE UNITED NATIONS' DECLARATION
OF THE RIGHTS OF MOTHER EARTH

Nowhere in the U.S. Constitution does the word "nature" appear. Instead, the Constitution "exalted the property-owning citizen beyond anything known previously in the history of political establishments," said the great philosopher-theologian Thomas Berry. He wrote that as part of the foreword to *Wild Law*, by Cormac Cullinan, in support of the proposed UN Declaration of the Rights of Mother Earth. "The difficulty is not with the rights granted to humans," said Berry, "the difficulty is that no rights and no protections were granted to any non-human mode of being."

Berry advocates that "any founding Constitution enacted by humans should state in its opening lines a clear recognition that human existence and well being are dependent on the well being of the larger Earth Community."

Such an idea sounds somehow impossible in a modern context, but it was not always so. Jason Marks reminds us in *Earth Island Journal* (spring 2012) that "the judges of ancient Rome recognized that certain biological principles—*jus naturale* in Latin—existed independently of the laws of men. Many Eastern religions assume the interconnectedness of all of nature's elements, including humans." And most indigenous communities over ten centuries have viewed the beings of the natural world in all respects to be equals, a concept that enabled a generational sustainability that continues to exist today in many parts of the world. Even in U.S. law, "the Endangered Species Act [signed by president Nixon] asserts that other beings have a right not to be made extinct," argues Marks.

Early in 2010 some 30,000 people gathered in Cochabamba, Bolivia, to draft a proposed UN Universal Declaration of the Rights of Mother Earth. It was formally submitted to the UN on April 22, 2010, with the backing of Bolivia, Ecuador, and other nations, plus dozens of environmental and indigenous-rights organizations, notably the Pachamama Alliance, Global Exchange, Council of

Canadians, and the Indigenous Environmental Network. It has not yet been voted on. If it is finally passed by the UN General Assembly, and then adopted by nation-states, it would be the second major international document that asserted support for a concept of human existence that is *not* superior to nature. The first was the UN Declaration on the Rights of Indigenous Peoples. Hopefully, this new document on Mother Earth rights would take its place alongside UNDRIP, as well as the UN's Universal Declaration of Human Rights, in establishing guiding principles and boundaries for future human behavior. The goal will then be to persuade all nation-states to adopt all these declarations as part of their domestic legal structures.

The fifty or so specific articles within the proposed Universal Declaration of the Rights of Mother Earth include the assertions that "we are all an interdependent part of Mother Earth," that Mother Earth is a living being with inalienable rights, and that all living beings share these rights equally.

2. The Primacy of Scale: Not Globalization, Localization

"There *is* a capitalist alternative gaining acceptance across the U.S. and throughout the world," says Michael Shuman, author of *The Small-Mart Revolution*, one of the country's leading localization activists. He proposes an alternative economic model rooted in local ownership and "import substitution."

The goal of import substitution is for countries and communities to become as fully self-sufficient as possible in all major aspects of an economy: food, energy, transport, light manufacture, etc. This was the popular trend among governments in smaller developing nations in the mid-1900s as they attempted to break free from their subservience to large powers and former colonial masters. Gandhi's India was the most well-known proponent of the trend. After World War II, the whole tendency was fiercely opposed by global corporations as potentially undermining the Bretton Woods system, as discussed in chapter II, and economic globalization. However, import substitution is now making a comeback, especially in South America.

Even if globalization were in every other way benign, its massive dependence on global transportation for nearly every step of the process would be enough to demand a shift to the local. As Bill McKibben wrote in his foreword to *The Small-Mart Revolution*, "If the average bite of food didn't have to travel two thousand miles before it reached your table, or if the power for the block where you live came from the windmill in the cul-de-sac; if the local bus was a pleasure to ride—think of the carbon that could be saved. It may be that shortening supply lines would help us ward off the worst effects of peak oil. It may also turn out to be the key to saving democracy . . . a town that takes real control of its economic and social lives, insulates itself from the corrupt decision making of the central authorities."

The most efficient mode of food production, says McKibben, is one in which local farmers grow food for their own communities and consume it locally. Also, there is much to be said for the intimacies, codependencies, and sense of solidarity that are built into such localized processes.

Some readers might view negatively the prospect that their lives would not be as filled with varieties of commodities from other countries. However, plenty of trade would persist for favored items, as it has for millennia. It's only that trade would not be mandatory, and local production would not be focused on export, and not run by a global corporate hierarchies.

The abiding principle in all this is "subsidiarity": whatever economic activity and governance can be achieved locally should be; if not locally, then regionally; if not regionally, then, and only then, nationally. The goal is to move power to control economy and politics as close as possible to the people. Ultimately, subsidiarity means that most economic priorities should shift to local agriculture, local manufacture, local resources, local energy, local currency, local banking, local governance, *minimum* trade. Outside investors must be strictly regulated; most profits must be retained locally. Full representation of local stakeholders on local corporate boards must be assured. Formal codification of "site here to sell here" policies; no local or regional companies moving manufacturing to low-wage countries.

Governance should *never* be globalized; there is no possibility for democratic function at a global level, though there is the possibility of cooperation. Decisions about global issues, including protections against pollution, international crime, the state of the oceans, or the appropriate cooperative means for wealth transfer from wealthy to poor may be discussed in cooperative international bodies.

In his role as coordinator for the Business Alliance for Local Living Economies (BALLE), Michael Shuman has pointed out some current struggles:

Ruthless chain stores like Costco, and major Internet retailers like Amazon, have steamrolled almost every local community's homegrown businesses. Five supermarket chains sell 42 percent of all our groceries. Home Depot and Lowe's account for 45 percent of all hardware and building supplies. Walmart now captures nearly 10 percent of *all* U.S. retail spending; it is the largest grocer in the country, the largest music seller, the largest jeweler, the largest furniture dealer, and the largest toy seller.

Currently, nearly all business subsidies in this country go to *non*-local firms. Subsidies to big business exceed $50 billion per year at the state and local level, and $63 billion per year at the national level, according to Shuman. That practice has to be reversed. But that is very difficult, since it's the big businesses that finance the election campaigns of the people who vote on the subsidies.

Local businesses continue to survive, without subsidies, because they continue to fulfill functions that large out-of-town enterprises cannot. The great majority of these smaller businesses are locally owned sole proprietorships, partnerships, and privately held small corporations. That they can sustain themselves is one sign of the viability of businesses that operate in their own communities. In fact, according to Shuman, in 2006, more than 20 million Americans generated $970 million of business with no employees at all. These businesses, many informal and home-based, generated more than 7 percent of the U.S. economy.

In addition, small local businesses are far more likely to serve as community "cash cows," recycling profits and wages among local beneficiaries and enterprises, while externally owned businesses export their wages and profits to some other place, out of state or out of country. "One hundred dollars spent at Borders," says Shuman, "would circulate thirteen dollars into the local economy; the same one hundred dollars spent at two local independent bookstores would circulate $45, three times more." For restaurants, the benefit is similar. Local restaurants offer similar advantages over chains. Labor standards are also likely to be higher, because the worker is your neighbor.

The question of maximum appropriate size would ideally be a point of discussion in communities seeking to transition to emphasize local scale enterprises. The goal, I think, is to retain a scale at which all employees can feel a personal relationship to management, and some ability and process for influencing it on key matters. During the 1960s, for example, the government of Cuba set the limit for private enterprises at "family size," with a maximum number of employees you could count on one hand. I think it is obvious that considerably larger privately owned enterprises than that can retain a community character, fit standards of community control, and retain effective workplace democracy. But if the maximum size rule means that all local businesses become too small for arms manufacture or oil exploration, then so be it.

Once set on the local-business pathway, communities can assist and accelerate the trend via policies favoring local purchasing, local product labeling, local currency, and similar supportive ventures. One already successful example is the rapid growth of the CSA (Community Supported Agriculture) movement— a highly popular arrangement in which urban customers support small organic farmers who supply them with produce.

DIRECT DEMOCRACY

The importance of *smallness* applies at least as much to the viability of democracy as it does to economic viability. Nearly everyone involved in political reform activity anywhere in the world claims to be acting on behalf of democracy. But definitions of "democracy" are highly varied.

The United States claims it is the world's greatest democracy, for example, though it is presently ruled by oligarchs, voter participation is lower than most other democracies', and actual public participation in policymaking is nil. The communist system, even under Stalin, described itself as democratic, and so did Maoism, because of community-level processes that theoretically enabled local control but in practice did not often do so.

Many other nation-states, even when they do not have a high level of control by their wealthiest classes, may be too large to be democratically managed. The effective control of the system has moved away from government to corporations and to oligarchs of great wealth.

When one family, the Adelmans of Las Vegas, can give Newt Gingrich $10 million to run ads in the Republican primaries in two states, is there any possible way of calling the process democratic? Meanwhile, Mitt Romney raised even more and was able to outspend Gingrich and the Adelmans, but we don't even know who gave him his money. There is no longer any requirement to report that fact. This is all thanks to the Citizens United Supreme Court decision of 2010, surely among the most democracidal court rulings in the history of the United States.

Even without such domination by the wealthy, "representative democracy" is nearly nonfunctional in political units beyond a certain size. The United States is an ideal example. We vote every few years for people we don't know and have never met, and whose communications with us are mainly through advertising (paid for by corporate and oligarchic interests), and over whom we immediately lose control and contact. This does not even begin to approximate functional democracy, by any definition. Clearly, voters are frustrated with this trend, as the United States consistently reports the lowest voter turnout of any "democratic" country in the world—an eloquent expression of systemic failure.

The larger the size of the population, and the larger the geographic scale of the system, the less likely any country can sustain any kind of definition of democratic function, and the more easily it can be dominated by centralized oligarchic, political interests.

If we are going to continue to tout ourselves as a democracy, we obviously have to completely separate money from politics. In most EU countries, for example, campaigns are publicly funded, no political advertising is permitted, media are required to provide equal free time/space for candidates, private donations are outlawed, and the campaigns run for specific relatively short periods, typically as little as four to eight weeks in northern European countries. In the United States, presidential campaigns may take more than one year and cost as much as a billion dollars for each side, thus increasing the role and power of very wealthy donors. No democracy can survive that.

Of course, the ideal goal would be to move closer to "participatory democracy" or "direct democracy"—where actual two-way communications could be sustained between all citizens (regardless of wealth), as part of the decision-making process. But to achieve this would certainly require shifting power to far smaller-scale political units.

Among modern nation-states, the closest example of participatory or direct democracy now takes place within the canton system of Switzerland, where a very high degree of local and regional decision making is undertaken at the community level and honored at the "national" level.

In *The Breakdown of Nations*, Leopold Kohr, the German-born, Welsh economist and philosopher, argues this way: "The small state is by nature internally democratic. In it, the individual can never be outranked by the power of government whose strength is limited by the smallness of the body from which it is derived. . . . The rulers of the small state, if they can be called that, are the citizen's neighbors. Since he knows them closely, they will never be able to hide themselves in mysterious shrouds. . . . The gap between him and government is so narrow, and the political forces are in so fluctuating and mobile a balance, that he is always able either to span the gap with a determined leap, or to move through the governmental orbit himself."

Kohr cites the case of the tiny country of San Marino, contained within northeastern Italy, where two consuls are chosen every six months. The result is that a high percentage of the citizenry actually gets to function briefly as their country's chief of state.

On the other hand, Kohr admits, "Neither the problems of war nor those relating to the purely internal criminality of societies disappear in a small-state world; they are merely reduced to bearable proportions."

Economic philosopher E. F. Schumacher wrote *Small Is Beautiful*, but in the end it is not an aesthetic matter. Small is also logical, manageable, survivable, and nonalienating—and far more personally engaging.

THE INDIGENOUS EXAMPLE

If we are going to use examples of direct democracy, such as Switzerland and San Marino, as expressing positive democratic virtues of smallness, I think it is imperative to discuss examples from indigenous peoples as well.

There are obvious variations in governance and economic structures among indigenous societies over many centuries, but they often share certain characteristics. Very rarely have they been economically expansive, for example, keeping their populations sufficiently small to live well within their traditional environments and resource base. Their small-scale philosophy has had a great deal to do with their ability to sustain themselves and their resources so successfully over many centuries, at least until they have been overrun by invading colonial powers.

While researching *In the Absence of the Sacred*, in the 1980s, I spent considerable time traveling among Indian communities, and especially among the Iroquois peoples, mostly in upper New York State. I was privileged to enjoy the guidance of Oren Lyons, faith-keeper of the Turtle Clan of the Onondaga Nation, outside of Syracuse, as well as John Mohawk (Seneca), who was lecturing at Buffalo University until he passed away. From all this, I learned that most (though not all) indigenous peoples of North America had in common three primary political principles: (1) All land, water, and forest is communally owned by the tribe; there is no private ownership of land or resources beyond the immediate household; (2) tribal decisions are made by consensus processes in open assemblies that include every tribal member, and (3) chiefs do *not*, in most cases, have hierarchal power, as we tend to think of them; they are more like teachers, advisors, or facilitators, and their duties are within specific realms (medicine, planting, war, relationships, ceremonies, etc.).

I also learned a great deal about the history of U.S.-Iroquois interactions, and specifically the degree to which, as many scholars now believe, the Iroquois Confederacy and the principles of its "Great Binding Law" influenced the creation and structures of the emerging U.S. confederacy and our form of confederated democracy.

Keep in mind that we are speaking of the early and mid-1700s, when the U.S. colonists were in very close contact with the Iroquois peoples who occupied most of the northeastern woodlands of what became the United States. Among non-indigenous societies at that time, there were *no* models of democratic governance. There had been some idealistic writings by Montesquieu, Hume, Kant, and a few others, though nothing about how to structure a democratic *confederacy* of states. Of course, there had been the examples, 1,500 years earlier, of Greece and Rome, which were functional "democracies"—at least among the ruling classes of the wealthiest men.

Several of America's Founding Fathers—including Benjamin Franklin, James Madison, John Adams, William Livingston, and Thomas Jefferson—were well acquainted with the Iroquois, who had been operating a successful "confederacy" of states, that had been functioning for two centuries, displaying highly developed democratic processes.

Try to picture the situation. The U.S. colonies were *small*. The biggest cities at that time were Boston, New York, and Philadelphia, which was the largest, with 13,000 people. These were small towns by today's standards. Between the cities were forests, and Indians, and several days of passage through their lands. So it was quite natural that people like Franklin, Madison, and Jefferson befriended many of the Iroquois "chiefs" and examined how they had successfully operated their confederacy of separate states for two centuries (including Mohawk, Oneida, Seneca, Onondaga, and Cayuga, joined later by Tuscarora). Their structures and processes began to inform the thinking of the colonists about the confederacy they were hoping to create. What were the rules? Who was in charge?

According to professor Donald Grinde, of the University of California,

Riverside, author of *The Iroquois and the Founding of the American Nation*, the Iroquois had significant influence on colonial leaders. Most Americans had "little knowledge of democratic governments," said Grinde, and saw Iroquois governance operating free of the kinds of abuses as were still routine among European monarchies at that time.

Grinde points out that James Madison made frequent forays to study and speak with Iroquois leaders. William Livingston was fluent in Mohawk and stayed with them over extended periods. John Adams and his family socialized with Cayuga chiefs on numerous occasions, and Thomas Jefferson and Benjamin Franklin wrote about them frequently. Franklin knew them particularly well, as he was often the printer and typesetter for Indian treaties, going back to 1736, and attended important tribal meetings. In 1754, when the Americans were trying to create the original Albany Plan of Union, forty-two members of the Iroquois Grand Council were invited to serve as advisors on how to operate confederate structures. Franklin's speech at that meeting included this: "It would be a strange thing . . . if six nations of ignorant savages [!!?] should be capable of forming such a union and be able to execute in such a manner that it has subsisted for ages and appears indissoluble, and yet that a like union should be impractical for ten or a dozen English colonies."

According to Grinde, Franklin later convened meetings of Iroquois chiefs in order to help "hammer out a plan that he acknowledged to be similar to the Iroquois Confederacy."

Nonetheless it remains one of America's unacknowledged national secrets that the Iroquois had any role at all in assisting these colonists in figuring how to achieve a new, confederated democracy.

What the colonists learned was that the Iroquois had formal democratic processes at every level. They included full suffrage and full inclusion for all people in the decision-making processes. Women had equal power. Each community did have "chiefs," who were usually (but not always) males, but they were appointed by a committee of women elders, and, as mentioned, the chiefs had no top-down authority. They were more like "leaders" or "managers." There was one chief for planting, for example, another for harvesting, and also a hunting chief. There was a chief for disputes, a ceremonial chief, a medicine chief, a war chief, and many others. Their tenures depended on the judgment of the women as to how they were performing; the women had the power to remove the chiefs, and often did if they were not doing a good job.

Within each of the six tribal societies, all major decisions were made by assemblies of the entire community, discussing matters as a group for as long as it took until a *consensus* was reached. According to Oren Lyons, there were no limits on individual speechmaking. Sometimes, if consensus was close but not achieved, the opposing party would voluntarily step aside on that issue, permitting consensus to be achieved. There were no filibusters.

Legislative discussions happened in two venues. The women met separately from the men, and each group made its own consensus decisions. Then they met together and tried for overall consensus. It was a bicameral process, not unlike the U.S. House and Senate, which, some say, was an attempt at imitation, except with only men involved. Sometimes this process took weeks. The people were not in a hurry, except in the occasional matter of military issues if things became urgent.

If a matter was discussed three times and no consensus could be reached, the matter was just dropped entirely. They took the view, said Lyons, that maybe it was not important enough to drive to a conclusion; anyway, there was the likelihood it would come up again some other time. As for criminal acts, the entire community sat in judgment for as long as the process took. When someone violated someone else in the community, the usual punishment was direct service to the people violated. The exceptions were for rape or murder, for which the punishment was likely to be permanent expulsion from the tribe, apparently a sentence worse than death.

Several times a year, there would be central gatherings of the entire Iroquois Confederacy, including most "chiefs" from all the tribes. Those discussions on "national" issues proceeded until consensus was reached. In the absence of a consensus, the "federation" had no powers over the individual "states," which retained a high degree of autonomy, a stipulation that Tea Partiers might approve of.

An important difference with the U.S. Constitution was that the Iroquois had no "executive branch." No Chief #1. The colonists, however, grew up under monarchies and apparently couldn't get used to the idea of no top dog. They added an executive branch to the U.S. Constitution to go with a judicial branch, and a bicameral all-male voting system, which did not add women for another century and a half. Each branch is supposed to have equal powers. Property rights are a primary focus in the U.S. version. So if the United States learned from the Iroquois how to construct a confederate government along democratic lines, we didn't learn quite enough.

3. Experiments in Corporate Values and Structure

The idea of a corporation is not intrinsically negative. There are likely to be operational advantages to communities if people organize themselves into groups, whatever their names, for collective purposes, agreeing on procedures, goals, rules, rewards, hierarchical form, etc. The problems have mostly come from the *mutation* of the model over the last century to formats featuring strict hierarchy and top-down management, unremitting focus on growth and institutional expansion, aggressive profit motives above all, subordination of any interest in the common good, obliviousness to any concern for impacts on the natural

world, corruptions of democracy through undue influence, and the encouragement of fantastic levels of inequity within the corporate structure, extending
to the wider society.

All of this is the direct result of the cardinal capitalist principle of *unending*
capital expansion as the primary motive for all activities and choices. A major
contributing factor has been the ability of large corporations to impact governments to serve corporate interests via endless special favors, rules, subsidies,
tax breaks, etc. By now it is as if the two—corporations and government—had
effectively merged. It is the primary problem we now face. If corporations do
not want positive change, how will their servants in government be able to
provide it?

This critique does not apply equally to all corporations. A small percentage
of the total are *worker-owned and operated* and perform under alternative sets
of guidelines, with far more equitable results. And there are some other legal
variations such as nonprofit corporations (501(c)(3) and 501(c)(4), and B Corporations, each of which has legally freed itself from the requirement that its
primary mission is to fulfill shareholders' profit expectations. And, again, *scale*
matters a great deal. Corporations operating only on a local and *small-scale* basis,
even when primarily seeking profits, do not routinely represent a significant
threat to community welfare, and when they do, they can be influenced locally
and directly.

REDESIGNING CORPORATE FORM

Activist groups and "new economy" think tanks are currently focusing on how
to control corporate behavior and impact. Here is an abbreviated list of some
of the most relevant reforms now being discussed and proposed:

- The legal purpose of the corporation should be to harness private interests
  to serve the public interest, rather than to seek profit. Corporate charters
  must specifically see the environment, local well-being and health, and
  welfare of working communities as *higher* values than distributed profits.
  Corporations shall accrue fair returns for shareholders, but not at the
  expense of the legitimate interests of other stakeholders in the local community and within the corporation.
- Corporations are *not* people, and do not have the First Amendment rights
  of people. They must *never* be permitted to donate funds or provide unpaid
  services to political campaigns; this produces inevitable inequities and
  distortions in the system. Neither should they ever be permitted to donate
  to or sponsor political campaign advertising. Citizens United must be
  repealed.
- Corporations must engage in "true cost accounting," including recognition and responsibility for all external harms from production. Once all

natural resources become part of a "natural commons," they are no longer private property and new rules and taxes will be applied to encourage controls on their use. Similar recognition applies to the use of "the intellectual commons" as part of the technological invention process. This, too, must be taxed at a meaningful rate.

- Boards of directors of corporations must include *at least* 50 percent of voting members from its own workers, and from other community stakeholders, such as environmentalists, public health officials, and community economic forecasters. Gus Speth, former head of the EPA, now teaching at the University of Vermont, calls this a transition from "shareholder primacy to stakeholder primacy" in *Orion* (March/April 2012.) Corporations shall be governed in a manner that is participatory, transparent, ethical, and accountable to workers and community stakeholders.

- Each corporation will have a maximum size, determined by the kind of business it is—e.g., a manufacturing businesses will usually be larger than a local bakery—and by the wishes of local communities, in recognition of local conditions.

- "Limited liability" for corporate shareholders and executives must be banned. Full liability for harms caused by corporate activity will apply to all responsible board or staff, and to shareholders as well.

- Communities may initiate "site here to sell here" policies. Corporations must orient their activities primarily to local needs and are not permitted to move to other communities without specific approval of local elected authorities. Mobility of corporate capital to other communities or other countries is not permitted. Globalized corporate activity is discouraged.

- Worker-owned corporations, as well as employee stock ownership plans (ESOPs), as well as activity by B Corporations and "not for profits" and other nonprofit forms of corporate activity, are encouraged and may be subsidized in certain cases.

- Ratios of salaries within corporations—from the highest-level executives to the lowest-level workers—which now average 185 to 1, must never exceed 10 to 1. In other words, that would still permit a top executive to make 10 times an average worker's salary, which might be $40,000, thus enabling the chief executive to be paid $400,000, a more than adequate salary for anyone, I think, in a world of diminished resources.

- Corporate "profits" above a fixed percentage of income should be understood as being "inefficient" from the point of view of the wider society, as we discussed in chapter VI. Such profits normally result from a combination of suppression of worker wages below levels of their actual economic contribution and inflated prices attempting to absorb everything the market will bear. Rules and formulas should be created to control such ratios in the interests of resource efficiency, worker rights, consumer rights, and overall fairness. Such profits should be conceived as "surplus profits" and taxed at higher-than-normal rates.

- Each corporation is chartered for only one kind of enterprise—e.g., manufacture of specific products, banking for public deposits, and/or local lending, etc. Banks are not permitted to buy other corporations.
- Fractional banking is banned. A small tax (.01%) should be levied on all financial transactions and currency speculations within the investment banking and trading system. Mergers of commercial and investment banks are not permitted. The size of banks must remain within strict limits. Transfers of banks from Wall Street operations to community banks are encouraged.
- Capital gains, investment income, and inheritance income must all be taxed at standard rates for ordinary income.
- Workers' rights to collective bargaining must always be honored. Flexible work schedules must be offered, as well as full health coverage, six-week maternity leaves, guaranteed pensions, and grievance procedures.
- To reflect environmental values, taxes should be levied on the basis of resource depletion and use and levels of pollution and waste, in addition to taxes on ordinary profits and, at a higher rate, excess profits. All corporate activity should follow the principle of "the polluter pays."
- In the case of new technology development, the "precautionary principle" must apply—i.e., all technology must be assumed harmful until it is proved safe.
- All corporate charters must contain specific recognition of the rights of nature. Protection and preservation of the natural world—in its full biological and genetic diversity, and all of its being—must be accepted as part of corporate purpose, as it is a necessity for a sane and sustainable system. Nature has inherent rights to exist in an undiminished, healthy condition, separate from services to humans, and this principle should be incorporated into local and national laws.
- Corporate charters should confirm an emphasis on conservation and the most efficient means in all aspects of economic activity; no economic activity may legally avoid that standard.
- Corporations judged to be operating against the public interest, by whatever standard, may be suspended or dismantled by the community, acting through a board authorized to assure the public welfare. Workers within corporations may also petition a public interest board to change behaviors of corporate management.

WORKER-OWNED COOPERATIVES

There are presently about 1.4 million "nonprofit" organizations in the United States registered with the IRS, accounting for about 5 percent of U.S. GDP. These organizations include everything from the Red Cross to various health, education, and human service organizations to some hospitals and universities and, of course, to most do-gooder campaign organizations, including environmentalists, social-justice campaigners, and left- and right-wing political action groups. These groups are generally qualified to raise "charitable" or other donations from the general public, or from grant-making foundations (which are themselves also 501(c)(3)s), or, in some cases, from government agencies wishing to support the groups' work.

More significant, perhaps, for the psychological and political challenge they represent to traditional corporations are worker-owned *cooperatives*. These are often "profit-seeking" entities, but, the businesses are *labor-managed* and operate through various forms of "workplace democracy." The workers in the business are themselves the owners, and often the collective financiers, and share in all proceeds. Workers set production policies, schedules, and working conditions, appoint and control managers and boards of directors, and regulate salary structures and ratios. They typically operate on one-worker/one-vote principles; all members are considered equal, and salary ratios vary very little from top management to production workers, typically in a range of three to one.

The most famous worker co-op in the world is the Mondragon family of enterprises in the Basque region of Spain, now including more than 100,000 workers in an integrated network of some 120 industrial service, construction, and high-tech businesses. The model has been copied extensively in Europe and is also seen in South America. It is especially popular now in Argentina, which has recently formed more than 200 such co-ops, and other, similar expressions that have grown out of the Horizontalist direct democracy movement in that country during the last decade.

According to Greg Macleod, author of *From Mondragon to America: Experiments in Community Economic Development*, the entire Mondragon enterprise was founded by an idealistic Christian activist, Don José María Arizmendiarrieta, in the mid-1950s. His earliest "experiments" with the form had taken place in 1943, while Don José María was working "with the youth of Mondragon in social-economic activities such as the Young Christian Workers, the Workers Fraternity of Christian Action, etc." Soon after, he founded a Poly-Technical School in Mondragon, leading to the businesses. MacLeod reported that "the intentions of Mondragon's founding group were altruistic and community-oriented . . . while the traditional capitalist corporations merge [with other

enterprises] in order to *reduce* jobs, the community-oriented Mondragon Corporation merges to *create* jobs."

Mondragon systems emphasize the equality of all workers—one vote to each
member—the distribution of "profits" to workers, and the "supremacy of decision making by the 'general assembly' of all workers."

The Mondragon experiment spread rapidly in Spain, elsewhere in Europe,
and in South America. In Valencia, for example, the Cooperative Entrepreneurial Group of Valencia includes over twenty co-ops. The goals of most of
these enterprises are stated as encouraging workplace democracy, alleviating
the alienation of the workplace, encouraging participatory or direct democracy,
restraining the growth of capitalism, and promoting the spread of the model
more widely.

Worker ownership has sometimes been described as a "Third Way"—not
capitalist, not socialist. There are differences between means and ends among
firms in which *capital controls labor*, or in which the *state controls labor and capital*. In this case, it is *labor controlling capital* to produce an alternative positive
outcome.

In the United States the worker co-op movement is still small, comprising
about 7 percent of employed workers, but it is advancing. In a 2011 article in
the *Nation*, Gar Alperovitz reports, "There are more than 11,000 companies
owned entirely or in significant part by some 13.6 million employees in the U.S.
Most have adopted Employee Stock Ownership Plans; these so-called ESOPS
democratize ownership, though only some of them involve participatory management."

He gives the example of Gore-Tex, which has roughly 9,000 employee
owners at forty-five worldwide locations and generates annual sales of $2.5
billion. And at Seventh Generation, one of the leaders in environmentally
friendly cleaning and personal products, no one can be paid more than fourteen times the lowest base pay or five times higher than the average employee.
Alperovitz also cites B Corporations, which no longer have to fear stockholder
lawsuits if the company decides to pursue social goals ahead of profits. King
Arthur Flour, for example, "can be explicit, stating that 'making money in itself
is not our highest priority.'" So far only four states have passed B Corporation
legislation—Maryland, Vermont, New Jersey, and Virginia—but "many others
are likely to follow," says Alperovitz.

In a previous article in the *Nation* (February 11, 2010), Alperovitz and Thad
Williamson described the Evergreen Cooperative Laundry, a new model of
large-scale worker-and-community-benefiting enterprise. An industrial-size,
worker-owned, "thoroughly green" operation in Glenville, it is the first of ten
major enterprises in the works in Cleveland, where the poverty rate is more than
30 percent and the population has declined from 900,000 to 450,000 since 1950.

Alperovitz and Williamson point out that the Evergreen model draws heavily from the Mondragon Cooperative. Additional applications of the model are being considered in Atlanta, Baltimore, Pittsburgh, Detroit, and a number of other cities around Ohio. "The model takes us beyond both traditional capitalism and traditional socialism. The key link is between national sectors of expanding public activity and procurement, on the one hand, and a new local economic entity, on the other, that 'democratizes' ownership and is deeply anchored in the community."

4. Hybrid Economics

To me, one of the most frustrating experiences of the present day is the "either/or" dynamic of the whole discussion. If you feel okay about capitalism, or most elements of capitalism, you'd better not say anything nice about some features of social democracy as practiced in Europe, which lets some socialism creep into its capitalism, and vice versa. Or about socialism. You may be ostracized. I have friends, economists, who will walk out of the room if someone says something appreciative of some aspect of socialism, or communism, for that matter, or of what some socialist country might be experimenting with.

Actually, I hear similar responses, in the reverse, from socialists. Some think that even small, privately owned neighborhood businesses are a grave threat to an otherwise orderly system. Such small profit-making businesses might eventually serve to train and feed instincts toward acquisition, growth, market domination, competition, and all those other bad things. Everybody has to choose, like picking sides for the Super Bowl game. But, we already lost the Super Bowl. The other side lost, too. Things are not working out for anybody but the 1%. This is a time to put aside the ideologies we cling to and look around for something else—at least let's see what's on offer.

Take the case of the Iroquois whom we just discussed in the last section. They had centuries of experience with democratic governance and economic systems, and with how to create federated structures, which they were pleased to share with Benjamin Franklin, Thomas Jefferson, and quite a few other Founding Fathers. How great it is that the Americans were open and receptive to experimenting with some of those offerings? This interaction surely at least partly influenced the U.S. Constitution that we all love, and that the Tea Party says came from God. We certainly got the idea of bicameral legislatures out of this, and some ideas about how to organize federalism and consensus processes (like, say, town halls?). Soon after, so did the Europeans, once they finally broke away from their monarchies.

But that raises another curiosity. Studies of the Iroquois and other successful non-hierarchical, North American matrilineal indigenous societies of that period by American anthropologist, legislator, and businessman Lewis Morgan (1818–1881) apparently *also* informed European thinking of the mid-1800s, particularly about processes like collectivity (collective ownership) and communalism (shared authority). Morgan's observations notably influenced Karl Marx and became the basis of Friederick Engels's 1884 classic, *The Origin of the Family, Private Property and the State*. So we have Franklin, Jefferson, and Morgan, et al., in the United States, and Marx and Engels in Europe, reflecting on the same indigenous sources for the formulation of their political ideas. If that's not an argument for openness, I don't know what is.

CENTRAL PLANNING?

Saral Sarkar is an economist born in India, now living and writing in Germany. He identifies himself as an "eco-socialist." In his book *Ecosocialism or Barbarism*, he offers a strong case for central planning as we try to find our way out of the mess we are in now. The title refers to the fact that he sees a breakdown coming soon, if we do not get together and figure out a productive common pathway incorporating both ecological and social values. He argues that capitalism cannot possibly save us.

> "We cannot have both ecological sustainability and the growth dynamics of capitalism. . . . No capitalist can willingly accept a low-level steady-state economy. Therefore, the *state* must take up the task of organizing the retreat. It must be a *planned* retreat; otherwise, there will be terrible chaos and calamity. The state must overrule the primacy of profit and the growth compulsion. That means an economic framework plan must consciously reach an agreement on what, how much, and how to produce, and how much energy and how many resources are to be allocated to what."

I agree with Sarkar on this. We have got to make a plan. And we need the kind of governance process that makes plans. But how do we make a government that works and is not as corruptible as all the others that preceded it?

Sarkar suggests that a "multiplicity" of forms of socialization could be tried—state ownership, worker co-ops, and also the continued private ownership of smaller local businesses, plus providing considerable autonomy for local economies. "But finance capital (banks and insurance companies) and the greater part of the means of production can no longer remain under private control." Such central enterprises would have to be "nationalized."

He is making the case for a modified socialism. Some call it democratic socialism. But how do we get from here to there? And how could we assure that a participatory democracy would prevail?

CAN WE LEARN FROM CHINA?

We hear often about what China is doing wrong. And its mere size certainly seems to disqualify it as any kind of future model society in a resource-depleted world. However, given the country's tremendous success in certain areas—for example, the growth of its middle class is faster than any country in the world—it seems prudent to at least get acquainted with some things it might be doing right.

In January 2012, I attended a San Francisco World Affairs Council lecture given by Ann Lee, a native of Hong Kong who grew up in the United States and is now a professor of economics and finance at NYU. Lee was discussing her new book, *What the U.S. Can Learn from China*. She was explicitly *not* suggesting that China had a better system, nor that Americans should try to emulate the Chinese system. But she suggested that the system had evolved over recent decades into a mixed system that combines socialism with various forms of capitalism. It retains traditional socialist activity, with nationalized planning and operations in crucial areas. There are also "state capitalist" enterprises—state-owned businesses that compete in the free market—and state-authorized but privately owned enterprises, and some entirely free-market private operations. And there are extensive, highly varied *local* experiments in diverse forms of individual profit seeking (particularly in agriculture).

Lee suggested that the United States was limiting itself by leaving nearly all important economic concepts and decisions to the free-market system, with very little long-term planning. The U.S. economy, she said, driven solely by the short-term profit motive and individual gain, might be missing the bigger picture. Every successful business venture makes long-term plans, so shouldn't governments do the same? Perhaps the failure to plan has helped lead us to a crisis point that we could have anticipated.

China has experienced 9–12 percent growth for nearly two decades, producing those huge middle classes. The growth rate is now apparently declining slightly—expected to be about 8 percent in 2012. A bubble may be leaking. A lot of the growth in the past was due to production by low-wage factory workers making U.S. iPads, iPods, and similar products, and just about everything you see at Walmart. Growth has also come from the government's focus on advanced technical training, and by leaping ahead in many high-tech industries, like solar energy.

Of course, limits to growth will soon apply as much to China as to the U.S. and everywhere else. Labor costs are now rising in China—a good thing. And resources are getting scarce. The Chinese seem to be well aware of this, judging by the extreme aggressiveness with which they are now buying up remaining lands and resources in Africa, South America, the Pacific, and elsewhere—a bad thing. As we have mentioned earlier, these land grabs, whether by Chinese or

American interests, are destroying viable susbsistence farming in certain areas of Africa. China is also making plans about how to deal with the effects of a lower growth rate.

Professor Lee pointed out that some of the recent success of the Chinese model has emerged from its increasing *flexibility*. This has simultaneously combined state-run pilot projects, five-year plans, and "special economic zones," among other testing processes. These experiments, deployed in different parts of the country, compare varieties of approaches for different economic activities. Sometimes they include tax incentives, or "carrots and sticks," tested against each other for efficiency and market viability. Sometimes one region of China will compete with another, to see which factors work best.

This willingness to experiment has led China to change many of its policies, says Lee. For example, when Premier Deng noted that certain government-sponsored rural experiments showed that farmers became more engaged and productive when they shared in the profits from their own work, he initiated new zones of rural, family-run, *privately owned* agricultural activities that are now thriving—in other words, a quiet shift toward a predefined area of local capitalism.

Government planning in China is also applied within university systems, Ann Lee said, enhancing their role in bringing forth appropriately trained professionals, especially in "green tech" areas. Lee discussed the role of "meritocracy" in choosing national political and economic leaders. A lot of advancement in China, she said, is now based on step-by-step, up-the-ladder promotions over decades, including "practical experience running large organizations, from state-owned enterprises to regulatory agencies." Also required are a series of competency tests and evaluations, although high levels of "cronyism" continue to persist in some aspects, as it does to a degree in all countries.

Lee pointed out that many U.S. professions, such as medicine, law, and even building trades and others, already require competency tests before people are permitted to practice—bar exams, state medical exams, etc. China applies similar systems to the testing for public officials, including government officials who rise anonymously—we rarely hear about them; then suddenly, there they are.

She suggested that the lack of a long-term plan in the United States and of long-term academic training in critical fields might be an important cause of our failure to compete successfully in many areas right now. Attending only to short-term-growth needs of the stock market may be a good formula for long-term failure.

NEW-ECONOMY MODELS

I have tried to keep up with the work of the new-economy think tanks to see what models they are emerging. Good information sources are the New Economy Network and the New Economy Institute (not related), which report on a very wide range of exploration that they update on websites and try to publish quickly.

As for comprehensive transitional governance plans, however, there have been very few published so far. Notable among them is *Occupy World Street*, by Danish/Canadian businessman turned eco-village entrepreneur Ross Jackson. It lays out an elaborate global and local set of governance options under the overall name of the Gaian League, merging some centralized socialist-style planning with more liberal social democracy and private enterprise. One provocative notion, I thought, was the creation of an executive body for the league, and effectively the world, composed of only *small* countries, reversing present global practices. Jackson suggested these might include the likes of Denmark, Bolivia, Sri Lanka, Costa Rica, Iceland, Norway, Venezuela, Senegal, Bhutan, New Zealand, Maldives, Tunisia, Mauritius, Malaysia, and Switzerland, representing very mixed ideologies, in different stages of development, but sharing strong interests in equity and sustainability.

Another useful report is *Prosperity Without Growth: Economics for a Finite Planet*, by Tim Jackson (not related to Ross Jackson), who is an economics commissioner for the U.K. Sustainable Development Commission. The book redefines the meaning of such key values as "prosperity," "well-being," and "growth" to show how human economic satisfaction can be achieved within predefined levels of sufficiency and sustainability, rather than acquisition in a resource-diminished postcarbon world.

The Tellus Institute of Boston has issued a series of relevant reports. One is called "Visions of Regional Economies in a Great Transition World," by Richard A. Rosen and David Schweickart (2010), a comparative analysis of some of the mixed systems we might explore, with their positive and negative points, and hints about how to merge their better ideas.

The report explicitly rejects U.S.-style laissez-faire capitalism as any kind of viable pathway toward sustainability or future equity. Can we all agree with that? It then presents summaries of three possible political scenarios for the future.

The first they call Agoria, which they also label "Sweden Supreme." Agoria is capitalist, says the report, "but it has been tamed by government regulations and oversight." Some large shareholder companies continue to exist, but the government sector is far larger and more economically proactive than twentieth-century social democracies, and it is guided by central principles that include long-range ecological planning, multi-stakeholder controls, zoning and land-use boards, very high taxes on pollution, and sparing use of resources.

The second model is Ecodemia, a form of socialism. In this model, the major means of production are owned by society as a whole, not by private individuals, and the country is run through a form of market socialism. It is meant to promote workplace democracy, efficiency, and innovation, and stakeholder guidance at the community level, including as to the allocation of investment.

Most businesses are governed by employees—one person, one vote—and a workers' council serves as the board of directors. Regulatory boards supervise each industry. Jobs and minimum wages are guaranteed by government. Environmental sustainability is a primary value.

The third model, which the authors call Arcadia, envisions a world of decentralized local economies, only loosely affiliated. It works "toward locally self reliant economies, direct democracy in decision-making," and gives nature utmost value. It is best suited to rural regions and features co-op farming while discouraging all export industries. It comprises mixed enterprises, including sole proprietorships, local retail co-ops, and township and village enterprise, with few larger ones. The inspiration for the model is E. F. Schumacher's *Small Is Beautiful*. It stands firmly against growth and unnecessary commodity consumption, and it favors the rules of "subsidiarity" and local control. It's "designed to maximize happiness." Let's all move there. The only thing missing is movie theaters.

However, in looking at the new-economy groups, I was alarmed at the absence of two important economic arenas: the control and role of the military, and the media. In the United States these giant industries operate mostly as private enterprises (operating with government authorization and, in the case of the military, considerable funding). Both therefore remain mostly driven by the built-in needs of corporations and their stockholders—expansion, profit, growth, new markets, freedom, etc. This is certainly not a good way to leave things.

We really do not want military contractors to any longer have incentives to persuade governments or populations that more armaments or wars are desirable for the welfare of the country, when corporations' primary concern is really the welfare of the corporations. New rules against lobbying on military policy and for military contracts, and against all campaign contributions from any corporation involved in military production, are certainly mandatory. Military planning and production must be limited to government-run agencies, rather than private enterprise. It would surely be cheaper, more efficient, less wasteful, and less driven by self-interest.

As for media, most democratic countries of the world have put a great deal more emphasis on public, noncommercial channels of communication than has the United States—this is certainly true of most countries in Europe, which are managed and controlled by independent public agencies and operate the airwaves as a public commons. This was once also the policy in the United States, but, as with most other aspects of society, the steady trend has been toward privatization. Now, a small number of giant corporations have control over most of the imagery and ideas that are projected into our brains day after day, excluding whatever, in their judgment, is not helpful to the primary purpose of their efforts: advancing commodity consumption. The question of the desirability and degree of continuation of commercial broadcast media, especially as to its dominance by advertising, needs to be included at the forefront of any transformative agenda.

Uncharted Territory

So, have we finally answered the question "from the audience" about a clear alternative model to capitalism? Maybe not. We don't yet see a fully evolved system ready to be locked into place, solving all problems. We need to create it. We are in uncharted territory.

Future success can come only once each of us separately, and also together as local communities and larger societies, comes face-to-face with the reality that we have been living within a set of false assumptions.

The world of endless abundance is gone. We need to become open to a new, less arrogant and dominant relationship with nature, which in the end is the only viable source of our survival and whose rules of balance, interaction, and good health will ultimately prevail. Once we succeed in this mental transition, we may look forward to some obvious benefits from it—the pleasures of nature's re-emergence in our awareness may prove surprisingly fulfilling, not to mention sustaining.

We also need to accept that our "way of life" is in inevitable decline. We cannot assume that the economic and financial worlds constructed around us can last for another generation. The economic model that our society accepted totally, and expected to be permanent, turned out to be viable only in the short term (two hundred–plus years), under conditions of a prevailing abundance that no longer exists. The current mad scrambling and squabbling among countries of the world to grab the last resources—food-growing lands, rare minerals, traditional energy sources, fresh water—must eventually give way to a recognition that scarcity has replaced abundance. So, *cooperation* must replace *competition*.

We need to act fast to purge from our consciousness the idea that there is any conceivable way to reorganize a sustainable society by leaving things to a free-market process. The paradigm of life as acquisition and consumption will eventually give way to the concepts of life as interaction, communication, community, and sufficiency, living within the capacities of nature. This is crucial to acknowledge. No capitalist society will ever give rights of nature first priority.

Also, some serious questions remain about whether any single new economic form is even desirable. Perhaps ultimately what we seek is a multiplicity, a mosaic, of local democratic forms that express diverse instincts and ideas that are appropriate to local places, peoples, and conditions and do not seek connections to any kind of larger central system and its propensity toward top-down control. This would certainly be consistent with our prior admonitions on scale. It would also be consistent with models of success and sustainability from many indigenous communities.

As of now, the state of discourse about any these matters in the United States is pathetic. As of March 2012, after twenty-three public debates during the Republican primary campaigns, not one question was asked of the candidates about environmental matters, except that Newt Gingrich was criticized for a photo eight years ago with Nancy Pelosi warning of climate change, and Mitt Romney was attacked for once mentioning climate as a problem, back when he was governor of Massachusetts.

The prevailing unconsciousness is stunning: The *New York Times* reported (February 5, 2012) that thousands of right-wing activists are now attending town council meetings to protest "local and state efforts to control sprawl and conserve energy. They branded any government action for things like public transportation or preserving open space, as part of a United Nations–led conspiracy to deny property rights and herd citizens toward cities." Tea Party members proclaimed it as part of the UN Agenda 21 plot against private property. The Republican governor of Maine, Paul LePage, has concurred, canceling a project to ease major highway congestion. (Agenda 21 actually is a nonbinding UN plan to "encourage nations to use fewer resources and conserve public land.")

The United States may not yet be fertile ground for *any* plan to save the world. We may need to work around it until things shift.

I think it would be a good idea for all of us to concentrate far more on learning about, creating, and supporting truly participatory democratic processes. We have touched on this only briefly with some examples of effective nonhierarchical democratic "assemblies" beginning with the Iroquois. Would that they could advise us further on such matters.

We could all doubtless learn more from the Occupy movement, whose assemblies have been revelations in small-scale democracy. And the Horizontalists from Argentina, who used similar public meetings successfully for nearly a decade, especially while occupying and reviving abandoned factories and other community workplaces. They created a variety of consensus-based processes among local communities, all of whom reject the idea of "power-over." I recommend the book *Horizontalism*, by Marina Sitrin, who herself was a discussion leader during Occupy Wall Street. The book contains dozens of interviews with participants elaborating on what they learned about working cooperatively without bosses. Sitrin also reports on similar groups, like the Zapatistas of Chiapas, and the Landless Peasant Movement that emerged in Brazil about a decade ago.

Those are all people who are actively exploring how to manage direct democratic processes, and whose skills may soon be in great demand. But there's a big problem. Such lessons in direct democracy tend to apply best to very small societies, able to control their local systems. Perhaps Leopold Kohr was right when he advised the "breakdown" of nations if we truly seek a meaningful new democracy, an opinion shared by E. F. Schumacher. But there are not many takers for such an idea. So far.

Meanwhile, for those who want to do something within their communities *right now*, it would be a very good idea for everyone to get acquainted with the work of the Transition Towns Network, begun in southwest England about a decade ago. That movement accepts the absolute necessity of a rapid transition to local economies, in response to the crises of peak oil and climate change. It is helping train local communities and local businesses in re-gearing themselves quickly toward new, powered-down, self-sufficient, democratically conceived sets of local standards. This may help withstand the future traumas we can now anticipate, and congeal a new sense of community within a new paradigm of local self-sufficiency. This is a movement that is growing very quickly, with more than one thousand affiliated small towns and communities in Europe, the United States, and Canada already engaged.

We have only just started. Personally, I think the long-term answers will surely lie with the evolution of a "hybrid" model, featuring aspects of all ideas and practices that have something to offer. I agree that at the same time that we need to give primacy to local systems and self-sufficiency, we also need a greater degree of central planning and management of crucial services—from healthcare to energy, transportation, media, disease control, education, environmental protection, social welfare, and the like. But this can be achieved only if we can recover a higher level of trust in government, free of corporate and oligarchic domination. In the interim, I think we could do worse than to look to the social democracies of Europe for short-term help in this process. They are not perfect, but they seem to be doing things better than others right now.

Over the next few years, it may be impossible to congeal a single new economic form—because of the global scale of our current problems, and the major conceptual and behavioral changes that are going to be necessary. A lot of things have to change, and in an organized manner. And we certainly cannot leave it to capitalists to engineer this one; it is not in their DNA.

I am afraid that it will not yet be possible to conclude this global conversation. But that's okay. Nobody yet has a final answer. We need to keep the process open. The chasm is still very wide from here to where we need to go, but we begin to see across to the other side. So let's put aside our ideologies, stay open, and keep talking.

Bibliography

Abram, David. *Becoming Animal: An Earthly Cosmology*. New York: Pantheon, 2010.

Alperovitz, Gar. *America Beyond Capitalism – Reclaiming Our Wealth, Our Liberty, and Our Democracy*. Hoboken: Wiley, 2005.

Anglemyer, Mary and Eleanor R. Seagraves, eds. *The Natural Environment: An Annotated Bibliography on Attitudes and Values*. Washington, DC: Smithsonian, 1984.

Anielski, Mark. *The Economics of Happiness: Building Genuine Wealth*. Gabriola Island, BC: New Society, 2007.

Bacevich, Andrew J. *Washington Rules: America's Path to Permanent War*. New York: Metropolitan, 2010.

Bagdikian, Ben. *The New Media Monopoly*. Beacon. 2004.

Barnes, Peter. *Capitalism 3.0*. San Francisco: Berrett-Koehler, 2006.

———. *Who Owns the Sky? Our Common Assets and the Future of Capitalism*. Island Press, 2003.

Barreiro, Jose', ed. *Thinking in Indian: A John Mohawk Reader*. Golden, CO: Fulcrum, 2010.

Boyle, David and Andrew Simms. *The New Economics*. London: Earthscan, 2009.

Brand, Stewart. *Whole Earth Discipline: An Ecopragmatist Manifesto*. New York: Viking, 2009.

Brands, H.W. *American Colossus: The Triumph of Capitalism, 1865-1900*. New York: Doubleday, 2010.

Brangwyn, B. & Hopkins, R. *Transition Initiatives Primer: becoming a Transition Town, City, District, Village, Community or even Island*. Totnes: Transition Network, 2008.

Bremmer, Ian. *The End of the Free Market: Who Wins the War Between States and Corporations?* New York: Portfolio, 2010.

Broad, Robin and John Cavanagh. *Development Redefined: How the Market Met Its Match*. Boulder: Paradigm, 2009.

Butler, Smedley D. *War is a Racket*. Port Townsend: Feral House, 2003.

Callenbach, Ernest. *Ecotopia*. Bantam. 1977.

Campbell, C.J. *Oil Crisis*. Brentwood: Multi-Science, 2005.

Capra, Fritijof and Hazel Henderson. "Qualitative Growth: A Conceptual Framework for Finding Solutions to Our Current Crisis That Are Economically Sound, Ecologically Sustainable, and Socially Just." 30 April 2009. The Capital Institute. 30 March 2011

Carson, Rachel. *Silent Spring*. Houghton-Mifflin. 1962.

Carlsson, Chris. *Nowtopia: How Pirate Programmers, Outlaw Bicyclists, and Vacant-Lot Gardners are Inventing the Future Today!* Oakland: AK, 2008.

Carlsson, Chris, ed. *Ten Years That Shook the City: San Francisco 1968-1978*. San Francisco: City Lights Books, 2010.

Chang, Ha-Joon. *Twenty-three Things They Don't Tell You About Capitalism*. New York: Bloomsbury, 2010.

Chomsky, Noam. *Hegemony or Survival: America's Quest for Global Dominance*. New York: Metropolitan, 2003.

Copy Workshop, The. *The Book of Gossage*. Chicago: The Copy Workshop, 2006.

Court, Jamie. *Corporateering: How Corporate Power Steals Your Personal Freedom . . . And What You Can Do About It*. New York: Penguin, 2003.

Curry, Patrick. *Ecological Ethics: An Introduction*. Cambridge: Polity, 2011.

Cavanagh, John and Jerry Mander, eds. *Alternatives to Economic Globalization: A Better World is Possible*. San Francisco: Berrett-Koehler, 2004.

Catton, Jr., William R. *Overshoot: The Ecological Basis of Revolutionary Change*. University of Illinois Press. 1982.

Cullen, Francis T., William J. Maakestad, and Gray Cavender. *Corporate Crime Under Attack: The Ford Pinto Case and Beyond*. Cincinnati: Anderson,1987.

Cullinan, Cormac. *Wild Law: A Manifesto for Earth Justice*. White River Junction, VT: Chelsea Green, 2011.

Curl, John. *For All People: Uncovering the Hidden History of Cooperation, Cooperative Movements, and Communalism in America*. PM Press. 2009.

Daly, Herman. *Beyond Growth*. Boston: Beacon Press, 1997.

———. *Ecological Economics and Sustainable Development*. Edward Elgar Publishing, 2008.

Daly, Herman E. and John B. Cobb, Jr. *For the Common Good: Redirecting the Economy Toward Community, the Environment, and a Sustainable Future*. Boston: Beacon, 1989.

Danaher, Kevin, Shannon Biggs, and Jason Mark. *Building the Green Economy: Success Stories from the Grassroots*. Sausalito: PoliPointPress, 2007.

Devall, Bill and George Sessions. *Deep Ecology*. Salk Lake City: Gibbs Smith, 1985.

Dobbin, Murray. *The Myth of the Good Corporate Citizen: Democracy Under the Rule of Big Business*. New York: Stoddart, 1998.

Douthwaite, Richard. *The Growth Illusion: How Economic Growth Has Enriched the Few, Impoverished the Many, and Endangered the Planet*. Tulsa: Council Oak, 1993.

Down, Douglas F. *The Twisted Dream: Capitalist Development in the United States Since 1776*. Cambridge: Winthrop, 1977.

Drucker, Peter F. *Post-Capitalist Society*. New York: HarperBusiness, 1994.

Duchrow, Ulrich. *Alternatives to Global Capitalism: Drawn from Biblical History, Designed for Political Action*. Utrecht: International, 1995.

Ekins, Paul and Manfred Max-Neef (eds.) *Real-life economics: Understanding wealth creation*. London: Routledge, 1992.

Engels, Frederick; edited by Eleanor Burke Leacock. *The Origin of the Family, Private Property and the State*. New York: International, 1972.

Foster, John Bellamy, Brett Clark, and Richard York. *The Ecological Rift: Capitalism's War on the Earth*. New York: Monthly Review, 2010.

Gandhi, Mahatma; edited by Judith Brown. *The Essential Writings*. Oxford: Oxford UP, 2008.

Gannon, Zoe, and Neal Lawson. *The Advertising Effect*. London: Compass, 2010

Gelbspan, Ross. *Boiling Point: How Politicians, Big Oil, and Coal, Journalists, and Activists Have Fueled the Climate Crisis—and What We Can Do to Avert Disaster*. New York: Basic, 2004.

Georgescu-Roegen. Nicholas, *The Entropy Law and the Economic Process*. iUniverse, 1999.

Gerson, Joseph and Bruce Birchard, eds. *The Sun Never Sets . . . Confronting the Network of Foreign U.S. Military Bases*. Boston: South End, 1991.

Gladstone, Brooke and Josh Neufeld. *The Influencing Machine: Brooke Gladstone on the Media*. New York: Norton, 2011.

Goodell, Jeff. *How to Cool the Planet: Geoengineering and the Audacious Quest to Fix Earth's Climate*. New York: Mariner, 2011.

Gray, John. *False Dawn: Delusions of Global Capitalism*. New York: New, 1998.

Greer, John Michael. *The Ecotechnic Future: Envisioning a Post-peak World*. Gabriola Island, BC: New Society, 2009.

———. *The Long Descent: A User's Guide to the End of the Industrial Age*. Gabriola Island, BC: New Society, 2010.

Greider, William, *The Soul of Capitalism, Opening Paths to a Moral Economy*. Simon & Schuster, 2004.

Hahnel, Robin. *Panic Rules*. South End Press. 1999.

———. *ABCs of Political Economy*. Pluto Press, 2003

Hamilton, Clive. *Growth Fetish*. London: Pluto, 2004.

Hartmann, Thom. *Unequal Protection: The Rise of Corporate Dominance and the Theft of Human Rights*. San Francisco: Berrett-Koehler, 2002.

Harvey, David. *The Enigma of Capital and the Crisis of Capital*. Oxford: Oxford UP, 2010.

Hawking, Stephen and Leonard Mlodinow. *The Grand Design*. New York: Bantam, 2010.

Hayes, Peter, Lyuba Zarsky and Walden Bello. *American Lake: Nuclear Peril in the Pacific*. Harmondsworth, UK: Penguin, 1987.

Hedges, Chris. *Death of the Liberal Class*. New York: Nation, 2010.

———. *Empire of Illusion: The End of Literacy and the Triumph of Spectacle*. New York: Nation, 2009.

Heinberg, Richard. *The End of Growth: Adapting to Our New Economic Reality*. Gabriola Island, BC: New Society, 2011.

———. *Peak Everything: Waking Up to the Century of Declines*. Gabriola Island, BC: New Society, 2007.

———. *Power Down: Options and Actions for a Post-Carbon World*. Gabriola Island, BC: New Society, 2004.

———. *The Party's Over: Oil, War and the Fate of Industrial Societies*. Gabriola Island, BC: New Society, 2003.

———. *Searching for a Miracle: "Net Energy" Limits & The Fate of Industrial Society*. San Francisco: International Forum on Globalization, 2009.

Heinberg, Richard and Daniel Lerch, eds. *The Post-Carbon Reader: Managing the 21st Century's Sustainability Crisis.* Healdsburg: Watershed Media, 2010.

Hertsgaard, Mark. *Hot: Living Through the Next Fifty Years on Earth.* New York: Houghton Mifflin Harcourt, 2011.

Hertz, Noreena. *The Debt Threat: How Debt is Destroying the Developing World . . . and Threatening Us All.* New York: HarperBusiness, 2004.

———. *The Silent Takeover.* New York: FreePress. 2002.

Hopkins, Rob. *The Transition Handbook: From Oil Dependency to Local Resilience.* Totnes, UK: Green Books, 2008.

Howe, John G. *The End of Fossil Energy and the Last Chance for Survival.* Waterford, ME: McIntire, 2006.

Hohn, Maria and Seungsook Moon, eds. *Over There: Living with the U.S. Military Empire from World War Two to the Present.* Durham: Duke UP, 2010.

Huesemann, Michael and Joyce Siegelman Huesemann. *Techno-Fix: Why Technology Won't Save Us or the Environment.* Gabriola Island, BC: New Society, 2011.

Hutton, Will and Anthony Giddens, eds. *Global Capitalism.* New York: New, 2000.

Huxley, Alduous. *Brave New World.* New York: Perennial. 1998.

International Forum on Globalization. *Does Globalization Help the Poor?* San Francisco: International Forum on Globalization, 2001.

———. *Outing the Oligarchy: Billionaires Who Benefit from Today's Climate Crisis.* San Francisco: International Forum on Globalization, 2011.

Jackson, Ross. *Occupy World Street: A Global Roadmap for Radical Economic and Political Reform.* White River Junction,VT: Chelsea Green, 2012.

Jackson, Tim. *Prosperity Without Growth: Economics for a Finite Planet.* London: Earthscan, 2011.

Jacobs, Michael. *The Green Economy.* London: Pluto Press, 1991.

Jantsch, Erich and Conrad H. Waddington, eds. *Evolution and Consciousness: Human Systems in Transition.* Reading: Addison-Wesley, 1976.

Johnson, Chalmers. *Blowback: The Costs and Consequences of American Empire.* New York: Holt, 2004

———. *Dismantling the Empire: America's Last Best Hope.* New York: Metropolitan, 2010.

———. *Nemesis: The Last Days of the American Republic.* New York: Holt, 2007.

———. *The Sorrows of Empire: Militarism, Secrecy and the End of the Republic.* New York: Holt, 2004.

Kahn, Herman, William Brown, and Leon Martel. *The Next 200 Years: A Scenario for America and the World.* New York: Morrow, 1976.

Kasser, Tim. *The High Price of Materialism.* Cambridge: MIT, 2002.

Kasser, Tim and Allen D. Kanner, eds. *Psychology and Consumer Culture: The Struggle for a Good Life in a Materialistic World.* Washington, DC: APA, 2005.

Kelso, Louis O. and Patricia Hetter. *Two-Factor Theory: The Economics of Reality.* New York: Vintage, 1967.

Kelly, Marjorie. *The Divine Right of Capital: Dethroning the Corporate Aristocracy.* San Francisco: Berrett-Koehler, 2001.

Klare, Michael T. *Blood and Oil: The Dangers and Consequences of America's Growing Dependency on Imported Petroleum. New York: Metropolitan, 2004.*

———. *Resource Wars: The New Landscape of Global Conflict*. New York: Holt, 2001.

Klein, Naomi. *The Shock Doctrine and the Rise of Disaster Capitalism*. New York: Picador, 2007.

Kohr, Leopold. *The Breakdown of Nations*. Totnes UK: Green, 2001.

Korten, David C. *Agenda for a New Economy: From Phantom Wealth to Real Wealth*. San Francisco: Berrett-Koehler, 2009.

———. *The Post-Corporate World: Life After Capitalism*. San Francisco: Berrett-Koehler, 1999.

———. *When Corporations Rule the World*. San Francisco: Berrett-Koehler, 1995.

Kovel, Joel. *The Enemy of Nature: The End of Capitalism or The End of the World?* London: Zed, 2002.

Krall, Lisi. *Proving Up*. SUNY Press, 2011

Kunstler, James Howard. *The Long Emergency: Surviving the Converging Catastrophes of the Twenty-First Century*. New York: Atlantic, 2005.

Lang, Tim and Colin Hines. *The New Protectionism: Protecting the Future Against Free Trade*. London: Earthscan, 1993.

Lehman, Chris. *Rich People Things: Real Life Secrets of the Predator Class*. Chicago: Haymarket, 2011.

Leonard, Anne. *The Story of Stuff: How Our Obsession with Stuff is Trashing the Planet, Our Communities, and Our Health – and a Vision for Change*. New York: Free Press, 2010.

Lietaer, Bernard. *The Future of Money*. Century; New edition, 2002.

Lovins, L. Hunter and Boyd Cohen. *Climate Capitalism: Capitalism in the Age of Climate Change*. New York: Hill and Wang, 2011.

Lutz, Catherine. *The Bases of Empire: The Global Struggle against U.S. Military Posts*. New York: New York University, 2009.

MacLeod, Greg. *From Mondragon to America: Experiments in Community Economic Development*. Sydney, N.S.: Univ. Coll. of Cape Breton Press, 1997.

Mander, Jerry. *Four Arguments For the Elimination of Television*. New York: Perennial, 2002.

———. *In the Absence of the Sacred: The Failure of Techonology & the Survival of the Indian Nations*. San Francisco: Sierra Club, 1992.

Mander, Jerry, ed. *Manifesto on Global Economic Transitions*. San Francisco: International Forum on Globalization, Institute for Policy Studies, and the Global Project on EconomicTransitions, 2007.

Mander, Jerry and Edward Goldsmith, eds. *The Case Against the Global Economy, and For a Turn Toward the Local*. San Francisco: Sierra Club, 1996.

Marx, Karl; edited by Max Eastman. *Capitalism and Other Writings*. New York: Random House, 1932.

Marx, Karl, and Frederick Engels; edited by Phil Gasper. *The Communist Manifesto*. Chicago: Haymarket, 2005.

Mayhew, Robert; *Essays on Ayn Rand's We the Living*. Lanham, Md: Lexington Books, 2004.

McChesney, Robert W. *Rich Media, Poor Democracy: Communication Politics in Dubious Times*. Urbana: U. of Illinois, 1999.

McKibben, Bill. *Deep Economy: The Wealth of Communities and the Durable Future*. New York: Times, 2007.

McLuhan, Marshall. *Gutenberg Galaxy*. University of Toronto Press, 1962.

———. *Understanding Media*. McGraw Hill. 1964.

Meadows, D. and J. Randers. Beyond the Limits: Confronting Global Collapse, Envisioning a Sustainable Future. White River Junction, Vermont: Chelsea Green, 1993.

Meadows, Donella, Dennis L. Meadows, Jørgen Randers. *Limits to Growth: 30 Year Update*. Chelsea Green. 2004.

Melman, Seymour. *The Permanent War Economy: American Capitalism in Decline*. New York: Touchstone, 1974.

Monbiot, George. *Heat: How to Stop the Planet Burning*. New York: Penguin, 2006.

Murphy, Pat. *The Green Tragedy: Leed's Lost Decade*. Yellow Springs: Arthur Morgan Institute, 2009.

Papworth, John. *Small is Powerful: The Future as if People Really Mattered*. London: Adamantine, 1995.

Payer, Cheryl. *Lent and Lost: Foreign Credit and Third World Development*. London: Zed, 1991.

Peters, Nancy J. *War After War*. San Francisco: City Lights, 1992.

Polanyi, Karl. *The Great Transformation: The Political and Economic Origins of Our Time*. 2nd ed. Boston: Beacon, 2001.

Porritt, Jonathon. *Capitalism – as if the world matters*. London: Earthscan, 2005.

Postman, Neil. *Amusing Ourselves to Death*. New York: Penguin. 2005.

Potter, Wendell. *Deadly Spin: An Insurance Company Insider Speaks Out on How Corporate PR is Killing Health Care and Deceiving Americans*. New York: Bloomsbury, 2010.

Princen, Thomas. *The Logic of Sufficiency*. Cambridge: MIT, 2005.

Prugh, T., R. Costanza and H. Daly. *The Local Politics of Global Sustainability*. Washington, D.C..: Island Press, 2000.

Quartiroli, Ivo. *The Digitally Divided Self: Relinquishing Our Awareness to the Internet*. Milan: Silens, 2011.

Rand, Ayn. *Atlas Shrugged*. New York: Signet, 1993.

———. *The Fountainhead*. New York: Signet, 1993.

———. *We the Living*. New York: Signet, 2009.

Robin, Corey, *The Reactionary Mind: Conservatism from Edmund Burke to Sarah Palin*. Oxford: Oxford UP, 2011.

Rochlin, Gene I. *Trapped in the Net: The Unanticipated Consequences of Computerization*. Princeton: Princeton UP, 1997.

Rogers, Heather. *Green Gone Wrong: How Our Economy is Undermining the Environmental Revolution*. New York: Scribner, 2010.

Ruiz, Dean, ed. *Defying Corporations, Defining Democracy: A Book of History and Strategy*. New York: The Apex Press, 2001.

Ruppert, Michael C. *Collapse: The Crisis of Energy and Money in a Post Peak Oil World*. Chelsea Green. 2009.

Sale, Kirkpatrick. *Human Scale*. New York: Coward, McCann & Geoghegan, 1980.

Sarkar, Saral. *Eco-Socialism or Eco-Capitalism? A Critical Analysis of Hiumanity's Fundamental Choices*. London: Zed Books. 2009.

Schor, Juliet B., *Plenitude: The New Economics of True Wealth*. Penguin Press, 2010

Schumacher, E.F. *Small Is Beautiful: Economics as if People Mattered*. New York: Harper, 1975.

Seligman, Martin. *Authentic Happiness*. New York: Free Press. 2002.

Shirer, William L. *Gandhi: A Memoir*. New York: Washington Square, 1979.

Shuman, Michael H. *Going Local: Creating Self-Reliant Communities in a Global Age*. New York: Free, 1998.

———. *The Small-Mart Revolution: How Local Businesses are Beating the Global Competition*. San Francisco: Berrett-Koehler, 2007.

———. *Towards a Global Village: International Community Development Initiatives*. London: Pluto, 1994.

Sims, Andrew, and Joe Smith, eds. *Do Good Lives Have to Cost the Earth?* London: Constable, 2008.

Sitrin, Marina, ed. *Horizontalism: Voices of Popular Power in Argentina*. Oakland: AK Press, 2006.

Smith, Adam. *An Inquiry into the Nature and Causes of The Wealth of Nations*. University of Chicago Press. 1977.

Smith, Adam, Knud Haakonssen. ed. *The Theory of Moral Sentiments*. Cambridge University Press. 2002.

Solomon, Norman. *Made Love, Got War: Close Encounters with America's Warfare State*. Sausalito: PoliPointPress, 2007.

Soros, George. *George Soros on Globalization*. New York: Public Affairs, 2002.

Speth, James Gustave. *The Bridge at the Edge of the World: Capitalism, the Environment, and Crossing from Crisis to Sustainability*. New Haven: Yale UP, 2008.

Spretnak, Charlene. *Relational Reality: New Discoveries of Interrelatedness That Are Transforming the Modern World*. Topsham, ME: Green Horizon Books, 2011.

Stiglitz, Joseph E. *Freefall: America, Free Markets, and the Sinking of the World Economy*. New York: Norton, 2010.

Tainter, Joseph A. *The Collapse of Complex Societies*. Cambridge: Cambridge UP, 1988.

Tormey, Simon. *Anti-capitalism: A Beginner's Guide*. Oxford: Oneworld, 2004.

Vanden Heuvel, Katrina. *The Change I Believe In: Fighting for Progress in the Age of Obama*. New York: Nation Books, 2011.

Victor, Peter. *Managing Without Growth*. Edward Elgar Publishing, 2008. Wallerstein, Immanuel. *World-Systems Analysis: An Introduction*. Durham: Duke UP, 2004.

Weatherford, Jack. *The History of Money*. New York: Crown, 1997.

Wilkinson, Richard and Kate Pickett. *The Spirit Level: Why Greater Equality Makes Society Stronger*. New York: Bloomsbury, 2010.

Williams, Chris. *Ecology and Socialism: Solutions to Capitalist Ecological Crisis*. Chicago: Haymarket Books, 2010.

Williamson, Thad, David Imbroscio, and Gar Alperovitz. *Making a Place for Community: Local Democracy in a Global Area*. New York: Routledge, 2003.

Wolff, Richard D. *Capitalism Hits the Fan: The Global Economic Meltdown and What to Do About It*. Northampton, MA: Olive Branch, 2010.

Wu, Tim. *The Master Switch: The Rise and Fall of Information Empires*. New York: Knopf, 2010.

Zerzan, John. *Future Primitive and Other Essays*. New York: Autonomedia, 1994.

Organizations

The following is an abbreviated list of organizations, and some publications, focusing on economic and environmental issues relevant to those in this book. Please consult their websites for further details.

350.ORG
www.350.org

ADBUSTERS
www.adbusters.org

BUSINESS ALLIANCE FOR LOCAL LIVING ECONOMIES
www.livingeconomies.org

CAPITALISM NATURE SOCIALISM
www.centerforpoliticalecology.org

CENTER FOR AMERICAN PROGRESS
www.americanprogress.org

CENTER FOR FOOD SAFETY
www.centerforfoodsafety.org

CENTER FOR A NEW AMERICAN DREAM
www.newdream.org

CENTER FOR A STEADY STATE ECONOMY
steadystate.org

COMMUNITY SOLUTIONS
www.communitysolution.org

COUNCIL OF CANADIANS
www.canadians.org

DARK MOUNTAIN PROJECT (UK)
www.dark-mountain.net

ECONOMIC POLICY INSTITUTE
www.epi.org

EARTH POLICY INSTITUTE
www.earth-policy.org

ETC GROUP
www.etcgroup.org

FOCUS ON THE GLOBAL SOUTH
www.focusweb.org

FOOD & WATER WATCH
www.foodandwaterwatch.org

GLOBAL EXCHANGE
www.globalexchange.org

GLOBAL FOOTPRINT NETWORK
www.footprintnetwork.org

GUND INSTITUTE FOR ECOLOGICAL ECONOMICS
www.uvm.edu/giee

INDIGENOUS ENVIRONMENTAL NETWORK
www.ienearth.org

INTERNATIONAL CENTER FOR TECHNOLOGY ASSESSMENT
www.icta.org

INTERNATIONAL FORUM ON GLOBALIZATION
www.ifg.org

INTERNATIONAL SOCIETY FOR ECOLOGICAL ECONOMICS
www.ecoeco.org

INTERNATIONAL SOCIETY FOR ECOLOGY AND CULTURE
www.localfutures.org

INSTITUTE FOR LOCAL SELF-RELIANCE
www.ilsr.org

INSTITUTE FOR POLICY STUDIES
www.ips-dc.org

LIA FUND
www.theliafund.org

MONTHLY REVIEW
www.monthlyreview.org

NATION INSTITUTE
www.nationinstitute.org

NAVDANYA
www.navdanya.org

NEW ECONOMICS FOUNDATION
www.neweconomics.org

NEW ECONOMICS INSTITUTE
www.neweconomicsinstitute.org

NEW ECONOMY NETWORK
www.neweconomynetwork.org

NEW ECONOMY WORKING GROUP
www.neweconomyworkinggroup.org

OAKLAND INSTITUTE
www.oaklandinstitute.org

OCCUPY
www.occupywallst.org

OIL DRUM
www.theoildrum.com

POLARIS INSTITUTE
www.polarisinstitute.org

POST CARBON INSTITUTE
www.postcarbon.org

PUBLIC CITIZEN
www.citizen.org

RESURGENCE MAGAZINE
www.resurgence.org

SOLUTIONS JOURNAL
www.thesolutionsjournal.com

SOUTH CENTRE
www.southcentre.org

STORY OF STUFF PROJECT
www.storyofstuff.org

SUSTAINABLE SCALE PROJECT
www.sustainablescale.org

TEBTEBBA
www.tebtebba.org

TELLUS INSTITUTE
www.tellus.org

THIRD WORLD NETWORK (TWN)
www.twnside.org.sg

TRANSITION TOWNS
www.transitionnetwork.org

UNITED FOR A FAIR ECONOMY
www.faireconomy.org

UNITED NATIONS FRAMEWORK CONVENTION ON CLIMATE CHANGE
www.unfccc.int

WORLD WATCH INSTITUTE
www.worldwatch.org

YES! MAGAZINE/POSITIVE FUTURES NETWORK
www.yesmagazine.org

Acknowledgments

So many people helped me on this book—and I am forever grateful to all. First to my family, my sons Yari and Kai, and Kai's family, Maria, Ezra and Eli, for their love and support. And to my wife, Koohan Paik, who read every draft of the book, contributed great ideas, editing, and more than a few of the better paragraphs, while keeping a joyful spirit in down-beat times.

Certain friends followed the development of this project closely from beginning to end and were constantly helpful with new approaches, concerns and criticisms. I would like to mention in particular, Ernest "Chick" Callenbach, Wes Nisker, Gar Smith, Annie Leonard, Jim and Marybeth Heddle, Andy Kimbrell, John Cavanagh, Jack Santa Barbara, Deborah Green, and Doug Tompkins.

Researchers included the tireless Sarah Weber, who found a mountain of important material over two years, even while finishing her studies and holding a Teaching Assistant job at Berkeley. Thanks also for great help in specific research zones to Alexis Halbert, Lilly Alvarez, and Kourosh Benham from IFG. And for logistical support throughout, to Katie Damasco, Anjulie Palta, and Eileen Hazel.

For their good suggestions, enthusiasm, encouragement and feedback over the past two years, thanks to my colleagues at IFG: Debbie Barker, Meena Raman, Martin Khor, Vicky Corpuz, Walden Bello, Vandana Shiva, Maude Barlow, Tony Clarke, Bing Gong, Anuradha Mittal, and Victor Menotti. Enormous appreciation as well to Richard Heinberg, David Korten, Gus Speth, and Patrick Bond for their critical, inspiring work and leadership over similar rocky terrain. And for being the most encouraging and supportive of friends, thanks to Elizabeth Garsonnin, Alvin and Sara Duskin, Stephanie Welch, Randy Hayes, Imok Cha, Albie Miles, Christine Ahn (and Jeju), Fred and Marge Dente, Ray Catania, Sharon and Kip Goodwin, Janet Ashkenazy, Lee Swensen, and Vijaya Nagarajan, as well as to my sister Anita Rosenstock, my niece Janet, and my nephew Rob Waring. And, my great appreciation to the gang at YakiniQ—Christy, Ray, Sahara, India, Roslyn, and everyone.

My longtime colleague Sharon Donovan introduced me to Counterpoint Press, the perfect small publisher I was seeking—thank you Sharon for that. Editors Roxanna Aliaga and Annie Tucker and production manager Emma Cofod were a tirelessly helpful and alert team; and thanks to the executive team of Jack Shoemaker and Charlie Winton for your wisdom and patience!

Last but not least, for financial support over more than two years, without which this would not have been possible, my heartfelt appreciation to Charlotte Levinson of the Levinson Foundation, and to the Foundation for Deep Ecology.